MAID IN THE U.S.A.

PERSPECTIVES ON GENDER

Pleasure, Power, and Technology: Some Tales of Gender, Engineering, and the Cooperative Workplace

Sally Hacker

Black Feminist Thought: Knowledge, Consciousness, and the Politics of Empowerment

Patricia Hill Collins

Understanding Sexual Violence: A Study of Convicted Rapists

Diana Scully

Feminism and the Women's Movement: Dynamics of Change in Social Movement Ideology and Activism

Barbara Ryan

Black Women and White Women in the Professions: Occupational Segregation by Race and Gender, 1960–1980

Natalie J. Sokoloff

15⁻⁹⁵

MAID IN THE U.S.A.

Mary Romero

Routledge
New York • London

Published in 1992 by
Routledge, an imprint of
Routledge, Chapman and Hall, Inc.
29 West 35 Street
New York, NY 10001

Published in Great Britain by
Routledge
11 New Fetter Lane
London EC4P 4EE

Sections of chapter 1 appeared in the following:
"Coping With Exploitation of Domestic Workers," In *Sociology*. Beth B. Hess, Elizabeth W. Markson and Peter Stein (eds.) pp. 322–23. New York: MacMillan Publishing Company (1991).
Sections of chapter 5 appeared in the following:
"Sisterhood and Domestic Service: Race, Class and Gender in the Mistress-Maid Relationship," *Humanity and Society* (1988) Volume 12, Issue 4, pp. 318–346.
Sections of chapter 6 appeared in the following:
"Not Just Like One of the Family: Chicana Domestics Establishing Professional Relationships With Employers," *Feminist Issues*. (1990) Volume 10, Number 2, pp. 33–41.
"Chicanas Modernize Domestic Service," *Qualitative Sociology*. (1988) Volume 11, Issue 4, pp. 319–334.
"Day Work in the Suburbs: The Work Experience of Chicana Private Housekeepers," In *Worth of Women's Work: A Qualitative Synthesis*. Anne Statham, Eleanor Miller and Hans Maulksch (eds.). pp. 77–91. Albany, N.Y.: State University of New York Press (1988).
    Abridged Version Reprinted in John J. Macionis and Nijole V. Benokraitis' *Seeing Ourselves Classic, Contemporary, and Cross-Cultural Readings in Sociology* pp. 174–180. Englewood, NJ: Prentice Hall (1989).
Sections of Chapter 1 and 6 appeared in the following:
"Domestic Work in Transition from Rural to Urban Life: A Case of La Chicana," *Women's Studies*. (1987) Volume 13, Issue 3, pp. 199–200.

Library of Congress Cataloging in Publication Data

Romero, Mary.
    Maid in the U.S.A. / Mary Romero.
        p.   cm.—(Perspectives on gender)
    Includes bibliographical references and index.
    ISBN 0–415–90611–3.—ISBN 0–415–90612–1 (pbk.)
    1. Women domestics—United States—History. 2. Hispanic American
women—Employment—History. 3. Minority women—Employment—United
States—History.   I. Title.   II. Title: Maid in the USA.
III. Series:
Perspectives on gender (New York, N.Y.)
HQ6072.2.U5R675   1992
331.4′8164046′0973—dc20   92–90
                                                                                        CIP

British Library Cataloguing in Publication Data Available on Request

CONTENTS

ACKNOWLEDGMENTS

This study would not have been possible without the constant support and encouragement of my husband, Eric Margolis. He has lived with the book as long as I have and willingly provided the everyday love and humor needed to write a book. He read every draft carefully and offered supportive criticisms and suggestions. We both knew the end of the book was near when we both preferred to do housework rather than to write, read, or talk about it.

I owe countless debts to my family, who have always given me their love and support and in every way enriched my life. My mother, Amalia Romero, my sister, Frances Romero, and my sister-in-law, Trinnie Romero, helped me make initial contacts with Chicanas currently employed as household workers and shared their own work experiences.

Many colleagues have contributed to the development of my ideas. I am particularly indebted to Arlene Daniels, who encouraged me to explore the importance of the labor process in workers' experiences of domestic service and their struggles and resistance against demeaning housework. Over the last six years, I have benefited from the ongoing dialogue with Judith Rollins, Evelyn Glenn, Phyllis Palmer, Elaine Kaplan, Bonnie Thornton Dill, and Margo Smith.

I appreciate the careful reading and valuable comments that Myra Marx Ferree offered on each manuscript draft. I am fortunate to have found a series editor who understood my concerns and offered important criticism to strengthen my arguments. I also want to thank Lisa Freeman for her extensive comments and constant encouragement throughout the project.

I want to thank Elizabeth Higginbotham, Louise Lamphere, and Arlie Hochschild for contributing generous amounts of time in reading various drafts of the manuscript; and Denise Bielby, Tomas Almaguer, and Ramon Gutierrez for extensive comments on early chapter drafts. I appreciate the comradely assistance of numerous friends who sent me newspaper articles, advertisements, and other items on housework.

The research on Chicana private household workers was supported by a Sally Butler Memorial Fund for Latina Research grant from the Business and Professional Women's Foundation. The visiting-scholar positions funded by the University of California President's Fellowship Program provided the support for writing several manuscript drafts. I am grateful for the support and assistance received from the Chicano Studies Department at the University of California, Davis, and the Sociology Department at the University of California, Berkeley. Special thanks to Adaljiza Sosa Riddel and Arlie Hochschild for their support during the fellowship.

Finally, I want to acknowledge the women whom I interviewed and thank them for sharing their experiences.

Chapter 1

INTERSECTION OF BIOGRAPHY AND HISTORY: MY INTELLECTUAL JOURNEY

A PERSONAL NARRATIVE ON THE DEVELOPMENT OF THE RESEARCH PROBLEM

When I was growing up many of the women whom I knew worked cleaning other people's houses. Domestic service was part of my taken-for-granted reality. Later, when I had my own place, I considered housework something you did before company came over. My first thought that domestic service and house-work might be a serious research interest came as a result of a chance encounter with live-in domestics along the U. S.-Mexican border. Before beginning a teaching position at the University of Texas in El Paso, I stayed with a colleague while apartment hunting. My colleague had a live-in domestic to assist with housecleaning and cooking. Asking around, I learned that live-in maids were common in El Paso, even among apartment and condominium dwellers. The hiring of maids from Mexico was so common that locals referred to Monday as the border patrol's day off because the agents ignored the women crossing the border to return to their employers' homes after their weekend off. The practice of hiring undocumented Mexican women as domestics, many of whom were no older than fifteen, seemed strange to me. It was this strangeness that raised the topic of domestic service as a question and made problematic what had previously been taken for granted.

I must admit that I was shocked at my colleague's treatment of the sixteen-year-old domestic whom I will call Juanita. Only recently hired, Juanita was still adjusting to her new environment. She was extremely shy, and her timidity was made even worse by constant flirting from her employer. As far as I could see, every attempt Juanita made to converse was met with teasing so that the conversation could never evolve into a serious discussion. Her employer's sexist, paternalistic banter effectively silenced the domestic, kept her constantly on guard, and made it impossible for her to feel comfortable at work. For instance, when she informed the employer of a leaky faucet, he shot her a look of disdain, making it clear that she was overstepping her boundaries. I observed other encounters that clearly served to remind Juanita of her subservient place in her employer's home.

Although Juanita was of the same age as my colleague's oldest daughter and but a few years older than his two sons, she was treated differently from the other teenagers in the house. She was expected to share her bedroom with the ironing board, sewing machine, and other spare-room types of objects.[1] More importantly, she was assumed to have different wants and needs. I witnessed the following revealing exchange. Juanita was poor. She had not brought toiletries with her from Mexico. Since she had not yet been paid, she had to depend on her employer for necessities. Yet instead of offering her a small advance in her pay so she could purchase the items herself and giving her a ride to the nearby supermarket to select her own toiletries, the employer handled Juanita's request for toothbrush, toothpaste, shampoo, soap, and the like in the following manner. In the presence of all the family and the house guest, he made a list of the things she needed. Much teasing and joking accompanied the encounter. The employer shopped for her and purchased only generic brand items, which were a far cry from the brand-name products that filled the bathroom of his sixteen-year-old daughter. Juanita looked at the toothpaste, shampoo, and soap with confusion; she may never have seen generic products before, but she obviously knew that a distinction had been made.

One evening I walked into the kitchen as the employer's young sons were shouting orders at Juanita. They pointed to the dirty dishes on the table and pans in the sink and yelled "WASH!" "CLEAN!" Juanita stood frozen next to the kitchen door, angry and humiliated. Aware of possible repercussions for Juanita if I reprimanded my colleague's sons, I responded awkwardly by reallocating chores to everyone present. I announced that I would wash the dishes and the boys would clear the table. Juanita washed and dried dishes alongside me, and together we finished cleaning the kitchen. My colleague returned from his meeting to find us in the kitchen washing the last pan. The look on his face was more than enough to tell me that he was shocked to find his houseguest—and future colleague—washing dishes with the maid. His embarrassment at my behavior confirmed my suspicion that I had violated the normative expectations of class behavior within the home. He attempted to break the tension with a flirtatious

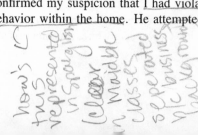

and sexist remark to Juanita which served to excuse her from the kitchen and from any further discussion.

The conversation that followed revealed how my colleague chose to interpret my behavior. Immediately after Juanita's departure from the kitchen, he initiated a discussion about "Chicano radicals" and the Chicano movement. Although he was a foreign-born Latino, he expressed sympathy for *la causa*. Recalling the one Chicano graduate student he had known to obtain a Ph.D. in sociology, he gave several accounts of how the student's political behavior had disrupted the normal flow of university activity. Lowering his voice to a confidential whisper, he confessed to understanding why Marxist theory has become so popular among Chicano students. The tone of his comments and the examples that he chose made me realize that my "outrageous" behavior was explained, and thus excused, on the basis of my being one of those "Chicano radicals." He interpreted my washing dishes with his maid as a symbolic act; that is, I was affiliated with *los de abajo*.

My behavior had been comfortably defined without addressing the specific issue of maids. My colleague then further subsumed the topic under the rubric of "the servant problem" along the border. (His reaction was not unlike the attitude employers have displayed toward domestic service in the United States for the last hundred years.)[2] He began by providing me with chapter and verse about how he had aided Mexican women from Juarez by helping them cross the border and employing them in his home. He took further credit for introducing them to the appliances found in an American middle class home. He shared several funny accounts about teaching country women from Mexico to use the vacuum cleaner, electric mixer, and microwave (remember the maid scene in the movie *El Norte*?) and implicitly blamed them for their inability to work comfortably around modern conveniences. For this "on-the-job training" and introduction to American culture, he complained, his generosity and goodwill had been rewarded by a high turnover rate. As his account continued, he assured me that most maids were simply working until they found a husband. In his experience they worked for a few months or less and then did not return to work on Monday morning after their first weekend off. Of course it never dawned on him that they may simply have found a job with better working conditions.

The following day, Juanita and I were alone in the house. As I mustered up my best Spanish, we shared information about our homes and families. After a few minutes of laughter about my simple sentence structure, Juanita lowered her head and in a sad, quiet voice told me how isolated and lonely she felt in this middle-class suburb literally within sight of Juarez. Her feelings were not the consequence of the work or of frustrations with modern appliances, nor did she complain about the absence of Mexican people in the neighborhood; her isolation and loneliness were in response to the norms and values surrounding domestic service. She described the situation quite clearly in expressing puzzlement over the social interactions she had with her employer's family: why didn't her employer's children talk to her or include her in any of their activities when she wasn't working? Her reaction was not unlike that of Lillian Pettengill, who wrote about her two-year experience as a domestic in Philadelphia households at the turn of the century: "I feel my isolation alone in a big house full of people." [3]

Earlier in the day, Juanita had unsuccessfully tried to initiate a conversation with the sixteen-year-old daughter while she cleaned her room. She was of the same age as the daughter (who at that moment was in bed reading and watching TV because of menstrual cramps—a luxury the maid was not able to claim). She was rebuffed and ignored and felt that she became visible only when an order was given. Unable to live with this social isolation, she had already made up her mind not to return after her day off in Juarez. I observed the total impossibility of communication. The employer would never know why she left, and Juanita would not know that she would be considered simply another ungrateful Mexican whom he had tried to help.

After I returned to Denver, I thought a lot about the situations of Juanita and the other young undocumented Mexican women living in country club areas along the border. They worked long days in the intimacy of American middle class homes but were starved for respect and positive social interaction. Curiously, the employers did not treat the domestics as "one of the family," nor did they consider themselves employers. Hiring a domestic was likely to be presented within the context of charity and good works; it was considered a matter of helping "these Mexican women" rather than recognized as a work issue.

I was bothered by my encounter along the border, not simply for the obvious humanitarian reasons, but because I too had once worked as a domestic, just as my mother, sister, relatives, and neighbors had. As a teenager, I cleaned houses with my mother on weekends and vacations. My own working experience as a domestic was limited because I had always been accompanied by my mother or sister instead of working alone. Since I was a day worker, my time in the employer's home was limited and I was able to return to my family and community each day. In Juanita's situation as a live-in domestic, there was no distinction between the time on and off work. I wondered whether domestic service had similarly affected my mother, sister, and neighbors. Had they too worked beyond the agreed upon time? Did they have difficulty managing relationships with employers? I never worked alone and was spared the direct negotiations with employers. Instead, I cooperated with my mother or sister in completing the housecleaning as efficiently and quickly as possible.

I could not recall being yelled at by employers or their children, but I did remember anger, resentment, and the humiliation I had felt at kneeling to scrub other people's toilets while they gave step-by-step cleaning instructions. I re-

member feeling uncomfortable around employers' children who never acknowledged my presence except to question where I had placed their belongings after
I had picked them up off the floor to vacuum. After all, my experience was
foreign to them; at the age of fourteen I worked as a domestic while they ran off
to swimming, tennis, and piano lessons. Unlike Juanita, I preferred to remain
invisible as I moved around the employer's house cleaning. Much later, I learned
that the invisibility of workers in domestic service is a common characteristic of
the occupation. Ruth Schwartz Cowan has commented on the historical aspect
of invisibility:

> The history of domestic service in the United States is a vast, unresolved puzzle,
> because the social role "servant" so frequently carries with it the unspoken adjec-
> tive *invisible*. In diaries and letters, the "invisible" servant becomes visible only
> when she departs employment ("Mary left today"). In statistical series, she appears
> only when she is employed full-time, on a live-in basis; or when she is willing to
> confess the nature of her employment to a census taker, and (especially since the
> Second World War) there have frequently been good reasons for such confessions
> to go unmade.[4]

Although I remained invisible to most of the employers' family members, the
mothers, curiously enough, seldom let me move around the house invisibly,
dusting the woodwork and vacuuming carpets. Instead, I was subjected to constant supervision and condescending observations about "what a good little girl
I was, helping my mother clean house." After I had moved and cleaned behind
a hide-a-bed and lazy-boy chair, vacuumed three floors including two sets of
stairs, and carried the vacuum cleaner up and downstairs twice because "little
Johnny" was napping when I was cleaning the bedrooms—I certainly didn't feel
like a "little girl helping mother." I felt like a domestic worker!

There were employers who attempted to draw parallels between my adoles-
cent experience and their teenagers' behavior: they'd point to the messy bedrooms and claim, "Well, you're a teenager, you understand clothes, books, papers, and records on the floor." Even at fourteen, I knew that being sloppy and
not picking up after yourself was a privilege. I had two brothers and three sisters.
I didn't have my own bedroom but shared a room with my sisters. Not one of us
would think of leaving our panties on the floor for the others to pick up. I didn't
bother to set such employers straight but continued to clean in silence, knowing
that at the end of day I would get cash and confident that I would soon be old
enough to work elsewhere.

Many years later, while attending graduate school, I returned to domestic
service as an "off-the-record" means to supplement my income. Graduate fel-
lowships and teaching assistantships locked me into a fixed income that frequently was not enough to cover my expenses.[5] So once again I worked alongside my mother for seven hours as we cleaned two houses. I earned about fifty

dollars for the day. Housecleaning is strenuous work, and I returned home exhausted from climbing up and down stairs, bending over, rubbing, and scrubbing.

Returning to domestic service as a graduate student was awkward. I tried to reduce the status inconsistency in my life by electing to work only in houses from which families were absent during the day. If someone appeared while I worked, I ignored their presence as they did mine. Since working arrangements had been previously negotiated by my mother, I had limited face-to-face interactions with employers. Most of the employers knew I was a graduate student, and fortunately, most seemed reluctant to ask me too many questions. Our mutual silence served as a way to deal with the status inconsistency of a housewife with a B.A. hiring an ABD to clean her house.

I came to El Paso with all of these experiences unquestioned in my memory. My presuppositions about domestic service were called into question only after observing the more obviously exploitative situation in the border town. I saw how vulnerable undocumented women employed as live-in domestics are and what little recourse they have to improve their situation, short of finding another job. Experiencing Juanita's shame and disgust at my colleague's sons' behavior brought back a flood of memories that eventually influenced me to study the paid housework that I had once taken-for-granted. I began to wonder professionally about the Chicanas employed as domestics that I had known throughout my own life: how vulnerable were they to exploitation, racism, and sexism? Did their day work status and U.S. citizenship provide protection against degradation and humiliation? How did Chicanas go about establishing a labor arrangement within a society that marked them as racial and cultural inferiors? How did they deal with racial slurs and sexist remarks within their employers' homes? How did Chicanas attempt to negotiate social interactions and informal labor arrangements with employers and their families?

AN EXPLORATORY STUDY

The Research Process

Intending to compare my findings with the research on U.S. minority women employed as domestics, I chose to limit my study to Chicanas, that is, women of Mexican descent born and raised in the United States. Although many women born in Mexico and living in the United States consider themselves Chicanas, my sample did not include women born outside the United States. My major concern in making this distinction was to avoid bringing into the analysis immigration issues that increase the vulnerability of the women employed as domestics. I wanted to keep conditions as constant as possible to make comparisons with the experiences Judith Rollins, Bonnie Thornton Dill, and Soraya Moore Coley report among African American women and with Evelyn Glenn's study of Japanese American women.[6] In order to duplicate similar residential and citizenship characteristics of these studies, I restricted my sample to Chicanas living in Denver whose families had migrated from rural areas of New Mexico and Colorado. All of the women interviewed were U.S. citizens and lived in Denver most of their adult lives.

I began the project by soliciting the cooperation of current and former domestics from my own family. I relied on domestics to provide entree into informal networks. These networks turned out to be particularly crucial in gaining access to an occupation that is so much a part of the underground economy. My mother, sister, and sister-in-law agreed to be interviewed and to provide names of relatives, friends, and neighbors. I also identified Chicana domestics in the community with the assistance of outreach workers employed by local churches and social service agencies. The snowball sampling was achieved by asking each interviewee to recommend other Chicana domestics as potential interviewees.

The women were extremely cautious about offering the names of friends and relatives. In most cases, they contacted the person first and only then gave me the name and telephone number. This actually turned out to be quite helpful. Potential interviewees had already heard about my study from someone who had been interviewed. They had a general idea of the questions I was going to ask and in some cases a little background information about who I was. However, on three occasions, I called women to ask for an interview and was confronted with resistance and shame. The women expressed embarrassment at being identified by their work—as a "housekeeper" or "cleaning lady." I responded by sharing my research interests in the occupation and in the relationship between work and family. I also shared my previous experience as a domestic.[7] One woman argued with me for twenty minutes about conducting research on an occupation that was low status, suggesting instead that I study Chicana lawyers or doctors, that is, "another occupation that presents our people in a more positive light." Another woman denied ever having worked as a domestic even though several women, including her sister-in-law, had given me her name as someone currently employed as a domestic.

The stigma of domestic service was a problem during the interviews as well. From the outset, it was very important for each woman to establish herself as someone more than a private household worker. Conducting nonstructured, free-flowing, and open-ended interviews allowed the women to establish multiple identities, particularly diffuse family and community roles.

The interviews were conducted in the women's homes, usually while sitting in the living room or at the dining room table with the radio or television on in the background. Although family members peeked in, for the most part there were few interruptions other than an occasional telephone call. From time to time, the women called to their husbands in the other room to ask the name of a street where they had once lived or the year the oldest son had been born in order to figure out when they had left and returned to work. The average interview lasted two hours, but I often stayed to visit and chat long after the interview was over. They told me about their church activities and plans to remodel the house and asked me for my opinion on current Chicano politics. Some spread out blankets, tablecloths, and pillow covers to exhibit their needlework. They showed me pictures of their children and grandchildren, giving me a walking tour of living rooms and bedrooms where wedding and high school portraits hung. As each one was identified, I learned more about their lives.

I conducted twenty-five open ended interviews with Chicanas living and working in the greater Denver metropolitan area. The most visible Chicano communities in Denver are in the low-income neighborhood located in the downtown area or in one of two working-class neighborhoods in the northern and western areas of the city. I interviewed women from each of these communities. I asked them to discuss their overall work histories, with particular emphasis on their experiences as domestics. I probed for detailed information on domestic work, including strategies for finding employers, definitions of appropriate and inappropriate tasks, the negotiation of working conditions, ways of doing housework efficiently, and the pros and cons of domestic service. The accounts included descriptions of the domestics' relationships with white middle class mistresses and revealed Chicanas' attitudes toward their employers' lifestyles.

All of the interviewees' families of orientation were from northern New Mexico or southern Colorado, where many of them had lived and worked on small farms. Some of the women had arrived in Denver as children with their parents, others as young brides, and still others as single women to join siblings and cousins in Denver's barrios. Several women recalled annual migrations to northern Colorado to pick sugar beets, prior to their permanent relocation to Denver. In some cases, the women's entire families of orientation had migrated to Denver; in others, parents and siblings had either remained behind or migrated to other cities. Many older women had migrated with their husbands after World War II, and several younger women interviewed had arrived at the same time, as children. Women who had migrated as single adults typically had done so in the last ten or fifteen years. Now they were married and permanently living in Denver. In the next section, I provide a brief historical discussion of the region as a way of contextualizing information about this particular Chicano subculture.

Historical Background

After the Mexican American War, Mexicans were given the option to maintain their Mexican citizenship and leave the country or become U.S. citizens. Many reluctantly choose the latter in order to keep their homes. Although the Treaty of Guadalupe Hidalgo was supposed to guarantee land grant provisions to those who chose to remain in occupied territory, legal and illegal maneuvers were used to eliminate communal usage of land and natural resources. Between 1854 and 1930, an estimated 2,000,000 acres of private land and 1,700,000 acres of communal land were lost.[8] In the arid Southwest, small plots were insufficient to continue a subsistence-based farming economy, thus the members of the Hispano community were transformed from landowners to wage laborers. Enclosure of the common lands forced Mexicans from their former economic roles, "freed" Mexicans for wage labor, and established a racially stratified labor force in the Southwest.

As early as 1900, the Hispano farming and ranching communities of northern New Mexico and southern Colorado began to lose their population. A combination of push-pull factors conspired to force rural Hispanos off the land and attracted them to urban areas like Denver. Rural northern New Mexico and southern Colorado experienced drastic depopulation as adults left to find jobs. During the depression, studies conducted in cooperation with the Works Progress Administration (WPA) noted the desperate situation:

> The Tewa Basin Study by the U.S. Department of Agriculture showed that in eleven Spanish-American villages containing 1,202 families, an average of 1,110 men went out of the villages to work for some part of each year prior to 1930. In 1934, only 157 men out of 1,202 families had found outside work.[9]

Migration in search of jobs became a way of life for many families. New Mexicans and southern Coloradans joined the migratory farm labor stream from Texas, California, and Mexico. World War II further depopulated the rural villages as people flocked to the cities in response to job openings in defense plants and related industries. Postwar migration from New Mexico was estimated to be one-fifth of the 1940 rural Chicano population.[10] This pattern continued in the following decades. For instance, Thomas Malone found that during the decade of the 1950s, only one of seven northern counties in New Mexico had not experienced a decrease in its former predominately Spanish-speaking population.[11] By 1960, sixty-one percent of the population had been urbanized,[12] and between 1950 and 1960, an additional twenty-four percent left their rural communities.[13]

Perhaps because research on population movement among Chicanos has been so overwhelmingly concerned with emigration from Mexico, this type of internal population movement among Chicanos has not been well studied. What research is available has focused primarily on male workers and the relationship between urbanization and acculturation.[14] Chicanas have been either ignored or treated simply as family members—mothers, daughters, or wives, accompanying male relatives in search of work—rather than as wage earners in their own right. Nevertheless, for many women migration to an urban area made it necessary that they enter the labor market. Domestic service became a significant occupation in the experience.

Profile of Chicana Household Workers

Only the vaguest statistical data on Chicana private household workers are available; for the most part these workers remain a doubly hidden population. The reasons are themselves instructive. Domestic workers tend to be invisible because paid domestic work has not been one of the occupations recorded in social science surveys, and the U.S. Census Bureau uses a single code lumping together all private household workers, including launderers, cooks, housekeepers, child-care workers, cleaners, and servants. Even when statistics on domestics can be teased out of the census and labor data bases, they are marred by the common practice of underreporting work in the informal sector. Unlike some of the private household workers in the East, Chicana domestics are not unionized and remain outside the "counted" labor force. Many private household workers are not included in the statistics collected by the Department of Labor. The "job" involves an informal labor arrangement made between two people, and in many cases payment is simply a cash transaction that is never recorded with the Internal Revenue Service (IRS).

Governmental undercounting of Chicanos and Mexican immigrants in the United States further adds to the problem of determining the number of Chicanas and Mexicanas employed as private household workers. For many, domestic service is part of the underground economy, and employing undocumented workers is reported neither to the IRS nor to the Immigration and Naturalization Service (INS), thus making another source of statistical information unreliable. Chicanos continue to be an undercounted and obscure population. Problems with the categorization of domestics have been still further complicated by changing identifiers for the Mexican American population: Mexican, Spanish-speaking, Hispanic, Spanish-surnamed, and the like make it impossible to segment out the Chicano population.

The twenty-five Chicanas whom I interviewed included welfare recipients as well as working-class women, ranging in age from twenty-nine to sixty-eight. Thirteen of the twenty-five women were between twenty-nine and forty-five years old. The remaining twelve were over fifty-two years old. All the women had children and the older women also had grandchildren. The smallest family consisted of one child, and the largest family had seven children. The average was three children. All but one of the women had been married. Five of the women were single heads of households, two of them were divorced and the other three were single, separated, or widowed. The married women were currently living with husbands employed in blue collar positions, such as construction and factory work. At the time of the interview, the women who were single heads of households were financially supporting no more than two children.

Educational backgrounds ranged from no schooling to completion of high school. Six women had completed high school, and seven had no high school experience, including one who had never attended school at all. The remaining twelve had at least a sixth grade education. Although the least educated were the older women, eight of the women under forty-two had not completed high school. The youngest woman with less than an eighth grade education was fifty-three years old. The twelve women over fifty averaged eight years of schooling. Three of the high school graduates were in their early thirties, two were in their early forties, and one was fifty-seven years old. Although one woman preferred to be interviewed in Spanish, all the women spoke English.

Work experience as a private household worker ranged from five months to thirty years. Women fifty years and older had worked in the occupation from eight to thirty years, while four of the women between the ages of thirty-three and thirty-nine had worked as domestics for twelve years. Half of the women had worked for more than ten years as private household workers. Only three women had worked as domestics prior to marriage; each of these women had worked in live-in situations in rural areas in Colorado. Several years later, after marriage and children, they returned as day workers. All the other women, however, had turned to nonresidential day work in response to a financial crisis; in the majority of cases, it was their first job after marriage and having children. Some of the women remained domestics throughout their lives, but others moved in and out of domestic work. Women who returned to domestic service after having other types of jobs usually did so following a period of unemployment.

The work histories revealed that domestic service was only one of several low paying, low status jobs the women had held during their lives. They had been hired as waitresses, laundresses, janitors, farmworkers, nurses aides, fast-food servers, cooks, dishwashers, receptionists, school aides, cashiers, babysitters, salesclerks, factory workers, and various types of line workers in poultry farms and car washes. Almost half of the women had worked as janitors in hospitals and office buildings or as hotel maids. About one-fourth of the women had held semiskilled and skilled positions such as beauticians, typists, and medical-record clerks. Six of the women had worked only as domestics.

Paid and Unpaid Domestic Work

In describing their daily routine activities, these Chicanas drew my attention to the interrelationship between paid and unpaid housework. As working women, Chicana private household workers face the "double day" or "second shift," but in their case both days consisted of the same types of tasks. Paid housework done for an employer was qualitatively different from housework done for their own families.

In the interviews, Chicanas described many complexities of domestic service. They explained how they used informal networks to find new employers for themselves and for relatives and friends. As they elaborated on the advantages and disadvantages of particular work arrangements and their reasons for refusing certain household tasks, I soon realized that these women not only knew a great deal about cleaning and maintaining homes, but they understood the influence of social relationships on household tasks. Analysis of the extensive planning and negotiation involved in the informal and underground arrangements of domestic service highlighted the significance of the social relationships surrounding housework.

Their work histories included detailed explanations of beginning, returning to and continuing in domestic service. In the discussions, I began to understand the paradox of domestic service: on the one hand, cleaning houses is degrading and embarrassing; on the other, domestic service can be higher paying, more autonomous, and less dehumanizing than other low-status, low-skilled occupations. Previous jobs in the beet fields, fast-food restaurants, car washes, and turkey farms did not offer annual raises, vacations or sick leave. Furthermore, these jobs forced employees to work long hours and to keep rigid time schedules, and they frequently occurred outside or in an unsafe work environment. Unlike the other options available, domestic service did have the potential for offering flexible work schedules and autonomy. In most cases, domestic service also paid much more. Although annual raises, vacation, and social security were not the norm for most Chicanas in domestic service, there remained the possibility that such benefits could be negotiated with employers. Furthermore, as former farmworkers, laundresses, and line workers, the women found freedom in domestic work from exposure to dangerous pesticides, poor ventilation, and other health risks. This paradox foreshadowed a critical theoretical issue, the importance of understanding the social process that constructs domestic service as a low-status occupation.

Stigma as a perceived occupational hazard of domestic service emerged during the initial contact and throughout most of the interviews. The stigma attached to domestic service punctuated the interviews. I knew that many women hid their paid household labor from the government, but I did not realize that this secrecy encompassed neighbors, friends, and even extended family members. Several women gave accounts that revealed their families' efforts to conceal their employment as domestics. Children frequently stated that their mothers "just did housework," which was ambiguous enough to define them as full-time homemakers and not necessarily as domestics.

Faced with limited job opportunities, Chicanas selected domestic service and actively sought to make the most of the situation. In comparison with other jobs they had held, domestic service usually paid more and offered greater flexibility in arranging the length of the work-day and work-week. Although other jobs did not carry the stigma of servitude, workers were under constant supervision, and the work was similarly low-status. Therefore, the women who chose domestic service over other low-paying, low-status jobs based their selection on the occupation that offered some possibility of control. Their challenge was to structure the work so as to reap the most benefits: pay, work hours, labor, and autonomy. Throughout the interviews, the women emphasized job flexibility as the major advantage of domestic service over previous jobs. Nonrigid work schedules allowed time to do their own housework and fulfill family obligations, such as caring for sick children or attending school functions. By stressing the benefits gained by doing day work, Chicanas diffused the low status in their work identities and emphasized their family and community identities. The ways in which they arranged both work and family revealed coping strategies used to deal with the stigma, and this drew me to analyze housework as a form of labor having both paid and unpaid manifestations.

The conventional social science separation of work and family is an analytical construct and is not found in the lived reality of Chicana domestics. Invariably the interviewees mixed and intertwined discussions of work and family. Moreover, the actual and practical relationships between work and family were explicit in their descriptions of daily activities: the reasons for seeking employment included the family's financial situation and the desire to raise its standard of living; earning extra money for the household was viewed as an extension of these women's roles as mothers and wives; arranging day work involved planning work hours around the children's school attendance, dentist and doctor appointments, and community and church activities; in some cases, young mothers even took their preschool-age children with them to work. The worlds of paid and unpaid housework were not disconnected in the lives of these women.

Attending to the importance of the relationship between paid and unpaid domestic work led me to ponder new questions about the dynamics of buying and selling household labor. How does housework differ when it is paid work? How does the housewife role change when part of her work is allocated to another woman? What is the range of employer-employee relationship in domestic service today? And is there a difference in the type of relationships developed by employed and unemployed women buying household labor?

The importance of attending to both paid and unpaid housework in researching domestic service became more apparent as I began presenting my research to academic audiences. When I read papers on the informal labor market or on family and community networks used to find work, some of my colleagues responded as women who employed domestics. Frequently question-and-answer sessions turned into a defense of such practices as hiring undocumented workers, not filing income taxes, or gift-giving in lieu of raises and benefits. Although I was aware that as working women, many academics employed someone to clean their houses, I was not prepared for scholars and feminists to respond to my scholarly work as housewives or employers. I was also surprised to discover that many of the maternalistic practices traditionally found in domestic service were common practices in their homes. The recurring responses made me realize that my feminist colleagues had never considered their relationships with the "cleaning woman" on the same plane as those with secretaries, waitresses, or janitors; that is, they thought of the former more or less in terms of the mistress-maid relationship. When, through my research, I pointed out the contradiction, many still had difficulty thinking of their homes—the haven from the cruel academic world—as someone's workplace. Their overwhelming feelings of discomfort, guilt and resentment, which sometimes came out as hostility, alerted me to the fact that something more was going on.

Although written over a decade ago, Margaret Mead's depiction of the middle-class woman's dilemma still seems to capture the contradictory feelings and attitudes that I hear among feminists today.

> Traveling around the country, I meet a great many young wives and mothers who are struggling with the problem that seems to have no solution—how to hold down two full-time jobs at once. . . . As I listen I realize how many of them—guiltily but wistfully—yearn for the bygone days of servants. . . . They are guilty because they don't quite approve of anyone's working as a servant in someone else's home.[15]

In a society that espouses egalitarian values, we can expect yearnings "for the bygone days of servants" to be experienced as a contradiction. A century ago, Jane Addams discussed the awkward feelings and apprehensiveness academic women feel:

> I should consider myself an unpardonable snob if, because a woman did my cooking, I should not hold myself ready to have her for my best friend, to drive, to read, to attend receptions with her, but that friendship might or might not come about, according to her nature and mine, just as it might or might not come about between me and my college colleague. On the other hand, I would consider myself very stupid if merely because a woman cooked my food and lived in my house I should insist upon having a friendship with her, whether her nature and mine responded to it or not. It would be folly to force the companionship of myself or my family upon her when doubtless she would vastly prefer the companionship of her own friends and her own family.[16]

In her book on black domestics and white employers in the South, Susan Tucker addresses the deeper psychological and class factors involved in hiring servants.

Most studies of domestic work maintain that the prime motivation for hiring a servant is the enhancement of the employer's image as a superior being. Yet, many women certainly must feel some discomfort, even when paying a decent wage, about the possibility of such a motivation. . . . There are many conflicting principles and traditions surrounding the employment of a socially and economically disadvantaged woman who goes daily into a wealthy home. One might feel discomfort if one were aware of any number of different types of ideas—feminist, egalitarian, religious.[17]

Domestic service must be studied because it raises a challenge to any feminist notion of "sisterhood." A growing number of employed middle- and upper-middle class women escape the double-day syndrome by hiring a poor women of color to do housework and child care. David Katzman underscored the class contradiction:

Middle-class women, the employers, gained freedom from family roles and household chores and assumed or confirmed social status by the employment of a servant. . . . The greater liberty of these middle-class women, however, was achieved at the expense of working-class women, who, forced to work, assumed the tasks beneath, distasteful to, or too demanding for the family members.[18]

Housework is ascribed on the basis of gender, and it is further divided along class lines and, in most cases, by race and ethnicity. Domestic service accentuates the contradiction of race and class in feminism, with privileged women of one class using the labor of another woman to escape aspects of sexism.

To identify its gender, racial and class dynamics, I explore domestic service through an investigation of both unpaid and paid housework. Relying heavily upon the words of women of color, I establish the ways in which class, race, ethnic, and gender hierarchies are reproduced in the home and create oppressive working conditions. By quoting their descriptions of working conditions, social relationships with employers and families, and strategies for survival and change, we come to understand the social constraints that shape the personal lives of women of color employed as private household workers in the United States.

Chicana voices also explain how they try to restructure domestic service to reduce the stigma associated with the occupation, to create a more humanistic working environment, and to raise their wages. On the basis of my interviews with twenty-five Chicanas, I argue that private household workers are struggling to control the work process and alter the employee-employer relationship to a client-tradesperson relationship in which labor services rather than labor power are sold. The struggle over the work process is aimed at developing new interactions with employers that eliminate aspects of hierarchy along the lines of gender, race, and class.

Before describing domestic workers in terms of particular processes and specific structural relationships, I discuss the broad theoretical implications of paid and unpaid domestic work. In the following chapters, I will explore housework as both a paid and an unpaid activity and consider the intersections of class, race, and gender. I show how the dialectic of domestic service is rooted in the structural positions and self-interests of both protagonists. Further, I establish the dialectic nature of the development of practices that have altered and continue to change the institution itself. Thus as domestic workers developed strategies and practices to open up new areas of freedom, employers developed new forms of control. I begin with historical overview to show that housework was not always "women's work," nor is domestic service today.[19] Chapter four uncovers the patterns and circumstances that shaped domestic service into an institution dominated by women of color in the United States. I then turn to a microanalysis of the structure of housework and social relationships in domestic service. The experiences of women of color employed as domestics presented in chapter five reveal the way in which cultural values supporting the systems of gender, class, and racial domination direct the structure of housework and the complex set of needs that domestic labor fulfills. Chapter six examines the strategies used by domestics to restructure the work to eliminate demeaning and degrading aspects and to redefine the social relationship between domestics and employers. Chapter seven reflects on the intersections of race, class, and gender in domestic work and speculates on the content and definition of sisterhood that will determine a struggle that transforms housework.

Chapter 2

WOMEN'S WORK IS NEVER DONE

Popular images of the family romanticize the allocation of household tasks; in the traditional Norman Rockwell image, smiling mothers wearing aprons place delicious meals on the dining room table, husbands carry trash to the curb once a week, and sons cheerfully mow the lawn while daughters bake cookies. Recently this image has been slightly modified as commercials and movies depict fathers and children stepping into the homemaker's role during mothers' absences. Family members are shown being challenged to learn new household skills but enthusiastically joining in the "fun" of cooking, shopping, and doing the laundry. However, despite the media's illusion of gaiety and excitement, most household chores are experienced as drudgery. There is little enthusiasm or competition to wash and iron clothes, scrub bathrooms, or vacuum and dust the living room. Furthermore, the media continue to reflect and reinforce the sexual division of domestic labor. Pronatalism is everywhere, motherhood is assumed for all women, and homemaking is treated as a vocation and the "true" woman's career.

No longer brushed aside as trivial, housework has been analyzed in its centrality by social scientists interested in the family, work, gender, and the exploration of the norms and values of everyday life. Family life, gender roles, and marital relationships are embedded in housework. The ways in which meals are prepared and served, clothes are laundered and ironed, beds are made, and carpets are vacuumed reveal how we as individuals and as families reproduce or change culture in our daily lives. Housework is recognized as a window into the joys, pain, resentment, pride, and confusion experienced by family members.[1]

In the past, studies of household labor have not generally considered the employment of domestic workers; concomitantly, studies of domestic workers have not drawn systematically from the voluminous literature on unpaid housework. Rather, two distinct literatures have developed: one analyzes the unpaid work of housewives, and the other examines the paid labor of domestic workers. One reason for this distinction is obvious: domestic workers are generally women of color, whereas studies of unpaid housewives almost universally address the situation of white middle-class women, or, more recently, the plight of dual-career couples. Constructing a theoretical framework to explain the dynamics of race, class, and gender in domestic service requires an analysis that includes both paid and unpaid domestic work.[2]

Most employed women experience a "double day" which includes paid and unpaid work, but only domestic workers do housework on both shifts. Descriptions of the daily activities of domestic workers force us to contrast reproductive labor for pay with the unpaid work of the housewife: How does domestic service affect the division of labor within the family? What is the role of the sexual division of labor? How are tasks allocated between the housewife and worker, organized, and carried out? What are the working conditions? What is the pace? How is the work planned? Who performs what tasks? How does hiring a domestic worker alter the daily chores done by family members, particularly women?

This chapter reviews the literature on household labor, beginning with an analysis of the gender-specific aspects of homemaking activity from the housewife's perspective, that is, of housework as unpaid women's work. It then reviews theoretical approaches to housework as paid labor. I have approached this task with two goals in mind: one is to bridge the gap between the discrete discourses on paid and unpaid housework; the second goal is to point the way toward the inclusion of ethnicity, race, and class in studies of housework.

Because the research on housework did not reflect the relationship between paid and unpaid housework that I found in the lives of Chicana domestic workers, my review of the literature is followed by an analysis of the "second shift" as experienced by Chicanas employed as private household workers. When I interviewed Chicana private household workers about their own housework, I was struck by the way in which their conversations interwove housework for pay and housework as homemaking. Instead of describing family and work as separate worlds, their accounts demonstrated how each activity affected and determined the other. As they recounted their employment histories within the context of their family lives, they raised my curiosity about structural connections between paid and unpaid housework. The essence of the double day is the social necessity for women to contribute to both economic and homemaking activities. Unlike other employed mothers, they not only had to clean their own homes, but shouldered the burden of cleaning employers' homes. Domestic workers thus present a unique situation for comparison because their double day consists completely of housework. By exploring similarities and differences between activities that Chicana household workers engage in at work and at home, we can better understand the structure of housework and the relationships surrounding that work.

GENDER AND HOUSEWORK

To underscore women's unpaid work, feminist rethinking of the role of women in the economy, stimulated intense theoretical debates about the relationship between housework and the economy. Embedded in the literature is the assumption that housework is the sole property of the housewife and that women's work in the home is the focal point of gender inequality.[3] Theorists have argued, as Ann Oakley[4] and Nona Glazer[5] did, that the housewife carries the burden of housework regardless of whether she actually does the work, because social responsibility for the work has not been shifted from her shoulders.

Housework overdetermines women's lives in the home, but, perhaps more importantly, the outside labor market exploits the social ideology and role expectations of women and reproduces the structure in a gendered work force.[6] Debates over "wages for housework" and women as an economic class were central to what has come to be termed the "domestic-labour debate."[7] Although the domestic-labor debate may appear to some as doctrinal squabble, proposing the conversion of housework into wage labor was an attempt to "unmask" the mystifying relationship of women's labor to the economic system.[8] Although the debate was engaged more fully in Italy and England, the demand of "wages for housework" influenced feminist thinking about housework in general.

Studies of gender stratification in the home confirmed women's common experience. Housework was defined as symbolic of women's oppression, and many feminists argued that the shared experiences of the role of housewife united all women. Empirical studies revealing that husbands actually contribute very little to household labor led Heidi Hartmann to conclude that "the rather small, selective and unresponsive contribution of the husband to housework raises the suspicion that the husband may be a net drain on the family's resources of housework time—that is, husbands may require more household work than they contribute."[9]

When assistance is obtained from family members, it tends to be sex-segregated by task: typically, husbands do minor repairs;[10] daughters wash dishes and sons carry out the trash.[11] Clearly, husbands and children, as well as every producer of cleaning detergent and household appliances, consider housework "women's work." Julie Matthaei has noted that men's participation in housework is always secondary to their jobs and careers.[12] Ann Game and Rosemary Pringle have observed that the situation may actually be worsening as a result of the "liberating effects of technology" which have eliminated such chores as chopping wood and have broken down the sexual division of labor into chores previously defined as masculine. Women's work is extended through "do-it-yourself" kits which have shifted certain tasks previously considered "men's work" to the housewife.[13]

The sentencing of women to homemaking has frequently been rationalized by their male partners. In her essay "The Politics of Housework," Pat Mainardi analyzed responses from "significant others" about why they do not share the housework. She found responses such as: "I don't do it very well" or "We should each do the things we're best at."[14] Probably the most common response is "She likes housework." Just such a statement incited Betty Friedan's germinal study of housewifery:

> With the vision of the happy modern housewife as she is described by the magazines and television, by the functional sociologists, the sex-directed educators, and the manipulators dancing before my eyes, I went in search of one of those mystical creatures.[15]

Instead, Friedan found women whose "voices were dull and flat, or nervous and jittery; they were listless and bored, or frenetically 'busy' around the house or community." Many were suffering from what she termed "housewife's fatigue."[16] In her study of housewives, Ann Oakley similarly found women depressed and suffering from low self-esteem.[17] These and other studies show how the stigma of housework has impacted women. Housework is generally characterized as "a series of unconnected tasks, none of which require the worker's full attention."[18] Housewives describe the work as monotonous, fragmented and socially isolating, lacking intrinsic satisfaction. Autonomy is wanting because it only "frees women from" housework rather than "frees them to" pursue activities outside homemaking.[19] They themselves generally consider housework to be low-status and are aware that it is socially devalued work. Perhaps because of this, full-time housewives are considered "uninteresting, worthless" people. Studies of housewives reveal that an overwhelming number of modern women resent both the drudgery of housework and the responsibility allocated to them on the basis of their sex. Not surprisingly, several researchers have found that many women prefer to work outside the home rather than to stay home and do housework.[20]

Housework as Unpaid Labor

Research boundaries continue to be predicated on the separation of work and family into separate spheres. The reasons for this are of critical importance. The first set of reasons have to do with the affective setting in which housework takes place. Housework is performed within the context of diffuse family roles in which women are mothers, wives, or both. Housework has thereby become fused with the roles of mother and wife. Since fulfilling mother and wife roles are not considered labor, many household tasks involving the maintenance of the family are simply not counted as work. Furthermore, the home is assumed to be an escape from the world of work and a haven for leisure activities and emotional warmth. In fact, activities in the home are sometimes confused with leisure; housewives are perceived as enjoying free time not available to employed women. Full-time homemaking has even been held up to women as preferable to employment outside the home because they can be their own boss.[21] Oakley captured the essence of this attitude: "the housewife role is a freely chosen occupation offering scope for individual creative skill. While one says that housewives are oppressed, the other says that housewives are free from the oppression of most workers—restrictions of personality and freedom consequent on the imposition of repetitive industrial work routines and work rhythms."[22]

Housework has further been disqualified as "real" work by referring to it as a "labor of love." Even housewives themselves do not always recognize housework as work and confuse the activity with leisure.[23] This confusion, Meg Luxton explained, lies in the fact that housework incorporates both the "skill as a worker and her affection for her family."[24] The fulfillment of housework obligations is thus tied to self-definitions of good mothers and wives. Observing the relationship between deskilling of housework and the modern emphasis on the emotional dimensions, Game and Pringle wrote:

> As it became fragmented and deskilled, housework took on an emotional weight apparently out of proportion to its own in kind value. Thus laundering became not just laundering but an expression of love; cooking and cleaning were regarded as "homemaking," an outlet for artistic inclinations and a way of encouraging family loyalty; changing nappies was not just a shitty job but a time to build the baby's sense of security and love for the mother; scrubbing the bathroom was not just cleaning but an exercise of maternal instincts, keeping the family safe from disease.[25]

The second critical separation between housework and "real" work is that the former is unpaid labor. Housework does not fit definitions of work as productive labor, it does not produce values which can be exchanged in the capitalist marketplace. Presented as a dichotomy, "work" and "home" automatically function to draw contrasts: "Housework is typified as non-work, women's paid work is regarded as marginal and temporary, thus working wives and mothers are 'problems.'"[26] In identifying three ways in which housework differs from other work, Oakley drew attention to how exclusive the traditional concept of housework is and attempted to reconceptualize housework as work:

It is private, it is self-defined and its outlines are blurred by its integration in a whole complex of domestic, family-based roles which define the situation of women as well as the situation of the housewife. Housework is an activity performed by housewives within their own homes. The home is the workplace, and its boundaries are also the boundaries of family life.[27]

One approach to legitimizing full-time housewifery involve renaming the work. Previously, unemployed women dreaded questions about their occupation, responding more often than not with the expression "*just* a housewife." Recently, two alternative titles offering higher status have appeared: "homemaker" and "domestic engineer." The profound difference in the meanings of these titles describes both the ambiguity of the housewife's position and the social debate over how the problem might be solved. On the one hand, the shift from the term housewife to homemaker presupposes the separation of work and family. "House," the name of a structure, is transformed into "home," which implies an affective relation. Similarly, "wife," which immediately directs our attention to the man's economic power as breadwinner, is transmogrified into "maker," which stands on its own and has powerful connotations of creativity and production. "Homemaker" thus redirects attention from the economics of work to "home" and "family," reducing stigma by highlighting the aspects of housewifery that involve diffuse "motherly" duties. In comparison with housework, the role of either mother or wife is cherished. The analysis of housework as an expression of an emotional relationship stems from an ideology that presupposes a separation between the spheres of work and family. This approach is incompatible with theories grounded in the observation that the home is the housewife's workplace.

The term "domestic engineer," on the other hand, pushes in the opposite direction. Like other efforts to relabel low-status occupations (sanitary engineer instead of janitor), this title emphasizes skilled labor and identification with a high-status profession.[28] More importantly, "domestic engineer" is a label used to reduce stigma by identification with workers who do similar tasks for pay. Lewis Coser's comment about the low status of housework illustrates an attack on this attitude by comparisons with paid labor: "Unlike traditional work, housework today demands only a modicum of skill since household needs are provided for in the form of processed consumer goods and labor-saving devices, and this in a society in which achievement based on skill is most highly valued."[29]

Other researchers argue that the problem is not that housework is low-skill but that it is not paid. As Rae Andre pointed out, it "is not considered 'real' work, even though it meets other criteria and even though it is hard to imagine that anyone would do it strictly for pleasure."[30] Being outside the economic sphere of activity socially defined as "real" work, housewives do not receive the "right to any financial benefit or reward."[31] Julie Matthaei further argued that as

women entered the labor force, they re-evaluated homemaking as a job and concluded that since the work is unpaid labor, it is not important.[32]

It is instructive to recognize that the same "unskilled" tasks that consume
housewives' daily energy and time are indeed considered productive labor when
performed as paid work in the labor market. Washing, ironing, cooking, and
babysitting are always treated as work when completed by persons employed by
laundries, restaurants, and day care centers. This economic perspective suggested a strategy for reducing the stigma of housework that transcended semantic
changes. Computing the monetary value of housework was an attempt to give
marketplace value to homemaking activity. Comparisons with occupations engaged in similar activities—cook, teacher, nurse, chauffeur, and the like—have
been used to calculate the exchange value of housework.

Economists base their calculations on the accumulated market values of each
household task; they suggest that housework is far from valueless but may actually be priceless.[33] Ivan Illich developed the concept of "shadow work" to
describe:

> a kind of toil which is not rewarded by wages, and yet contributes nothing to the
> household's independence from the market. As "shadow work" household labor is
> unrecognized by either society or family members. In fact, the shadow work of the
> housewife in her non-subsistent domestic sphere is a necessary condition for the
> family wage earner to exist.[34]

In view of societal reluctance to accept housework as real work having worth
and value, it is not surprising that feminists are critical of former definitions and
have reconceptualized work in their struggle to understand the situation of
women. Naomi Gerstel and Harriet Engel Gross have argued that "for feminists,
the issue has been to make visible the unpaid efforts and activities involved in
'house' and/or 'domestic' and/or 'family' work."[35]

The Housework Dilemma

Although attempts to either refocus on "homemaking" or professionalize the
wide range of skills involved in housework may have served to elevate some
women's self-esteem, there were negative consequences as well. Time management studies have found that housework expands to fill the day: unemployed
women average eight hours a day and part-time workers average six hours a day
while full-time employed women average about five hours.[36]

In *The Feminine Mystique*, Betty Friedan analyzed the amount of housework
done by employed and unemployed women. She found that full-time housewives, even some who hired private household workers, frequently expanded
domestic labor to a sixteen hour day. In contrast working women managed to

accomplish the job in less time and to maintain a job or career. Friedan asserted that full-time housewives are deceived into doing more work. "The more a woman is deprived of function in society at the level of her own ability, the more her housework, mother-work, wife-work, will expand—and the more she will resist finishing her housework or mother-work, and being without any function at all."[37] Oakley also investigated the impact that social norms and values have on the actual amount of work done by women. She found that self-defined home-makers have an "extreme concern with the physical appearance and cleanliness of the home" and "an inbuilt tendency to raise standards and elaborate routines; those made redundant by machines, or by the factory production of domestic commodities, are replaced by new, more intricate, more sophisticated patterns of behavior."[38]

Similarly, efforts to establish housework as a vocation by upgrading standards and skills may have increased expenditures of time and energy. Women employed outside the home have not fared much better than "homemakers" and certainly have not escaped the burden of housework. Although the participation of husbands and children in household tasks varies according to the researcher's measurement,[39] their contributions remain minimal and, like full-time home-makers, employed women continue to be responsible for the housework.[40] One of the reasons that household chores have not shifted to other family members is because reproductive labor remains women's priority. Employment is always treated as the second career, whereas homemaking and motherhood continue to be socially defined as the major and primary career in women's lives. Consequently, many women feel guilty about their participation in the labor force and their choice not to be full-time homemakers. Some women respond by doing more housework rather than accepting assistance from husbands and children, thus defending their homemaking territory.[41] Women committed to both home and work attempt to be "superwomen" by overachieving in both careers.

Various solutions to women's housework burden have been proposed. Conservative groups and religious fundamentalists have resurrected the "cult of domesticity," arguing that the sexual division of labor in the home is natural and established by God. Advocates of this view call for women to accept their roles as mother and wives and to find happiness and fulfillment accordingly.[42] However, most women enter the labor force out of necessity and increased demands on their time force them to seek ways to restructure housework. Changes in the traditional structure of housework include limiting family size, working a different shift from their spouses, reducing housework standards, and purchasing labor-saving commodities and services. Women may also seek jobs that are less demanding and offer flexible schedules. Frequently chores and responsibilities are reallocated to husbands and children. For some households, the solution is to hire someone to do the work.

DOMESTIC SERVICE: PAID HOUSEWORK

Sociologists, anthropologists, and historians have termed domestic service in the United States "a peculiar occupation." Not only has the occupation continued for centuries, it appears to have survived the transformations of various economic systems—slavery, feudalism, and capitalism. To account for its persistence, some researchers have defined domestic service as a remnant of premodern or preindustrial social formations. They treat the occupation's peculiarities as simply the vestigial remains of slavery and feudalism.

Historical overviews of the specific situations of the domestic labor of white immigrant women and women of color have generated several theoretical constructs. One such construct, adopted from modernization theory, suggests that domestic service is a vanishing occupation. Another concept, put forth by Marxists who recognize slave and feudal roots in domestic service, analyzes the occupation as currently embedded in a capitalist economy. They define domestics as wage laborers. Various "midrange" theories emerge from each theoretical framework to account for the obvious race, class, and gender distinctions of the occupation.

Modernization Theory

Lewis Coser, one of the foremost proponents of modernization theory, characterized domestic service as becoming extinct because household labor had been modernized and the work was no longer useful in an industrialized and developed economy. His view is based on several assumptions about the changing needs of household labor. First, Coser began with the proposition that modern employers have needs different from those of their predecessors that can be fulfilled without domestic workers. He emphasized the fact that modern technology replaced the domestic by reducing the amount of necessary household labor and by making it easier. In the past, household work such as laundry and food preparation required heavy physical labor. Laundry, for example, was one of the chores to be transformed by an entirely new social and economic division of labor. It was subjected to twin processes: the changing social division of labor moved it outside the home and into the economic marketplace, while simultaneously the technological division of labor revolutionized the remaining tasks into a capital-intensive and mechanized job. Similarly, food preparation moved from hearth to market when much of the preparation of raw foods was concentrated, centralized, and mechanized. As technology advanced and the social division of labor progressed, the housewife's burden lessened. Modernization theorists concluded that American families would soon be able to maintain a respectable life-style without a private household worker and therefore servants would no longer be a necessary status symbol.[43]

Modernization theorists built their model in explaining the decline of domestic service at the turn of the century. They argued that the decline in the number of household workers evidenced the occupation's unnecessary role in modern society. This interpretation was given an air of inevitability when aspects of the occupation were characterized as preindustrial and thus not likely to survive the transformation into an industrialized economy. Among the traits that Coser identified as premodern are the following: the emphasis upon particularism over universalism, ascription over achievement;[44] "tasks that are defined as menial and hence below the dignity of the master and his wife";[45] and live-in arrangements that blurred the boundaries of the working day.[46]

Thus Coser characterized the employee-employer relationship found in domestic service as "premodern" and considered it to have retained many traits from the traditional master-servant dynamic. That is, domestic service preserved and was inseparable from the powerful economic, social and psychological relations—superior-inferior, dominant-subordinate, powerful-weak, rich-poor, and sometimes male-female—that defined and determined the master-servant relationship itself. Lewis Coser, David Chaplin, and others maintained that neither the Victorian aristocratic servant role nor the mistress-maid hierarchical relationship was consistent with our democratic society. Aaron Levenstein argued that the decline in household help manifested the workers' refusal to engage in servitude and was "evidence of a change in the American character."[47]

A subset of modernization theory emphasized the changing composition of the domestic labor force. The "changing-character" thesis was supported by pointing to the overrepresentation of immigrant and African American women in domestic service. Coser went so far as to assert that "only persons suffering from marked inferiorities and peculiar stigmas can be induced to enter it."[48] Levenstein claimed that the pool of household workers can "be obtained through immigration" only and argued that "the servant class was never native American; even in colonial days domestics came as indentured servants who ultimately moved up to higher status jobs once their service was over."[49] The "changing character" thesis is also apparent in studies alluding to a casual relationship between the poor working conditions found in domestic service and the composition of the work force (immigrants and minorities). For instance, Harold Wool contended that the poor status of domestic service as menial work is directly related to the number of immigrants and African Americans.[50] More recently, Susan Tucker drew the same conclusion, arguing that both African American and white women contribute to the devaluation of housework through their shared definitions of femininity. Incredibly, she declared that "both black and white women generally do not think that domestic work, particularly child-rearing, is a job that should be compensated by more than the minimum wage."[51] Advocates of modernization theory paid little attention to the fact that domestic service lagged behind other occupations in workers' rights and benefits; the focus was on the servitude nature of the work. Coser went so far as to speculate that even if working conditions were improved and minimum wage, social security, and other benefits were granted, the occupation would continue to be stigmatized as servile and workers would continue to reject the work.

The occupation has long been described as an entry level position for immigrants which offers social mobility to foreign-born women and their children to move on to higher-status and better-paying jobs. Studies of intergenerational social mobility among European immigrants led theorists to term domestic service a "bridging occupation."[52] Reformers and scholars praised the work experience for furnishing rural, traditional immigrant women with exposure to the modern world in a protected and supervised environment.[53] As reformers would have it, by offering opportunities to learn middle-class values and skills, domestic service prepared immigrants to enter the formal labor market. As a transitional occupation into the formal sector, domestic service was not only a sure way of modernizing traditional, rural, ethnic women but also offered the means for social mobility. In this model the mistress-maid relationship was depicted as one of benevolent maternalism, inculcating "new work disciplines and middle-class norms and values."[54]

Race Relations

Studies on women of color refuted many of the theoretical concepts derived from the experiences of white European immigrants. Rather than finding domestic service to provide a bridging or transitional occupation or a path to social mobility, women of color experienced it as an "occupational ghetto." To explain this phenomenon research focused on analyzing the racial and sexual division of domestic labor in which both employee and employer are women. From the days of slavery and feudalism, race and gender domination have been characteristics intrinsic to domestic service. Scholars examining the situation of women of color have found in the domestic situation a microcosm in which to study how gender, class, and racial inequalities are reproduced and reinforced. Housework provides a fertile area to study inequalities between groups of people because the act of cleaning up after others is frequently assigned to subordinates. Lenore Davidoff, for example, noted that sweeping and scrubbing floors is assigned to humiliate and punish inmates in the army, prisons, orphanages, and mental hospitals.[55]

Researchers have disputed the "changing character" thesis as well as the "bridging" model. For instance, in their analysis of the employer-employee relationship in domestic service, Linda Martin and Kerry Segrave discredited Harold Wool's argument that the low status of domestic service was a result of women of color entering the occupation. They pointed out that his argument placed the cart before the horse. Wool argued that the occupation was at one time neither low-status nor menial but became so only after the field was overrun by nonwhites and aliens. However, a more logical, less racist and xenophobic theory recognized that powerless and unskilled immigrants and minority groups were shunted into the lowest and poorest-paid positions. Thus, Martin and Segrave marshalled data to prove that the occupation was always low-status and that groups left the service as soon as other opportunities were available. Only immigrant and minority women remained because they had no alternatives. Women of color "did not enter an 'average' status occupation and in some mysterious way degrade it to 'low' status."[56]

Recent studies of women of color have been heavily influenced by social psychological perspectives. Several studies of domestics have ignored the structure of the work itself or have treated the structure as a reflection of the hierarchical employee-employer relationship. Conflicts between employees and employers have tended to be analyzed as struggles to maintain dignity and self-worth rather than as symptoms of structural race, class and gender conflict. Judith Rollins and other researchers have discovered ways in which women of color counter racist perceptions and create their own positive self-images.[57]

In one prominent example, Rollins investigated interpersonal relationships between white women employers and African American domestic workers. In her analysis, white middle-class women enhanced their own feelings of power and escaped the stigma of housework by employing a working-class woman of color. As Rollins explained, "The domestic is . . . an extension of, surrogate for, the woman of the house."[58] Not only are workers expected to do household chores previously done by the housewife, but they frequently are expected to fulfill the psychological needs of their employers and families. Hiring women of color functions both to relieve white middle class women from the burden of housework and to enhance their own feelings of race and class superiority.[59]

In social psychological explanations, relationships between employer and employee are subsumed beneath the abstract and general category of relationships of domination involving a personal and asymmetric nature. Rollins summarized the perspective in her argument that the personal nature of the relationship takes priority over all other aspects of domestic employment and "allows for a level of psychological exploitation unknown in other occupations."[60] In her analysis of domestics entitled "stories of resistance," Bonnie Thornton Dill similarly relied upon psychological explanations of employees' behavior. She described various ideal types, including confrontation, chicanery, and cajolery, and analyzed them as "interpersonal skills" used by household workers to manage employer-employee relationships. These techniques were used "to define what they would and would not give to their employers in the way of time, commitment, and personal involvement."[61] Whereas Rollins developed the concept of *ressentiment*, which emphasized domestics' domination by circumstances, Dill turned the coin to describe the workers' ability to create options and strive to "make the job good yourself." Dill pointed out attempts to resist and the coping strategies used to maintain dignity and self-worth. → shows strain in Spanglish

Although strategies of resistance and struggle are prevalent in studies on women of color, researchers have tended to interpret workers' actions within the context of personal management styles and other individual characteristics. Interpersonal relationships were thus given priority in the setting of working conditions.

Marxist Perspectives

In marked contrast to theorists like Coser and Rollins who defined domestic service as inevitably tainted by relations of domination and the low-status nature of the occupation, Marxist theory explains race and gender oppression as embedded in social relationships, not intrinsic to the work itself. Marxist theorists have emphasized five aspects of the domestic labor relationship: (1) race and gender oppression is not intrinsic to the occupation; (2) the occupation is part of capitalism; (3) domestic work involves physical and ideological reproduction; (4) reproductive labor is devalued because of social divisions of labor; and (5) housewives and domestic workers are both part of the reserve army of the unemployed and thus serve a vital function in the capitalist economy.

The historical-structural analysis of domestic service acknowledged it as a capitalist relationship in which race, class, and gender inequalities are part and parcel of the capitalist system of production, not simply residues of slavery or feudalism. The sexual division of labor which ascribes to women the primary role of housewife also functions to keep housewives and domestics in the industrial reserve army from which they can be drawn into the formal economy during times of labor shortage and into which they can return during recessions. Moreover, although women are all subject to the imperatives of the market and to sexual domination, their actual experiences reflect their class positions. The cheap domestic labor of women of color is one means by which white middle-class women escape oppressive aspects of their domestic roles. Their liberation is achieved at considerable cost to poor and working class women of color. Jacklyn Cock, in her study of domestic service in South Africa, explained why it is appropriate to analyze the work as taking place under conditions of capitalism: "Feudalism is not the dominant mode because workers have been separated from ownership of the means of production; nor is slavery because the appropriation of surplus assumes no rights of ownership over, or responsibilities for, the person of the exploited."[62]

Building on the domestic labor debate, Marxist feminists studied the mode of production to understand the division of the classes and specific forms of exploitation.[63] Marxism, as well as providing a fruitful paradigm for investigating domestic service as an occupation located within the class structure of a particular historical situation, provides another tool. Because the work takes place within the home, domestic service is part of the societal reproduction system. As such, it exercises superstructural as well as basic economic functions. Louis Althusser identified two modes by which superstructure institutions function. Those that function primarily with recourse to force and violence he termed the "repressive state apparatus"—for example, the police or army; those that function primarily by socialization he termed "ideological state apparatus." If one ignores the heavy Stalinist influences in Althusser's language, a fundamental understanding remains. It is not force which holds capitalism together; capitalism survives because it is able to reproduce the system without recourse to force.[64]

The family is the archetypical ideological apparatus. Its goal is reproduction in a physical sense but, more importantly, the family oversees the reproduction of the basic ideological forms—class, race, age, and gender ideologies, social expectations, folkways, mores, norms, and the like. Domestic workers participate both in the physical and ideological aspects of the reproduction of labor in their own families and in those of the dominant class. Although both classes of women—employees and employers—are devalued because they engage in reproductive labor, by hiring a domestic a middle-class woman is freed to pursue her own occupation, that is, employment that earns a salary much higher than the amount she pays the worker.[65] Moreover, clean clothes and dinner make it possible for the white middle-class man to present himself at the office and for the middle-class child to obtain the advanced schooling and socialization that are necessary parts of the reproductive of the bourgeois family.

Although the labor process in domestic service is somewhat different from that found in other work settings, domestics are engaged in battles similar to those of other employees. Women who employ domestics attempt to lengthen the workday, increase the work load, and restrain wages, while the worker struggles to do the opposite. However, differences in the labor process affect the character of the conflict. Karen Hansen has described some of the aspects of domestic service that hinder collective action:

> The labor process in domestic service is hierarchical, asymmetric, and deeply charged with idiosyncratic factors. The privatized nature of the job, its special locus in the employer's household, where most servants labor in isolation from other workers when on duty, do perhaps accentuate a servant's sense of personal dependence on the employer's goodwill. This sense in turn may adversely affect the servant's experience of sharing identity with other workers, particularly if he or she resides on the employer's property in a high-income residential area, further distanced from the mass of ordinary workers.[66]

Whereas on the factory floor class struggle, and racial and gender conflicts are structured, rule-governed, and collective; between the housewife and the

[handwritten annotations: "isn't see wider ramifications", "→ look @ ...", "see wider Ramifications"]

domestic worker, class and race antagonisms are played out at an interpersonal level. Even though employers traditionally set wages and working conditions, there is evidence that domestics in fact enter into a negotiating relationship with employers in which they informally agree upon a working arrangement. Exploring these negotiations and the ways in which domestics reorganize the work to "make the best of the situation" illuminates the structural as opposed to interpersonal relationship between the work process and employee-employer relationships. The conflict between employer and employee takes place primarily over the work process.[67] Employers typically determine the labor arrangement, and employees can negotiate from a position of strength only when they have other employment alternatives. Domestics resist employers' control over the work by shifting to nonresidential day work, working simultaneously for several employers, quitting jobs with employers who stay home to supervise, or defining the job by task rather than by time.

Discussion

The economic role of household labor has not been well conceptualized because of the categorization and separate analyses of the work as paid and unpaid labor. Even when researchers have acknowledged that housewives may not actually do the work, this narrow division has persisted. As paid labor, the work itself became overshadowed with concerns about the race and class relationships between employers and employees and was generally analyzed outside the usual work and occupational framework. Assumptions were made about the intrinsically "dirty" nature of domestic service and the personalism and asymmetrical relations between employer and employee in the occupation. As unpaid labor, housework has been analyzed solely from the housewife's point of view and made to symbolize the oppression of all women. Even though classical feminists recognized that some women hire someone else to do the work, the major focus of analysis remained the unpaid nature of the work. On an ideological level, some feminists advocated wages for housework as a solution to the problems of low status, disregard for women's unpaid labor at home, and the consideration of housework as an expression of women's nature.[68] Many feminists did realize that wages for housework "is a reform that does not challenge the basic division of labour and thus could never eradicate the disastrous psychological and cultural consequences of that division of labour."[69] However, the same argument has not directed researchers' attention to the ways in which household tasks are distributed and structured when the work becomes another woman's paid labor. By turning from the plight of the "wageless housewife" to a discussion of the occupation of domestic service-housework as paid labor—we move toward a new understanding. Domestic service provides a window into the relationship of housework to the economy per se.

CHICANA PRIVATE HOUSEHOLD WORKERS
AS WORKING MOTHERS

As working mothers, the Chicana private household workers that I interviewed experienced firsthand the issues addressed in the literature review. However, the emic perspective of these women workers differs because they engage in reproductive labor outside their homes for other women. Not caught up in the etymology of "homemaking" versus "household engineering," they called all of it housework. A profile of their double day, in which they clean both their own homes and the houses of other women, will set the stage for exploring broader issues of the influence of gender, class, ethnicity, and race on domestic labor.

The appropriate metaphor for housework is Hercules mucking out the Aegean stables. Women in their own homes experience it as the work they can neither stop nor finish. Chicana domestics like Mrs. Lucero know the frustration well:

> You can work all day at your house and by the time your kids come home from school—it doesn't look like you did anything. By four o'clock it looks the same as it did when you started.

It does not seem possible, but, for women employed as private household workers, even more of their lives is taken up by household chores and child care. Inquiries about daily and weekly routines revealed schedules organized around homemaking and housework. As I asked them about their own housework, it was obvious that the separate spheres of work and family, so frequently employed as analytical categories in both social science and popular literature, had little relevance to these Chicanas' lives. Unlike characterizations in the literature that portray working mothers in conflict between worlds of work and family, these Chicana working mothers described their employment as an extension of their homemaking activities. That is, they cleaned other women's houses to support their own household.

Not only was their day dominated by housework, their work histories reflected life cycles organized around the demands of housework and child care. Like most women, they used events such as children's births or entrances into grade school to recall their own work histories. It became clear in their accounts that leaving and returning to the labor market were regulated by the family cycle. For example, the three women who worked as domestics prior to marriage left their occupations upon marriage and later returned as day workers when their children entered school. The following description of Chicanas' experience as housewives and working mothers illustrate how employment as a household worker functioned as an extension of and strategy for fulfilling their homemaking responsibilities.

For Chicana private household workers, having a job meant doing paid housework during the day and returning to do unpaid housework in their own homes. At home or on the job, there was no respite from housework. Notice the language that Mrs. Castro, mother of five, used to describe her double day. The word "and" connects her thoughts on housework in a never ending series:

> And then I go to clean houses and I come home and it's a drag when you come home and your house is a mess, cause you just came from a clean house. It really upsets me.

Mrs. Lucero expressed a similar attitude but found relief in the fact that "at least I'm not there [at the employer's home] to see things get messy again." Differences from the paid housework done for employers were further distinguished by the structure of their unpaid housework in their own homes.

> It's [housework] so different in your own home because in your own home you don't only clean. You're doing laundry. You're keeping up with the kids. My phone is constantly ringing. . . . It takes me all day to do my house.

These women understood all too well the plight of working women. Homemaking activities ranged from the usual housecleaning, cooking, laundry, and shopping to endless errands, nursing, and child care. Although tasks and the amount of work differed among families, mothers with younger children were faced with additional tasks related to child care, including extra laundry, cooking, and housecleaning. Child care duties were frequently socialized to other family members by women who lived near their families of orientation; babysitting nephews, nieces, and grandchildren was not unusual.

Five of the women were caring for aging mothers or other relatives. For Chicanas, limited Spanish-speaking services for older folks required bilingual Chicanas to accompany their monolingual Spanish speaking relatives to various government and public offices. Lack of convenient and safe transportation similarly created demands on women caring for elders. Mrs. Sanchez cleaned houses for a living, did her own housework, and helped her mother with her house. She addressed the difficulty that extra chores and errands generate in an already overburdened schedule:

> If I don't work Monday and I plan on cleaning [my] house that Monday or whatever day it falls [that] I'm not working. It gets hard sometimes because I have my mother and I do a lot of errands for her and she knows she is after me. [laughter.] So sometimes I have to tell her that I'm going to do something so I can do my own [housework and errands].

Like most working-class families living from paycheck to paycheck, Chicana housewives were constantly seeking ways to reduce expenses. Many of the "modern conveniences" were eschewed "to make ends meet." Thus, in order to keep food costs down, Chicanas engaged in time-consuming food production to avoid the higher costs of ready-made, premixed, or frozen foods. One woman even passed up the ready-made *masa* for tortillas because flour and lard were cheaper. A few women canned fruits and vegetables, not as a hobby but because it saved on food expenses. Almost all the women roasted and froze green chiles. Most women assisted in the family garden. Other types of money-saving practices included hanging the laundry outside to dry rather than using the clothes dryer, darning socks, and patching clothes. Middle class people generally use the phrase "time is money" to justify buying convenience food and labor-saving devices. In the lives of these women, whose time was not highly valued in the marketplace, it meant the opposite—saving money by spending time.

In many cases the women arranged the job so that they were always at home when their families were there. Husbands' and children's schedules were rarely inconvenienced or altered. Consequently, husbands were not faced with the need to change the division of household labor. Like so many other mothers and wives, Chicanas were expected to cook, wash, iron, vacuum, dust, and care for children. For the most part, they did not escape the sexual division of labor that dominates household work today.[70] About half of the women described a rigid sexual division of labor in household duties. One of the most extreme cases was described by thirty-two-year-old Mrs. Ortega, mother of two.

> I don't pick up anything in the yard. I don't take care of any of the vehicles or nothing. I don't even have to worry about gas in the cars. He knows the inside of the house is my job and the outside around the house and the vehicle is his job.

All of the women approved of their husbands helping with housework, child care, cooking, and other household chores; yet this did not mean that they voiced dissatisfaction with the division of labor between wife and husband. To some degree, the issue of equity was related to the husbands' perceived position as breadwinners. The women tended to discount the importance of their economic contributions to the family, characterizing their wages as "pin money." They described their wages as providing "extras" not afforded by their husbands' incomes. Objectively, however, the items included food, clothes, tuition, and bills. Clearly, the "extras" purchased by these wage-earning mothers are necessities rather than extras. They may not indeed be necessary for survival, but these items, which husbands' paychecks cannot cover, would be considered necessary by most middle-class families.

Despite their traditional orientation, these women did not define their husbands' contributions to the family and home as limited to bringing home a paycheck. In discussing the allocation of household chores, the women were quick to cite a long list of their husbands' activities.[71] Husbands' tasks included gardening and yardwork, chopping wood, hunting and fishing, and house repairs. Two-thirds of the husbands maintained and repaired the family vehicles, thus saving on labor costs and limiting transportation expenses to gas and the purchase of parts. One-fourth of the homes used wood burning stoves to curtail heating bills, and husbands were responsible for chopping wood and keeping the fire going. House repairs mentioned by the women were not limited to minor do-it-yourself projects; they included building a garage, a deck, and remodeling the kitchen.

Although hunting and fishing were considered recreational activities, one-fifth of the husbands packed their freezers with meat and fish that supplemented the family's diet and reduced the yearly food bill. Husbands took responsibility for the work related to hunting and fishing, including butchering deer and elk, cleaning fish, and smoking or freezing their catch. Some made *carne seca* (jerky). Similarly, gardening was approached as serious productive activity. Husbands usually did the initial heavy work of tilling and planting, but both husbands and wives shared in the ongoing weeding and watering. Although these husbands' activities were not different in kind from the hobbies and Saturday chores of middle class men, the former approached the tasks with a seriousness rooted in economic necessity.

Unable to purchase the same amount of commodities and services as middle-class men, many of these working-class fathers engaged in supplementary economic activities at home, producing commodities or providing services for the market. As well as working full-time, a few husbands worked odd jobs. For instance, one husband made and sold wrought-iron doors, fences and window bars. Another hired out his construction skills around the neighborhood, and yet another paid for the rototiller he bought to turn his garden by providing a tilling service on weekends. Nonetheless, regardless of the chores that husbands performed, their work rarely equaled the never ending labor their wives faced every day.

Most of the women whom I interviewed actively pushed for a more equitable distribution of family labor. The only ones to accept the division of labor as unchangeable were married to husbands who disapproved of their employment. Despite cultural stereotypes about male roles in the Chicano community, most husbands approved of their wives' employment. Of the four husbands who wanted their wives to quit, three wanted their wives to be full-time homemakers; the fourth disapproved not of his wife's working per se but of her employment in domestic service. These four husbands expressed their dissatisfaction and pressured their wives by refusing to help with household chores. All four women accepted the unequal division of labor as the price they paid to work outside the home. Mrs. Lovato described her husband's tactic:

> He'll pick up his clothes and take it down to the hamper but he won't help me clean. He won't pick up a dish. He won't fry himself an egg—nothing.

Husbands who wanted their wives to quit working frequently showed their disapproval by creating more housework. For example, Mrs. Salazar's husband objected to her working and tried to discourage her from continuing her job by increasing her housework at home:

> He feels I don't have to go out and work. . . . He's the man and he should support me. He always felt that way. . . . He felt if I want to work outside the home, I should be able to keep up my home. And he makes it hard for me. He left his clothes scattered, like, normally he'll pick up his clothes and put them in the hamper but when I'm working his clothes lay where he takes them off, until I can pick them up. And if I leave my vacuum cleaner in the middle of the living room, when I got home from work my vacuum cleaner was there for me to pick up. He wouldn't pick it up for me. . . . He's pretty good about helping me if I'm home all the time. He's an old Mexican man [laughter]. He's tough like that.

As "shadow work," domestic service was relegated to the peculiar nonwork status commonly given to housework. Even when husbands and other family members did not discourage the women from entering or continuing domestic service, their behavior indicates that they did not value housework as "work." Not only was work done by wives in their own homes not considered "real work" by their families, five of the women said that their employment as household workers was not treated as a "real job" by their families. This attitude was particularly common in families in which mothers worked part-time.[72]

These Chicanas recognized that their employment directly benefited the children. Their employment as household workers paid medical bills, tuition, house and car payments, as well as bought school clothes, books and music lessons. Like other working women Chicanas gained "privileges," such as relief from household tasks, only when their employment was defined as financially necessary.[73] The amount of assistance they received from their husbands and children was partially related to the families' attitudes toward their employment as private household workers. Several women pointed out to their husbands and children that their paid labor provided an additional contribution to the family; thus, they expected help with the housework on a regular basis. Mrs. Salazar's husband reinforced this attitude.

> I guess he [husband] made the kids really buckle down and he helped them. I told them [children] since I started working that if you guys want me to work you guys got to help me because I can't do it and sometimes I feel really pressured you know.

My inquiries about husbands helping with housework were usually interpreted as having to do with child care. Descriptions of the ways in which husbands "helped out" were almost uniformly the same: when wives were not home, husbands were responsible for the children. They watched the children and sometimes fed them if the wife had prepared food before she left. However, "watching the kids" did not necessarily involve the broad range of tasks such as bathing or cleaning up after the children. Husbands were more likely to supervise older children and make sure that their chores were done. In fact, most of the married women with school age children mentioned that their husbands helped with the housework by telling the children to do their chores. Mrs. Segura's response was typical:

No he don't [do housework]. He'll tell the kids "that doesn't go there," "pick it up and take to the hamper" or "put it in your room."

A few husbands were noted for cooking at barbecues or occasionally preparing a favorite recipe, however, only four women said that their husbands "started dinner" if they came home from work first. The difference between "starting dinner" and "making dinner" typified most husbands' activities in the home. That is, they were more likely to be described as "helping out" with a particular task rather than undertaking the entire job. They were more likely to reheat leftovers than to cook, and they helped with the laundry by removing the clothes from the washer and placing them into the dryer. Taking responsibility for doing the entire activity of cooking or laundry tended to occur only under unusual circumstances. Mrs. Chavez gave an example of such an event:

The only time he cooks is when I've been in the hospital [laughs]—when he knows I'm not going to come home for the rest of the evening and figures I might as well get busy and do some cooking. . . . then he'll cook. But not just because I'm working, no he doesn't cook.

Husbands were more likely to do the grocery shopping, vacuuming, and picking up if they were retired, unemployed, or worked different shifts. Mrs. Gallegos said that she had argued with her husband for years over the household chores. As a construction worker, he experienced long periods of unemployment during the winter. After fifteen years, he finally assumed most of the housework during his layoffs, including cooking and laundry.

The sexual division of labor found among husbands and wives did not necessarily extend to sons and daughters. Not one of these Chicanas voiced a belief in "men's" or "women's" work in reference to their children. Both sons and daughters were expected to help with housework, particularly washing dishes, feeding pets, and picking up after themselves. These mothers expressed the importance for both male and female children to learn homemaking skills. Mrs. Garcia voiced the shared consensus that learning skills was an important part of children's socialization and assured their later independence as adults.

> When I was working he [her son] could do some of it [cooking] too. Even when he was young. I taught my children how to take care of themselves, how to fix themselves a meal. Things like that cause I figured that they're not going to have me forever. . . . Everyone helped. They had their chores. Like my boy had his chores.

All of the women expected their children at least to pick up after themselves, and most expected regular assistance in various household chores, like setting the table, washing dishes, folding clothes, throwing out the trash, feeding the pets, and vacuuming. Mrs. Lujan taught her children to cooperate in maintaining a tight schedule:

> My kids get their school clothes ready at night and I do their lunches at night and I fix lunch for my husband at night, you know everybody is in bed and then I get up early in the morning you know, and it is very easy you know, we are very organized. My whole family works with me though. I mean they're not dependent upon me to do everything for them.

These Chicana mothers expressed the belief that everyone in the family needed to pitch in and share household chores. Mrs. Rojas concluded that if everyone worked together to do the housework on Saturday mornings, the work would soon be done and the entire family could spend a leisurely weekend:

> On weekends—never did want to work weekends, we'd all pitch in and clean house. Everybody would take a room.

Although not as sex stereotyped as adult roles, the division of labor among children was influenced by the age of the child and the number of children.[74] Older children were expected to babysit younger brothers and sisters and were responsible for more household chores. Women with female children usually acknowledged that their daughters did more housework than their sons, but they did not exempt boys from household chores. The general situation seems to be: if the daughter(s) was the oldest child at home, she frequently did more than her brothers. For example, Mrs. Chavez described the allocation of chores between her daughter [the oldest child] and three sons:

> My daughter does a lot of it [housecleaning]. My boys—I have them vacuum their room and have them help me change sheets, fold clothes and things like that.

In homes in which there were only male children, the sons did more housecleaning and cooking.

> I always used to have the boys help me with the housework here at home. They used to do all general housework here at home—vacuuming, cooking. When they got old enough I would leave the food in the refrigerator all prepared and they would cook it. By the time me and their dad would get home they had everything [dinner] ready.

It is critical to understand, however, that despite the allocation of various household chores to both sons and daughters, mothers retained full responsibility for the work and did more than other family members. The only exceptions were found in homes with unemployed or underemployed older daughters. For instance, Mrs. Quintana was a single head of household with two daughters. Her older daughter worked full-time and contributed financially to the household. The younger daughter was unemployed and was therefore responsible for all the cooking, laundry, and housecleaning. In return, she received financial support from her mother and sister. Mrs. Quintana and her daughters were each responsible for ironing their own clothes, making their own beds and picking up after themselves. They shared equally in many other homemaking activities, such as grocery shopping and washing dishes.

In sum, the division of household labor left all these women with the double day. Like many other working mothers, Chicanas did not have enough help with housework, child care, laundry, and cooking. Mrs. Chacon voiced a wish to be able to afford to hire someone to help her with the spring-cleaning in her own home.

> I would appreciate someone—to be able to afford someone to come in and help me instead of taking one or two weeks to do the job. Instead you'd be able to pay someone to come in and have it done the way you want it done too.

Unlike higher-paid workers, they were unable to gain relief from the double day by replacing their labor with the labor of another. As workers in a poorly-paid occupation, Chicana household workers had limited resources and certainly could not afford the same solutions as middle-class women. Rarely could they afford to take the family to restaurants, order take-out, or fill the refrigerator with expensive frozen or precooked food. Nor could they afford to pay for child care. The cost of day care can be a burden for middle class women; it is especially onerous for low-paid workers. The lack of bilingual and bicultural services was also a problem in purchasing child-care services.

Faced with limited financial resources, they pursued other alternatives. Extensive organization and planning was a major strategy adopted by all the women.

To keep on top of the daily demands of housework and to fulfill the endless family obligations, these working mothers devised comprehensive plans. Mrs. Chavez's description of her daily activities throughout the week illustrates the constraints under which she operated.

> When I work [outside the home], [there are] dentist's and doctor's appointments that I have to be after four and grocery shopping in the evening. Washing clothes takes me two days out of the week to do it because I only do it in the evenings or on Saturdays, on Saturday's mornings and if I do it only Saturday morning it takes me most of the day. . . . You always have to give yourself sometime to fix dinner and leave it at least cooking while you take one of the kids to the doctor or dentist appointment. . . . when you come back you just set the table and everybody eats. So everything has to be after four.

For the majority of women whose extended families lived in the city, female relatives were an important resource. Relatives—particularly grandmothers and sisters—were frequently called upon to care for the children during the day.[75] Five of the women mentioned exchanging child-care services with relatives and neighbors. Relatives were especially helpful in preparing for the holidays. However, only women residing fairly close to their relatives were able to obtain regular assistance. More frequently, relatives were a source of aid only during a crisis. Sisters and mothers provided help during sickness, childbirth and emergencies. And, of course, relatives dropping in from out of town often created additional housework rather than provided additional help.

The Chicanas that I interviewed represented their choice of employment as a conscious strategy. When I asked, "Why did you start doing housework?" their response was not, "I couldn't find any other job." Rather, they began by comparing housework with previously held unskilled jobs. Jobs as line workers, nurse's aides, waitresses, or dishwashers had fixed schedules. Taking days off from fast-food restaurants, car washes or turkey farms jeopardized their employment. Explanations about the way in which domestic service was compatible with taking care of their families followed.

They emphasized that domestic service allowed them to arrange their own hours, and they could easily add or drop employers to lengthen or shorten the workweek. As private household workers, they were able to arrange hours and the workweek to care for sick children, to attend PTA meetings, or to take children to the dentist. The flexible schedule also permitted women to participate in school functions or be active in church and community activities. Having control over their own schedules permitted the women to get their children off to school in the morning and be back home when school was over. Domestic service did not demand rigid commitments of time, nor did the occupation force women to make the job their first priority. Mrs. Garcia explained:

You can change the dates if you can't go a certain day and if you have an appoint-
ment, you can go later, and work later, just as long as you get the work done. . . .
I try to be there at the same time, but if I don't get there for some reason or another,
I don't have to think I'm going to lose my job or something.

Two-thirds of the interviewees said that they selected domestic service over
other low-paying jobs because the occupation offered the flexibility to fulfill
family obligations. As Mrs. Lopez related:

That's one thing with doing daywork—the children are sick or something, you just
stayed home because that was my responsibility to get them to the doctor.

Mothers with preschool children preferred domestic service over other low-
paying jobs that they had held in the past. Unable to afford a sitter or day-care,
domestic service offered an alternative. Mrs. Rodriquez, a thirty-three-year-old
mother of two, took her preschool children to work with her:

I could take my kids with me. There were never any restrictions to taking the
children. Most of the people I've worked for like kids, so I just take the kids with
me. It's silly to have to work and pay a sitter. It won't work.

Mrs. Cordova also mentioned this aspect of domestic service as grounds for
selecting the occupation:

So that's what I enjoyed about housework is that I could take the kids along and
not worry about not having a reliable baby-sitter. So that's mainly the reason I did
it [domestic service], because I knew the kids were going to be all right and they
were with me and they were fed and taken care of.

Flexibility was not an inherent characteristic of domestic service. Neither was
taking children to the job. Provisions for both had to be negotiated in informal
contracts and labor arrangements with employers. Employers who requested
workers to stay longer—for instance, to do extra household work, babysit, or
wait for repairmen—complicated arrangements made for child care. They were
often dropped in favor of employers who were agreeable to working conditions
compatible with their child care needs. If the women had young children, they
were not likely to continue working for employers who did not allow children
to accompany them. If they had to be home at the end of the school day, they
did not keep employers who were unwilling to let them leave work at the specified time. Mrs. Lopez voiced this concern:

I always arranged with the ladies [employers]—always told them I had children
and that I had to come home early. I had to come home early. I'd just get so much

of that stuff [work] done and if I had to go in the next day to finish I would. But I would never leave my children alone.

Although cultural values regarding traditional sex roles appear to be a major factor in selecting domestic service, a closer look reveals other operative factors, including social and economic conditions that circumscribe and limit Chicanas' choices. The two oldest women interviewed (sixty-eight and sixty-four years old), attributed to discrimination and racism the limited job choices they had experienced throughout their lives. Mrs. Portillo did day work for thirty years. She stated:

> There was a lot of discrimination and Spanish people got just regular housework or laundry work. . . . There was so much discrimination that Spanish people couldn't get jobs outside of washing dishes, things like that.

Younger interviewees tended to blame themselves, citing lack of experience and education before opportunity as obstacles they had encountered in the labor market. After nine years of working in domestic service, Mrs. Fernandez identified lack of skills and other experience as limiting her employment options. With four children, this thirty-five-year-old woman with an eleventh-grade education pondered her future if she were to become head of household:

> I'm not qualified to do much you know. I've often thought about going back to school and getting some kind of training. I don't know what I would do if I really have to quit housework because that wouldn't be a job to raise a family on if I had to. So I would have to go back and get some training in something.

CONCLUSION

The literature on domestic service universally reports that women find the stigma attached to the role painful. Chicanas' descriptions of domestic service as a strategy for fulfilling both economic and homemaking activities, while true, masks the fact that their accounts also serves as mechanisms to cope with the stigma attached to the occupation. A few of the people that I approached for interviews declined, manifesting embarrassment and anger at being identified by their employment. Those who did agree to be interviewed were at least somewhat defensive about their work and dissembled by drawing attention to the benefits associated with flexible work schedules, autonomy, and the like.

Emphasizing aspects of domestic service compatible with traditional roles of mother and wife was another way in which they coped with the personal pain of being domestics. Highlighting benefits to her family shifted the woman's social identity from work roles to family.[76] Instead of viewing employment as a second career, they treated paid housework as an extension of their family obligations. Working was not considered the path to fulfillment or even upward mobility. They worked to contribute financially to the family. Unlike the common image that working mothers feel guilty about not being full-time homemakers, most Chicanas defined their paid labor as raising the family's living standard and, thus, as an extension of their obligations as mothers and wives. Since the status of motherhood is much higher than that of a domestic worker, identification with the traditional family role minimizes the stigma attached to the work role.

Analyzing the situation of the "wageless housewife" as well as private household workers directs our attention again to centripetal factors and social practices that assign women to housework and unite women over the housework issue. There are also centrifugal factors which fragment the consciousness of sisterhood into ethnic, racial, and class antagonisms. Domestic workers and their employers are caught up in a complex dialectic in which they construct and reconstruct the organization of housework.

Housewives and domestics encounter each other over housework, which is culturally defined not as work but as a "labor of love." As women, both employer and employee are responsible for housework in their own homes. In a sense both could be considered powerless victims. Although the burden of housework unites women, however, the completion of its tasks defines women's class differences. Poor working-class women are unlikely to have the financial resources to hire other people to do the work. Consequently, they can gain relief from the burden of housework only by reallocating tasks to other members of their families, frequently other females in their households. Hiring a woman from a different class and ethnic background to do the household labor provides white middle-class women with an escape from both the stigma and the drudgery of the work. White middle-class women not only benefit from racial and class discrimination which provides them cheap labor but actively contribute to the maintenance and reproduction of an oppressive system by continuing to pay low wages and by not providing health insurance, social security, sick pay, and vacation.

Relationships between white women employers and minority women are strained by the nature of the work domestics are expected to do. Women of color are hired to perform not only physical labor but emotional labor as well, and they are used to fulfill psychological needs. Housewives, whose work is defined as an expression of love, expect a domestic to possess similar emotional attachment to the work and to demonstrate loyalty to her employer. It follows that the more personal service is included in the domestic's daily work, the more emotional labor is extracted and the more likely the employer will insist that the domestic is "one of the family." Conflict arising from the extraction of emotional labor may be related to the employer's refusal to pay for fulfilling psychological needs. To understand the way in which emotional labor is tied to the structure of housework, we need to consider the employer-employee relationship in domestic service within the broader labor process. The structural approach turns our attention away from narrow psychological views of "personalism and asymmetry" as unique features arising from interactions among women toward more comprehensive and universal questions of how employers extract emotional labor from workers.

The critical analysis of gender within the work setting draws our attention toward new interpretations of interpersonal conflicts between women employers and employees. We come to understand that the home is one of the *sites* of class struggle and that sisterhood is one of the *stakes* of class struggle. The content and definition of sisterhood are determined in the struggle and by the victor. Describing in specific detail the methods used by domestics to minimize control and personalism—particularly as these relate to the work process—makes it possible to identify class conflict in the home. Recognizing the opposing class positions of the women involved transforms sisterhood either into another means for employers to extract emotional and physical labor, or, conversely, into the means for employees to improve working conditions and increase pay and benefits.

In order to discover how systems of race and gender domination manifest themselves in the capitalist wage labor of domestics, we need a clear understanding of the connection between the structure of the work and the social relationship. A consensus that gender accounts for many of the oppressive aspects of the structure of housework is emerging among researchers. As Oakley claimed, "Some of housework's low status is due to the low status of the people who do it—women."[77] Similarly, Rollins attributed some of the experience of oppression to gender issues: "the origins of household work are with women."[78] Certainly gender accounts for some of the low status of housework—but not all.

It is important for the development of feminism to transcend simplistic notions that housework is "naturally" dirty work resulting in stigma.[79] I agree with Ellen Malos that the structure of housework is determined by a variety of social factors, and housework in itself is "not necessarily menial and uninteresting. . . . but that it is the context in which [the tasks] are carried out that makes them oppressive."[80] By expanding the discussion of domestic work to include both paid and unpaid labor, the structure of housework becomes visible. We can begin to describe the historical processes that transformed the work into "women's work" and, in the case of domestic service, into "black" or "Mexican women's work." We can also glimpse the form in which capitalist relations transformed housework, submitting domestic workers to scientific management and other forms of manipulation and subjugation. Juxtaposing paid with unpaid housework issues reveals additional cultural and structural components of housework under capitalism.

Household work remains socially devalued. As Julie Matthaei stated so succinctly: "The impact of work on the social position of the worker has never been determined by the importance of that work to the economy; rather, work's social meaning is determined by the constellation of social relationships within which the work takes place."[81] Not only must the wage structure change but the relationships surrounding the work must be restructured as well. We know little about the way in which the structure of housework influences the relationships between employees and employers in domestic service. Many questions about the structure of housework and the social relationships surrounding the work remain unanswered.

Structure of housework. Why does housework continue to be devalued work even after it is sold in the marketplace? Is the low status and devaluation of housework a consequence of being labeled "women's work" or "minority work"? What aspects of housework are allocated to domestics, and has this changed the status of housewives? What components of housework are retained by housewives when they hire a domestic? Why? Does the restructuring of housework into paid and nonpaid tasks affect the monetary value placed on the work? Does housework change when completed by a paid laborer?

Social relationships. Do some housewives transfer the stigma and low status of housework to domestics by devaluing the work and the worker? How are race and class reproduced in the intimate setting of the employer's home? What is the relationship between the type of informal labor arrangement and the type of employer-employee relationship that develops? What are the sources of conflict between employer and worker? How do workers struggle to better their working conditions? Under what conditions are housewives willing to treat domestics with the respect and dignity given other workers and honor the limitations of the work agreement or contract? Can housework concerns be reconciled with the domestic's rights as a worker?

Chapter 3

GENDER AND CLASS IN DOMESTIC WORK

The process that moved economic activity outside the family and isolated women in the home also brought working-class and middle-class women into direct conflict over homemaking activity and definitions of womanhood.[1] Changes in the economy that created domestic activity as a woman's sphere directly affected the activity of paid household workers. All women were not able to achieve the ideal state of woman as unpaid homemaker. Class differences determined that many women would continue to work for a living, in fact many lower-class women found themselves doing housework for higher-class "homemakers." To the present day, homemaking has had contradictory meanings for women of different class backgrounds. Nowhere is this more apparent than in the interaction between mistress and maid.

EUROPEAN ORIGINS OF DOMESTIC WORK

A brief overview of the development of the family economy in Europe establishes a context in which to discuss the colonial family economy in the United States. Precapitalist economies were based in large part on family labor. The household was a commodity production unit. Marriages were arranged around economic motives. Early inventions such as the spinning wheel, which was widespread in Europe by the 1530s, were incorporated in the family economy.

Under the "putting-out system," both men and women produced commodities to be sold in the market as well as goods for home consumption. Production certainly involved a division of labor between men and women, between young and old. However, the different work done by men and women was not exclusive; wives, husbands, sons, and daughters were co-workers in the family production unit. As Tilly and Scott explained: "The labor needs of the household defined the work roles of men, women and children. Their work, in turn fed the family. The interdependence of work and residence, of household labor needs, subsistence requirements, and family relationships constituted the 'family economy.'"[2] According to Rhonda and Robert Rapoport, economic ventures were integral to family life; that is, "work and family structures tend to be linked as parts of an integrated cultural whole."[3]

The developing market economy and the capitalist production which it spurred alienated family activity by dividing it into one sphere of commodity production and one sphere encompassing all other activity. Factories replaced the home as the center of production for exchange. By the late 1600s, weaving mills with hundreds of employees were clattering alongside European streams. In her germinal economic history of women, Julie Matthaei illustrated the effects of the burgeoning capitalist economy on the labor of men and women. Similar work came to be structured into different activities: "Weaving and sewing were done by both men and women; however, men wove or sewed for money as craftsmen, fine weavers, or fancy tailors, whereas women wove and sewed at home, for their families."[4] Husbands, the property-owners, moved capital production outside the home, increasing their property by producing goods or services to sell in the market. Wives, on the other hand, engaged in self-sufficient production to fulfill the family's basic subsistence needs.[5]

Domestic service has roots in both slave and feudal economies, the traditions and customs surrounding domestic service in Europe influenced the occupation's history in the United States. Domestics were employed by high-status women to eliminate the drudgery of housework in their personal lives.[6] Aristocratic women and men ran households with large staffs, whereas the emerging merchant and professional classes had merely one or two servants.[7] Divisions of labor among the household staff of the aristocracy were quite elaborate, including coachmen, cooks, bakers, butlers, nursemaids, valets, gardeners, chambermaids, and laundresses. Although the internal hierarchies were based on the specialization of household tasks, they reproduced the sexual and age divisions of labor in the society at large; that is, male servants occupied higher-status positions than women and children. The principle of demarcation, based on skill, was maintained through variations "in wages, living conditions, food, dress, use of leisure time, amount and quality of contact with the employer, and, of course, prestige."[8]

Through centuries of tradition, a paternalistic relationship had developed between masters and servants and was codified in legal relationships. Paternalistic behavior toward servants was transmitted and later institutionalized in the New World and in Third World countries under colonialism. Paternalism is at root a familial relation, and masters expected servants to demonstrate filial loyalty and obedience in return for protection and guidance. One of the ways in which the treatment of servants as family members manifested itself was payment by in-kind services and clothing in lieu of wages. Even though traditional domination gave way to institutional forms, the paternalistic authority of a master over his household servants remained concretized in attitudes toward servants as childlike and dependent.[9] The master-servant relationship that remained the norm in Europe and America until the rise of industrialization[10] is illustrated in the advice given to masters in *The Complete Bachelor*:

> To be on familiar terms with one's servants shows the cloven foot of vulgarity. . . . Encourage your servants now and then by a kind word, and see that they have good and wholesome food, clean and comfortable quarters. Once in a while give them a holiday, or an evening off, a cash remembrance at Christmas, and from time to time some part of your wardrobe or cast-off clothing. They are just like children, and must be treated with the rigor and mild discipline which a schoolmaster uses toward his pupils.[11]

Divisions between economic and family enterprises not only impacted the wageless domestic work of family members but simultaneously generated changes in the demographic characteristics of domestic service. Enclosure laws in England and France had accelerated changes in the domestic work force by pushing landless peasants into urban areas. Rural migrants were favored for domestic service over the urban poor. The preference for hiring servants from rural backgrounds was in part based on the bourgeoisie's dislike for and distrust of the urban proletariat. Despite earthshaking rural-urban migrations that resulted from the industrial revolution and the rise of capitalism, there were shortages of servants. The master-servant relationship itself was subjected to intense pressure from the money economy. Men were the first to take advantage of the expanding work options available in the industrial economy, and fewer and fewer accepted employment as servants.[12] Operating within a seller's market, those men who remained in the occupation were criticized for their air of "independence and insubordination."[13] Pamela Horn described how male servants forced the issue by demanding tips and fixing rates on services. The breakdown of traditional relationships is clear in this master's complaint that appeared in the *London Chronicle* in 1767:

> Can a master expect fidelity, love or gratitude from a servant who is always grumbling when the house is not filled with vail-giving company; and lives with him

with such uncertainty, that his staying or going from quarter to quarter depends mainly on the number and disposition of visitant?[14]

Employers seeking servants began to hire women to fill the gap created as men turned to other occupations. The transition to a predominately female domestic labor force was accompanied by declining status and wages. In Theresa McBride's analysis, domestic service became the "major setting for female urban labor force participation during the transitional stages of industrialization."[15] The general pattern of the "feminization" of domestic service, which McBride described as occurring in England and France, is indicative of the changes transmitted to the colonies:

> Domestic labour becomes commercialized and absorbs a large segment of the unskilled labour which migrates to the urban centers. Gradually, however, the men move into the modernizing sectors of the economy, leaving the females confined to the service sector by restrictive social values and by their lack of training.[16]

Economic, political and social upheavals that revolutionized Europe during the 17th and 18th centuries not only weakened traditional systems of servitude but strengthened the standing of the middle classes. The expanding bourgeoisie had recently acquired the means to hire help and elevated servants to an important status symbol. Thus, the growth of domestic service among the middle class fulfilled specific needs that were unique to this class. For instance, servants played an important role in providing status to the *nouveau riche*. Commenting on this function, Theresa McBride wrote, "These new men from modest rural families had worked their way up to become the heads or managers of commercial and industrial enterprises. They now created a great demand for household servants as the symbol and the record for their success."[17] Employers willingly increased their work loads to earn enough money to maintain domestic servants. Unlike the upper classes, the middle classes themselves may have been only one generation away from servanthood. Uncomfortable with their position, the middle classes found it necessary to draw rigid class lines between master and servant. Management manuals and the use of livery appeared simultaneously with a barrage of propaganda against the moral values of the servant class.[18] This development exacerbated class tensions between master and servant.

The structure of the work itself underwent changes as the middle classes joined in the ranks of those "keeping servants." Unlike the aristocracy, the middle classes could not afford to employ large staffs. Instead, middle-class houses were staffed with fewer servants or, more commonly, one "maid-of-all-work." Increased work loads imposed upon fewer servants living in smaller quarters intensified master-servant relations.[19] Judith Rollins has pointed out an important change in the occupation. Household servants differed from their predecessors because they "were hired to supplement or take over what were considered the wives' responsibilities and during this period middle-class wives came to have primary responsibility for the hiring, deportment, and work assignments of servants."[20] Similarly, Theresa McBride analyzed the middle class acquisition of household servants as a significant factor in establishing the housewife as "the mistress of servants. . . . because it represented a clear concession of sphere of power which was specifically female."[21]

DOMESTIC WORK IN COLONIAL AMERICA

For the most part, the family economy that developed in England was transplanted to the United States. Colonial America was typically an agricultural-household economy that used household service to assist in both the production of commodities for the market and family maintenance. During America's period of colonization, most servants—slaves and indentured laborers—were not free. Indentured servants signed a contractual labor arrangement to repay transportation from England. Black slaves were also used as household servants. Over time the institution of slavery replaced the indentured system in the South while whites and free laborers replaced indentured servants in the North. In the first major study of domestic service in the United States, Lucy Salmon informed us that the period following the American Revolution saw a dramatic rise in the hiring of "help" or "hired girls." "Help" was employed to assist the homemaker, the two women often working side by side. Young women were commonly hired during busy times, especially harvest season, and during events that increased homemaking activity, such as illness or the birth of a child.[22] Glenna Matthews described housewives in colonial-American homes as being "in charge of a team that kept the household supplied and functioning. Many housewives had help from a 'hired' girl even if they had no full-time servants, and they could count on regular assistance from their own families."[23]

The changing division of labor was beginning to appear when the English settled along the eastern coast of the United States. On both sides of the Atlantic, capitalism promulgated sex-typed activities for men and women. Five years before the Declaration of Independence, Richard Arkwright invented the first spinning mill in England. As the new mode of production continued to expand, the family economy gave way to the factory system, creating job options and social mobility unknown to previous generations. Men's work further turned to commodity production, service provision, or ventures to accumulate capital. Products produced by women in the home, once exchanged in the economy, sank back into simple use value. As commodity-producing activity in the family was replaced by industrial production, women's labor turned from production to consumption.[24] Christine Stansell dates the transition to 1770s:

Except for the rural hinterlands, there were no 'pure' household economies—where women themselves crafted all domestic necessities—by the time of the Revolution. In many families, domestic production was only makeshift (a bit of spinning here, a little soap making there), as family resources in land and household declined. Finally, women of the strolling poor were entirely uprooted from household production.[25]

Women's and men's activities were channeled into separate divisions of labor, reflecting their different relationships to the mode of production.[26]

Social changes in family structure accelerated after the American Revolution. Household tasks were redefined and new familial relationships evolved. Mothering was no longer limited to the physical bearing of children but increasingly emphasized their teaching, nurturing, and the psychological development. Christine Stansell illustrates the relationship between the new imagery of motherhood and republicanism: "If virtue was necessary to citizenship, they proclaimed, then women could play a part in the new republic as mothers who educated their sons in republican values."[27] Homemaking became more and more woman's exclusive domain. She alone was allocated responsibility for child care, cooking, nursing, and clothing the family. Family life as private and centered in the home isolated women from each other, discouraging cooperative approaches to housework.[28] At the time that women's lives were limited to the home, men took more exclusive ownership of public life.[29] Beliefs about women's innate ability for domestic chores and men's constitution for the marketplace developed. Social attitudes and values developed to support the evolution of two distinct and unrelated spheres: "the public world of work, based on economic relations and the private world of the family household, based on love relations."[30]

The evolution of household technology and the division of labor, as well as changing attitudes toward children, concluded the privatization and domestication of women. But class contradictions and conflicts prevented the evolution of a universal experience for women. Rather than make women's lives more similar to each other through the gender-specific activity of homemaking, social class accentuated their differences. A closer analysis reveals that even though women's homemaking activity was distinct from men's economic activity, the husband's class position determined the structure of women's activity,[31] governing his wife's ability to purchase household items and to hire domestic workers. In his famous study of the leisure class, Thorstein Veblen defined "conspicuous consumption" as the key class distinction within the women's sphere of family life. "It had become almost the sole social function of the lady 'to put in evidence of her economic units' ability to pay.' She was 'a means of conspicuously unproductive expenditure,' devoted to displaying her husband's wealth."[32]

Working-class men still depended upon the homemaker to reduce family expenditures by producing essential commodities, "limiting their families' consumption of commodities," and "finding other sources of income."[33] Out of necessity, poor families continued many of the practices of the precapitalist family economy, including home production for exchange and the employment of children as workers. Unlike those in the middle-class homes described by Veblen, children and women were unable to exist as consumers; they were part of a family that could survive only as a productive unit.[34] Homemaking for poor women meant struggling to "make ends meet," and this frequently involved taking in boarders, raising food, and doing "putting-out" work. "A ceaseless round of scraping, crimping, borrowing and scavenging came in some measure to dominate the housekeeping of all working-class women."[35]

While working-class women struggled for survival, upper- and middle-class women transformed homemaking into a profession. As the urban women of the bourgeoisie were relegated to homemaking activities within the safety of the "home" in a private sphere, working-class women toiled in the urban neighborhoods for their survival. As Stansell explains:

> The solitary housewife would not emerge within the urban working class until the late 1920s, when cheap utilities first became available in the tenements. In the first half of the nineteenth century, the boundaries between private and public life were fluid and permeable. Laboring women made their lives as wives and mothers on the streets as much as by their hearthsides.[36]

The eventual price working-class women would pay for bourgeois women's new homemaking activity was not an unforeseen consequence. Ralph Waldo Emerson wrote about the oppression of women that the new standards of housekeeping caused in his essay on "Domestic Life": "A house kept to the end of display is impossible to all but a few women, and their success is dearly bought."[37] Class differences in homemaking can be most clearly discerned in what came to be called the "cult of domesticity."

THE CULT OF DOMESTICITY AND DOMESTIC SERVICE

Through the first half of the nineteenth century, capitalism flexed its muscles. Gas lighting enabled factories to add a night shift, and the whirring mills and looms churned out consumer products at an ever-increasing rate. While steam-powered ships and locomotives hauled streams of new commodities to markets worldwide, newspapers and advertising media began to whet the public's appetite for manufactured goods. Technological advance brought about by the industrial revolution significantly impacted household labor in two major waves. In the first wave, men were absorbed in wage labor outside the home while women continued to cook, bake, clean, do laundry, and nurse family members at home. In the second wave, technological advancements including household appliances and a wide range of new products restructured household labor. In 1810, a Frenchman named Francois Appert developed processes for canning food, setting the stage for a revolution in food preparation. Within the next decade, gas lighting opened up the family evening to productive activity. Elias Howe patented the sewing machine in 1846. The hardship of housework was lessened by hundreds of small modern conveniences for heating, lighting, cleaning, and cooking. However, even though new skills were acquired, a general "deskilling" of housework occurred.

The first half of the 1800s saw a concomitant shift in the social ideal of women's homemaking activity: "The true sphere of a wife and mother is not merely that of a ministering servant to the physical wants and necessities of her family; it is to be the enlightened instructor and guide of awakening minds, her husband's counsellor, the guardian and purifier of the morals of her household."[38] This ideology, which the historian Barbara Welter termed the "cult of domesticity," called upon middle-class women to professionalize homemaking activity and to devote themselves to the vocation of enriching family life, thereby improving society at large.[39] The ideology of the private sphere not only consisted of "turning the domestic drudge into a 'homemaker'" but emphasized the elevation of "her family's status by her exercise of consumer functions."[40] The new women's vocation expanded homemaking activity and helped to redesign middle-class family life around consumption.

Upper- and middle-class women were not only expected to purchase commodities to fulfill family needs, they were encouraged to hire servants. *The Ladies Repository*, *Harper's Bazaar*, and the other women's magazines of the day strongly urged housewives to supervise the work of servants rather than engage in housework themselves.

> Being a lady, in fact, meant *not* doing certain kinds of housework. "It is not genteel for mothers to wash and dress their own children, or make their own clothing," observed Lydia Maria Child, who arrived in New York in 1841. Neither did a lady scrub her own floors, do her own washing, make fires or empty slops. "Women might work, but not ladies; or when the latter undertook it, they ceased to be such," a contemporary explained.[41]

Faye Dudden explains that this ideology redefined middle-class housewives' duties: "Domesticity's new view of women's roles, while implicitly assigning the domestic to drudge work, called employers to 'higher' tasks and to supervision."[42] Middle-class women elevated their status by supervising the work of servant and shifted to roles of "authority and activity, rather than passivity and isolation."[43]

Changes in the composition of both the hiring class and the servant class led to the unfolding of new and different social relationships. The growth of the middle class meant that many more women were able to employ domestic workers, and the hierarchy of control that was common in aristocratic homes devolved into a one-to-one relationship between mistress and maid. Most domestics were now maids-of-all-work, which translated into working alone on the job. Their isolation was worsened by being treated as invisible, and domestics complained of loneliness even when they were surrounded by people in the employer's home. Homemakers came to think of themselves as supervisors, restructuring homemaking activity to emphasize the consumption of commodities and the service of domestics. Harriet Robinson's diary, for instance, reflects that her everyday housewife duties were primarily managerial rather than manual.[44]

Nineteenth century reformers urged middle-class women to adopt the modern employer-employee relationship found in the office and factory. But supervision was modified to fulfill the new definitions of womanhood. As Faye Dudden explained, "supervision permitted both middle-class and affluent women to forge an accommodation between the work ethic and leisure, to enjoy a measure of luxury and self-indulgence while retaining the moral authority essential to true womanhood."[45] Both benevolent and entrepreneurial versions of supervision developed around the cult of domesticity. However, each differed somewhat in their effects on domestics.

Supporters of benevolent approaches viewed domestics less as workers and more as apprentices or students. During the second decade of the nineteenth century, an economic crisis in the British Isles caused large-scale immigration to America. An ideological formulation developed that household service was a beneficial apprenticeship for young rural or immigrant women to learn skills of housewifery and to learn to read and write. Having equated bourgeois standards of housekeeping with "vocations of womanhood," Stansell explains that "they [mistresses] saw the sloppiness of their domestics as something more than the notorious idleness and laziness of the poor. Supervising servants became in itself something of a reforming vocation. . . . The servant's social life, personal affairs, dress and appearance came under examination."[46] The cult of domesticity offered middle-class women opportunities to practice "good works" without leaving their own homes. Dudden's review of Helen Munson Williams' papers uncovered a plan for "home missionary work." One objective of the project was "to restore the right relationship between classes, and to bring them nearer to each other in the ways appointed by God and nature."[47] Overall

the plan calls for each family to take a fifteen-year-old girl from a "respectable" home "to lodge, board, clothe and instruct in the business of housekeeping, including cooking and laundry work, for two years in return for her services without wages." At the end of two years she will be rewarded with a diploma and the ability to earn wages—i.e., work as a domestic.[48]

Entrepreneurial models of supervision concentrated on improving efficiency, raising standards of cleanliness, and developing the middle-class woman's own supervisory skills. Quoting Eunice Beecher's advice column, Faye Dudden illustrated how extreme the new standards of cleanliness became: "All utensils should be examined thoroughly, rinsed with hot water and wiped dry each time you taken them out for use, if only to remove what dust may settle on them while in the closet." [49] The housewife qua supervisor was concerned about maintaining moral as well as performance standards. Mrs. Beecher "warned that domestics might be guilty of such crimes as using dishtowels for potholders, or failing to close the kitchen door, not to mention forging recommendations and filching supplies." [50]

Swept along by the momentum of capitalist development, middle-class women applied capitalist management principles to the home, including relationships with domestic workers. The fervor with which advocates promoted scientific management is visible in this 1865 advice printed in *The Ladies' Repository*: "There's more room for science and thought, and skill in managing a household properly than you'll ever find in your dry-goods store, with a bank and a grist-mill thrown in." [51] Household tasks became specialized, thus encouraging the commercialization of household goods and the replacement of homemade goods with store-bought items. Housework was increasingly "rationalized" to resemble the "scientific" management principles of capitalist production. The emphasis upon professionalizing was so great that advocates of domesticity considered housewives amateurs in the scientific practice of home economics. In order to redefine the work that once had been considered women's natural domain, previous experience and knowledge had to be rejected. Matthews illustrates the change: "If the goal was to set standards, then people had to be taught not to trust their own tastes. Further, if people were to follow the advice of experts, they had to be taught to despise tradition and the advice of older women." [52] Tasks were depersonalized and reduced to a form that required only labor power rather than skilled-labor services. Matthews reflects that "work began to be valued most when it was most abstract, most devoid of emotional content, most male-oriented." [53]

Building on the capitalist approach to labor, middle-class women launched a movement for scientific homemaking that attempted to rationalize "those aspects of homemaking that resembled commodity production." [54] The movement incorporated principles of "scientific management" and the latest technological advances and techniques for efficiency. Matthaei's account of Lillian Gilbreth, a movement crusader, emphasized the close relationship between "scientific homemaking" and the development of capitalist production:

> Lillian Gilbreth, was the wife of the pioneer of time-motion studies, Frank Gilbreth. She worked at applying to the home the principles her husband used in the

factory—if scientific management made *commodity* production rational and effi-
cient, it could do the same for *home* production. The result was "scientific homemaking" or "home economics," a movement which treated the home as a factory
and the homemaker as a worker and/or administrator.[55]

The application of scientific management was based on the model of capitalism—domestics being workers and mistresses being administrators. Middle-
class women attempted to subject domestics to many of the same forms of control as factory workers, including the standardization of work procedures and
speedups. Domestics were reduced to unskilled labor and subjected to constant
supervision. As in the factory, the scientific management model served to increase the level of drudgery in household work, which became restructured to
eliminate creative aspects. Just as managers disregarded workers' experience,
skill and judgment in the factory, mistresses rejected the skill of domestics in
their attempts to gain control over them. Household workers became increasingly replaceable, because all they brought to the relationship was their ability
to work rather than particular skills.

Unable to oversee every housekeeping detail, employers instituted a variety
of supervisory techniques. Eunice Beecher proposed monthly inspection tours
of every room, drawer and closet.[56] She advocated checking the domestic's performance, as well as her honesty, by leaving objects or money—depending on
the type of "test"—under the carpet. Suspicion drove some employers to lock
away food and drink (preferably with patent locks), thus eliminating the likelihood that a skeleton key might be used.[57] Previously, domestics had enjoyed a
great deal of autonomy in making decisions concerning the completion of the
work and its pace. In order to increase their control over domestics' labor,
middle-class women redefined the labor arrangement on the basis of time rather
than tasks. Faye Dudden has emphasized the change from task to time as a
critical transformation: instead of "having a certain amount of work to do, as
help had, domestics were expected to be at work constantly unless explicitly
'off'".[58] The switch served to further lengthen the workday. Dudden's distinction, which I will term the shift from labor services to labor power, figures
prominently in the ongoing struggle of domestics. The nineteenth century wom-
en's movement to professionalize homemaking sought to control the work process by restructuring the worker's labor from skilled labor services to unskilled
labor power. Later, the dynamics of the struggle changed when labor shortages
resulting from industrialization created conditions that allowed workers to negotiate from a position of strength. Modern attempts by domestics to return to
contracts based on labor services are discussed in detail in chapter 7.

Overall, the cult of domesticity negatively impacted the working conditions
of domestic service. Middle-class women reserved the challenging, creative, or
emotionally rewarding homemaking activities for themselves, assigning to do-

mestics only the most menial and physically difficult work. Matthews notes that "a housewife with adequate help might turn over the day-in and day-out preparation of meals to a cook and reserve the baking for special occasions to herself."[59] New standards for cleanliness increased the work load for domestics. Upgraded standards of cookery and cleanliness such as the "need" to change and wash sheets once a week, to polish the silver every Thursday, or to prepare balanced and creative meals,[60] resulted in additional work[61] and increased the number of hours spent on housework. Frequently, regular maintenance cleaning was replaced with "ritual cleaning," which Lucy Salmon defined as "the tradition that silver must be cleaned on Thursdays, sweeping done on Fridays, and all sleeping-rooms put in order before nine o'clock in the morning."[62]

Finicky supervision subjected domestics to "the meanness, unpleasantness, disorganization or arbitrariness of mistresses."[63] David Katzman has described the unpredictable nature of the labor arrangement: "Nothing except the conscience of an employer and her self-control protected a servant against her mistress's wrath."[64] The lack of respect shown by employers was so severe that Lucy Salmon claimed that no reform in domestic service was possible unless employers changed their attitudes toward the work. She cautioned domestic workers against "those employers who 'despise housekeeping,' who 'cannot endure cooking,' who 'hate the kitchen,' who 'will not do menial work'".[65]

Elevating supervision to a vocation effectively demoted hired domestics to unskilled labor that could be molded according to the homemakers' demands. Middle-class women were interested in hiring domestics not on the basis of prior knowledge or skills, but rather on subjective grounds such as personality and the degree of docile and obedient behavior displayed during an interview. If domestic work was to be downgraded to unskilled labor, tasks involving judgment, direction, or sentiment had to be eliminated or changed.[66] For many domestics, the workday began with orders about what tasks to accomplish, the order in which the tasks were to be performed, and detailed instructions about how to complete them. Supervision stripped domestics of their expertise and imprinted the work with signs of inferiority, deference, and servility. Changes in the quality of work and social relationships introduced by the "cult of domesticity" overlapped with transformations resulting from industrialization. The following section discusses the impact of industrialization on the homemaker and domestic workers.

THE SHRINKING HOUSEHOLD: THE LATE NINETEENTH CENTURY

After the Civil War, the pace of technological and social change accelerated. The decade of the seventies saw the development of the meat packing industry and

the pressure cooking method of food preservation. Canned fruits and meats began to appear in stores. The invention of the ice machine and refrigeration
opened local food markets to national and international trade. In the 1880s,
electric lights, phonographs and telephones began to change the tenor of family
life. However—in a curious dialectical reversal—instead of lessening woman's
household labor, "labor-saving devices" actually increased housework and led
to the expansion of domestic labor. Technological innovation often created more
work, viz, coal furnaces and gas lights, and still spread coal dust, ashes, and
grime through the house.[67] Laundering became more difficult and time consuming as a result of new fabrics and factory-made clothes,[68] and housecleaning
became more burdensome thanks to "machine-made upholstery, drapery fabrics,
carpeting, and heavily carved furniture."[69] Innovations such as ice-boxes and
indoor bathrooms increased labor through required maintenance. Alongside new
products and appliances, industrialization introduced new standards that added
time and energy to housework.[70] Public health reformers called for higher standards in cleanliness that similarly contributed to the demands upon household
labor.[71] Ironically, studies have confirmed that mechanization has little impact
on the amount of time housework takes.[72]

Ann Oakley, in her book *Subject Women*, identified three factors contributing
to the increasing burden of housework: (1) "existing household equipment is not
designed with maximum efficiency in mind"; (2) "technological innovation. . . .
acted against the 'rational' application of science and technology to housework
from the very beginning"; and (3) "increasing division of labour and increasing
routinization are the almost inevitable products of general technological 'im-
provements' in the work process, and what *these* lead to for the worker is an
intensified sense of powerlessness, not a feeling of freedom from the bondage
of work."[73] Furthermore, household technology was developed for individual
use, thus assuring privatization of housework rather than, for example, encouraging the development of cooperatives to decrease women's work.[74]

In situations in which labor costs are low, there are few incentives to mecha-
nize. Technological advances in household appliances and products thus did not
necessarily translate into labor-saving devices for domestics. As a matter of fact,
reformers of the day argued that mistresses relied on cheap domestic labor to
avoid the capital costs of modernizing their homes.[75] David Katzman stated that
"the presence of servants probably retarded modernization in the household, and
domestics would benefit little from its belated appearance in the home."[76] Nevertheless, technological advance contributed to the changing structure of domestic
service. The upgrading of housekeeping standards produced by household technology was more likely to occur in middle-class homes employing domestic
workers. Faye Dudden explained the relationship: "Families with domestics
could acquire the products associated with rising standards of living without
experiencing the burdensome necessity of caring for the incoming tide of furni-

ture, carpeting, and clothing."[77] As Dudden noted: "Since part if not all of their household work was actually performed by domestics, middle-class women were encouraged to use technological advances to raise housekeeping standards, especially those associated with cleanliness."[78] Stansell's description of the domestics' perspective on changing housekeeping standards illustrates the negative results for those actually doing the household labor:

> The profusion of detail and carving meant more surfaces to polish and cracks to dust. Possibilities for disorder increased with the number of objects. There were more possessions to be kept in place, more ornaments that could be broken. . . . Doilies had to be set right, mementoes placed correctly, pictures straightened, crystal polished. Fashionable appointments called for special care. Cushions had to be plumped up, houseplants watered and vases filled with flowers. Brussels carpets, *de rigueur* for the parlors of all women with a love for domestic niceties, were brushed several times a week on hands and knees.[79]

The subjective criteria used to evaluate workers added to the "opportunities for disagreement" between domestics and mistresses. Middle-class women responded by ignoring the validity of the labor issues involved and shifting the argument to one of standards. Consequently, mistresses' concern for developing and maintaining standards in homemaking led some middle-class women to advocate training schools as a solution to conflict with domestics. The School of Housekeeping in Boston was actually established by the Domestic Reform League and offered courses in "House Sanitation," "Chemistry of Foods," "Domestic Economy," and the "Principles of Housework."[80] In New York, the Children's Aid Society established industrial schools and lodging houses for working-class girls to teach sewing, cooking, and housecleaning.[81] As new opportunities for working-class women arose in the twentieth century, domestics began to gain a few rights as workers.

THE SERVANT PROBLEM:
THE EARLY TWENTIETH-CENTURY

While middle-class women stepped up their efforts to professionalize homemaking and elevated supervision to a vocation, industrialization was creating a shortage of household workers. The industrial expansion of the late nineteenth century increased employment options for women. Just as male servants turned to new occupations, women also left domestic service as soon as the job market expanded. Once other options were available, young women were unwilling to submit to "the drudgery, the regimentation, the unbecoming clothes and the coarse, work-reddened hands and arms which were their lot as domestics, preferring instead to seek employment in shops, offices and factories."[82] The shortage of household workers brought on by industrialization began a general decline in domestic service in the United States. In 1870, fifty percent of employed women were servants and washerwomen. By 1900, domestic service accounted for only one-third of all employed women.[83] Middle-class women referred to the situation as the "servant problem." George Stigler commented on the degree of concern the shortage caused: "Indeed one can hardly escape one or both of two inferences from the perennial complaints about the servant problem: either domestic service is a disappearing occupation or rivals the weather as a major conversational subject."[84]

Domestic service was distinctly different from other forms of employment. Although some praised the living conditions provided domestics, the reality was a far cry from the accommodations of the employer's family. Stansell describes how the servants' bedrooms "on the top floor were low-ceilinged, ill ventilated, badly heated and shabbily furnished."[85] Even access to modern utilities was denied to household workers.

> Water closets and bathtubs appeared on the second and third floors where the family slept, but not on the top floor where the servants' bedrooms were located. Domestics continued to use chamber pots and backyard privies and to take their baths in the kitchen. The family drew water for washing in their rooms, but servants still carried their own basins up the stairs and their slops back down.[86]

In an attempt to keep workers from leaving the service and to lure others, middle-class women preached its praises. Domestic service was extolled as the ideal occupation for girls because they were protected from urban neighborhoods and the work was based on feminine skills. As waves of Southern and Eastern European immigrants reached America's shores, reformers once again emphasized domestic service as the ideal place in which to expose rural and immigrant women to middle-class American culture and to instill middle-class values, particularly work discipline.[87] Obsessed with their mission to reform immigrant and urban women to proper feminine ways, mistresses restricted the type of clothes they wore and their leisure activities.[88]

Commenting on the particularly extreme working conditions—isolation, long hours, and the physically demanding nature of the work—Lucy Salmon described how they locked women into the occupation by eliminating resources that might be used to obtain other employment. Domestic working conditions lessened the possibility of having normal social relations or the time to develop new skills to obtain employment outside domestic service.[89] Unlike other occupations that changed under the impact of unionization and political pressure, domestic service lagged in gaining the eight-hour day, fringe benefits, and the minimum wage.

Training and certification was offered as a solution to the "servant problem." Household-training schools emerged along with home economics in high school. Mistresses thought of training and certification as a way to "weed" through applicants, as one observer claimed, to assure that only "attractive, intelligent girls capable of holding other jobs but liking housework" were hired.[90] Some domestics also advocated vocational training as a way of gaining respect and status. Training and certification were perceived as a route to upgrade housework to skilled labor; certification would elevate the status of household workers and increase their wages. However, training did not solve the problem. As one report concluded, "domestic workers with special training for their jobs received no higher wages than those without it. . . . It may therefore be concluded that the wages of household workers are determined by forces largely beyond the control of the workers themselves."[91]

Katzman pointed out a contradiction: the decision to choose work other than domestic service was not always "rational" in the capitalist sense, because domestic service frequently offered "earnings higher than most other comparable occupations."[92] Women employed as domestics typically received higher annual incomes than women employed in similar unskilled and semiskilled occupations. Moreover, live-in domestics were able to save additional money that was not spent on room and board. Yet even with the extra incentive of more money, women avoided the work or left the occupation at the first opportunity.[93]

Women's magazines voiced the middle-class housewives' view of the servant problem, "overlooking themselves as precipitating causes of the problem."[94] However, domestics pointed to the mistress-maid relationship as a major drawback in the occupation. Condescension and the lack of respect given to domestics by employers defined the low status of housework. Yielding to the complaints of domestics, a variety of proposals addressed the homemaker as the problem and pressed for a new relationship between domestics and middle-class homemakers. Domestics themselves pushed for working conditions resembling the businesslike relationship between worker and boss in the factory or office. Stansell found that even recent immigrant women in New York City began to negotiate certain working conditions as a result of their interaction with other experienced young women seeking jobs through the intelligence offices.[95] In 1915, the YWCA established a Commission on Household Employment and published a bulletin that advised how to establish housework as a business by "systematizing the work, regulating the hours, granting the worker sufficient time and freedom to live a normal life among her own people."[96]

Some reformers advocated establishing a formal and contractual employer-employee relationship. The Legal Aid Society of New York and Boston's Domestic Reform League were two organizations that attempted to institute the use of contracts between housewives and domestics.[97] Whatever specific recommendations were made to modernize domestic service, the personal nature of the mistress-maid relationship was recognized as a problem. I. M. Rubinow used a variation of the "vestigial" thesis to summarize the situation: "The peculiarities of the servant's position are due to the survival of medieval terms of contract."[98]

World War I and its aftermath brought a general prosperity, improving working conditions and opening employment opportunities for women. The war also slowed immigration, reducing the pool of women available for domestic service. Between the turn of the century and 1920, the percentage of employed women who worked as domestics had been cut in half to 16 percent. Perhaps because of the depression, the figure increased slightly to 20 percent over the following decade.[99] As always, domestic work attracted women with few other employment options. For those women who remained in the service, the shortage of household workers provided an opportunity to regain a measure of autonomy. A seller's market offered some leverage for changing the most oppressive aspects of the occupation. Furthermore, the rights gained by workers in the manufacturing and service economy established expectations that benefited domestic workers in their negotiations. The most significant change resulting from the burgeoning labor market was the reduction of work hours and the shift to day work, which were eased by the increased urbanization that permitted domestics to travel daily to and from work.

On average, domestics worked two or more hours per day longer than other working women and many worked seven days a week. Katzman estimated that "nearly all domestics in the nineteenth century worked at least ten hours a day, with a full working day averaging eleven to twelve hours."[100] Live-in domestics found it especially difficult to place limits on the length of the workday. Shifting to day work removed the domestic from the beck and call of the mistress and her family. In her study of the transition from live-in to day work among African American women in Washington, D.C., Elizabeth Clark-Lewis captured the significance of the shift to day work: "The women saw the change as a step toward autonomy and independence, and away from the dependency and indignity of live-in work. It was the difference between a 'job,' or 'work,' and 'serving.'"[101] Of course, autonomy and independence explains the opposition of mistresses to the shift from live-in to live-out; their ability to monitor domestics' loyalties, interests, and ideas was weakened.

Day work provided workers with the option of quitting unreasonable employers and replacing them with others less demanding. Quitting, or even threatening to quit, was a useful strategy to regain autonomy and improve working conditions. Domestics employed on a live-in basis were particularly vulnerable because they depended upon their employment for room and board. Consequently, finding a new employer and moving were more problematic and difficult. Day workers were able to replace employers at lower personal cost and could afford to be less tolerant of poor working conditions, importunate employers and low pay. Still, developing a working relationship with a new employer was not without its problems and domestics therefore quit employers only as a last resort.[102]

The importance of the twentieth century shift to day work cannot be overestimated. Day work changed the structure of domestic service by placing boundaries on the labor arrangement, increasing autonomy, providing the means to leave oppressive working conditions, and establishing a trend toward an eight hour day. As day workers, domestics were no longer dependent upon the employer and her family for companionship. Fewer hours spent in the employer's home reduced the degree of personalization in the mistress-maid relationship. Katzman identified the long term influence that day work had on domestic service by recognizing that "the day worker herself was the forerunner of the modern domestic cleaning woman who divides her work among a number of employers."[103] Domestics gained negotiating power and consequently were able to influence employer-employee relations.

THE DOUBLE DAY:
THE LATE TWENTIETH CENTURY

The transformation of homemaking activity from production to consumption became more complete and led to new developments for homemakers after World War II. Family needs were increasingly fulfilled through commodities or services purchased in the market. The proliferation of consumer goods and services deeply altered family life. Consumer goods and services not only fulfilled family needs but new ones. Household appliances and conveniences that were once considered luxuries became necessities. By midcentury, most families required the following commodities as basic necessities of life: air conditioners, refrigerators, washing machines, vacuum cleaners, clothes dryers, electric mixers, dishwashers, telephones, automobiles, radios, and televisions. In the waning years of the century, we have added stereos, microwave ovens, videotape machines, compact disc players, personal computers, and a host of other gadgets.

For many families, the rising standard of living created expectations beyond the husband's income. As consumers, homemakers felt pressured to purchase items necessary to fulfill their families' rising expectations. They struggled to provide for the family by saving, finding sales, and shopping for the most durable products. Nevertheless, many full-time homemakers were unable to fulfill their homemaking obligations without bringing in extra income. Consequently, middle-class homemakers joined working-class women in the labor force as a means to fulfill their families' needs. Employment was not so much a career

choice as an extension of their homemaking activities. Married women continued to define themselves first as homemakers. Women's life cycles reflected
periodic entrances and exits from the labor force as they patterned employment
around family life.

Not all women were forced into the labor force to fulfill their responsibilities
as homemakers. Needs are class-linked, and upper- and middle-class men were
still able to purchase the commodities and services required to maintain their
wives as full-time homemakers. Full-time housewifery remained a status symbol
for many men. However, in the process of developing homemaking into a profession, some women of the upper and middle classes became more involved
in public life through volunteer activities. Unable to find self-expression and
self-development in homemaking, many turned to careers outside the home.
Matthaei has emphasized this distinction: "The career woman. . . . wished to
leave the home sphere not for the good of her family, but rather for her own self-
development and fulfillment."[104] However, even privileged, educated women
with the training to pursue careers were faced with an either-or choice of family
or career.

Both working- and middle-class women's entrance into the work force contributed to the general upward trend of women's employment in the twentieth
century. Shortages of workers during the world wars encouraged married women
to work for the war effort, providing many with a smooth entrance into the labor
force. Postwar prosperity provided homemakers with additional job opportunities. The overall labor force participation rates for married women have increased consistently from 11.7 percent in 1930 to 15.6 percent in 1940. By
1950, 23 percent of married women were employed outside the home. The proportion reached 31.7 percent in 1960, 40.2 percent in 1970, and, by 1980 fully
half of all married women were employed.[105]

The increasing economic activity of women was one half of a social revolution. The male dominated sphere of production has in large part been opened to
women, but this has not resulted in a redefinition of homemaking. Although the
popular press and some researchers celebrate "househusbands"—the occasional
observation of men engaging in aspects of homemaking—the fact that this phenomenon is cause for comment indicates the extent to which family and home
are still thought of as the "woman's sphere." The "double-day" syndrome origi-
nated from the social expectation that employed women would fulfill their families' needs through daily activity in the work force and in the home. Instead of
confronting the problem head on, many working mothers seek relief from household chores by purchasing precooked, premixed, and frozen food, washable,
permanent-press clothes, and all means of labor-saving devices. Employed
homemakers find themselves in a treadmill situation; they must work to provide
commodities and services to fulfill needs that were previously satisfied by their
own labor as full-time homemakers. More and more working women find that

the ultimate way to avoid the double-day syndrome is to hire private household workers.

The major feature of domestic service in the twentieth century has been a continuing labor shortage. Matthaei noted that in 1900 there were 95.6 female servants per one thousand families; by 1960 the number had dropped to 33.3.[106] Homemakers continued to complain about the "servant problem," lamenting the passing of the days when they had had more control over the domestics in their employ. The labor shortage created a less docile work force, leading homemakers to complain about the laborer's attitude or quality of work as the "problem." Commenting on the ambiguous meaning of the "servant problem," George Stigler wrote: "Does it mean—as one often suspects—that a good servant cannot be hired at the wage rate one's parents paid?. . . . Or does it mean that the market mechanism does not work—that the offer of the going rate of wages does not secure a servant because servants do not move to the highest bidder?"[107]

Even though domestic service has become less oppressive since the turn of century, women are reluctant to enter the occupation. In some cases, this is related to employers assuming a traditional "mistress" role in which they attempt to train and supervise the worker as unskilled labor. Martha Sterns's 1951 article, "Castle in the Air with Maid," illustrated the persistently condescending attitude—once called paternalism—which might be termed "maternalism" now that women hired and supervised most domestic workers:

> It seems to me that the advantages of domestic service are many. Not everyone is born with an executive gift or can work well without direction. And yet many girls are born with a natural love for nice things, of physical well-being.
>
> By their own efforts they might not attain to the finer things of life, but it might be something to live in a house where they could see and care for such things, have comfortable living quarters and good food, and be paid a salary over and above. . . . Many of us know nice girls with clever hands who might be encouraged to train themselves for dignified and useful work for others, instead of forcing themselves into a separate life in an unfriendly world with which it is hard to cope. It is a release from the feeling of drive and competition to work under direction, or within a simple code of rules—we might say under protection. If not a white collar job, it is at least a white-uniform one.[108]

Regardless of the introduction of modern conveniences, the shift from live-in to day work, or the eight-hour day, domestic service remains undesirable work and only women with no other options enter the occupation. The overriding contradiction between mistress and maid is captured in the following statement made by a domestic: "Our employers trust us with their children, their valuables, their household appliances, their automobiles, the preparation of their food, their health and their safety. Yet, we are the lowest-paid workers in the U.S."[109]

In his study, David Chaplin found that a major source of worker frustration was having to satisfy employers' personal demands rather than meeting some objective standard. Despite their isolation, some workers were able to form personal ties to employers that could later be used to improve working conditions.[110] But the nature of the relationship between homemakers and private household workers was idiosyncratic. Linda Martin and Kerry Segrave described the situation as follows: "The domestic could never be certain of what would please or displease her mistress, since the job criteria were so subjective. She also never knew if what pleased her employer one day would displease her the next."[111] Workers continue to complain about employers' lack of consideration for them as human beings. For instance, one domestic recognized the source of the lack of respect in an article from 1960 entitled "Are Women Bad Employers of Other Women?":

> The women who induce hostile attitudes in their employees appear to despise housework as menial and low. . . . How, then, can they respect those who perform them [household tasks] for their living? I venture the suggestion that perhaps women still do not really like themselves and their status; that there exists in their subconsciousness, at least, a feeling of inferiority with its roots in the long centuries during which their marital and social position was, very definitely, inferior to that of men, and that this influences their attitude toward other women.[112]

In some areas of the United States, a seller's market makes it possible for domestic workers to demand more money and autonomy. The shift to day work has provided new alternatives in the occupation. Increasing numbers of middle-class women hire a private household worker on a schedule—once a week or even every other week. Many domestics employed as day workers have regular systems for maintaining a number of employers. Workers are thus able to replace employers with more ease than they could previously, and this increases their autonomy.

Nevertheless, domestic service remains in the informal sector of the economy, and the number of undocumented workers employed as domestics is expanding. In the late twentieth century, both minimum-wage and social security legislation have been extended to cover most types of domestic work, but many employers fail to comply and many employees prefer to work "off the record." Even though organizations such as the National Committee on Household Employment (NCHE) have enjoyed some success in publicizing the plight of household workers, unionization efforts have not yet had a demonstrative effect upon the occupation. For most domestics, the occupation continues to be regulated by community norms and values that determine informal-labor arrangements between the private household worker and her employer. Alejandro Portes's definition of the informal sector describes the current condition in domestic service:

It is work that is unstandardized and unorganized, requires no formal training and from which employees may be fired for lack of cause. Its workers are not included in the protective legislation covering wages, illness, accidents or retirement. And its labor is far more "elastic"; hired in good times and discharged during bad; hired for unspecified periods and fired without notice.[113]

Since the American Revolution, the number of workers hired per household has declined steadily. Some researchers point to this decline as evidence of a vanishing occupation. For instance, Matthaei argued that domestic service is a "vestige of the family economy within capitalism" and claimed that working mothers no longer need private household workers.[114] In part, her argument is based on the claim that commodities, labor-saving devices, and the reallocation of household tasks to family members eliminate the need for household workers. However, Rosanna Hertz's study on dual-career marriages found a preference for private household workers because day-care centers did not offer the personal services and flexibility in hours to accommodate the demands of the corporate world and in many cases were more expensive.[115] Statistics may not necessarily support the vanishing occupation thesis but may reflect the occupation's adaptation to America's late-twentieth-century family structure. The shift to day work made it possible for domestics to work for more than one employer. Today, most private household workers are employed in a different home every day of the week. Since most of their wages are unreported to the IRS, firm statistics are not available. However, a recent estimate indicated that 43 percent of employed women hired household workers.[116] Research on labor force participation of immigrants identifies domestic service as an important occupation in many women's work histories. Thus, the condition of domestic service is of much more than historical interest.

DISCUSSION

Relations between middle-class employers and household workers replicated class tensions and structured contradictions between capitalist and proletarian. Class struggle was played out as middle-class homemakers and domestics confronted each other over the length of the working day, the pace of work, and the expropriation of surplus value. As in industry, employers attempted to extract more labor for less pay while workers strove to work less for more pay. Chronic labor shortages resulted from women leaving the service to work elsewhere. Voting with their feet, women domestics transformed the occupation. They left live-in situations in favor of day work and quit employers whose direct supervision reduced their skilled labor services to simple labor power. Advice columns discussing the "servant problem" illustrate the ongoing conflict between mistresses and domestics over control and autonomy.

Homemakers and household workers have structurally different interests in homemaking activity. Unlike housewives, domestics have nothing to gain in making the work a full-time obligation. However, as several researchers have observed, unpaid housework carries an emotional dimension that merges the work with the internalized definition of good wife and mother. The ideology of domesticity connects women's identities to their roles as wives and mothers. This catches the homemaker in a dilemma; housework is drudgery that is instrumental to her identity. A homemaker who has her identity tied up in home and family cannot simply hire another woman to care for her family's needs without threatening her self-image. Thus, when private household workers are hired to maintain a particular life-style, many homemakers feel obligated to retain control even though they do not actually perform the work. By the act of supervision, the homemaker's home becomes a showpiece, a symbol of *her* womanhood as well as of her husband's success. As domestic service becomes increasingly dominated by women of color, particularly immigrant women, the occupation that brought women of different class backgrounds together in the women's sphere is now bringing race relations into the middle-class homemaker's home. The struggle between women that was once based on different class interests now has the added dimension of race and ethnic conflict. The following chapter looks at the role played by race and ethnicity in domestic service in the United States.

Chapter 4

DOMESTIC SERVICE AND WOMEN OF COLOR IN THE UNITED STATES

Census figures reveal that the percentage of women employed in domestic work has dropped steadily since the turn of century. In 1900, 28.7 percent of the female labor force was employed in domestic work, but in 1970, only 5.1 percent worked in the occupation. Although the percentages have declined, the racial and ethnic composition has remained much the same. Minority and immigrant women are overrepresented in the occupation. During the great period of immigration—1900 to 1915—large numbers of foreign born women took work as domestic servants. Today Latinas constitute the largest category of women entering the occupation.[1] Caribbean and Latin American immigrant women, many of them undocumented workers, are employed in private households throughout the United States. Thus the racial and ethnic stratification that marked domestic service at the turn of the century persists today.

Unlike the European experience of domestic service, the occupation in the United States not only involved class differences between employer and employee but racial and ethnic differences as well. In South Carolina, employers typically expect to hire African American women as domestics; in New York, employers may expect their domestics to be Caribbean immigrants; however, in Los Angeles and Chicago they can expect to hire undocumented Latin American immigrants. Racial, class, and gender stratification so typifies domestic service that social expectations may relegate all lower-class women of color to the status of domestic. Audre Lorde's account of an experience in New York poignantly illustrates the distinctiveness and transparency of racial and ethnic stratification:

"I wheel my two-year-old daughter in a shopping cart through a supermarket in Eastchester in 1967, and a little white girl riding past in her mother's cart calls out excitedly, 'Oh look, Mommy, a baby maid.'"

Lorde's account reflects our segregated social world—obviously the little white girl encountered African American females only as maids. Although most adult white women in this country would not be so naive as to verbalize such a statement about an African American child, employers do have a clear idea of whom they will hire. Whites are frequently socialized with role expectations that women of color will clean up after them, prepare their meals, wash and iron their clothes, and care for their children. Susan Tucker spoke to a number of African American women in the South who had actually been approached by white women in public places asking them if they were looking for work because they needed a domestic.[2] Martha Calvert, an African American Southern woman, understood the role expectation all too well: "So you're looking at me, and you can see I'm black and you know I'm from the South, so you know domestic work is something I know about, right? Just given those things about me."

This chapter investigates the situation of women of color in domestic service. The first section presents a broad overview of historical trends and regional differences that characterize racial stratification in the occupation. Special attention focuses on the Southwest, exploring specific policies and practices in the region that established and maintained domestic service as a racially segregated occupation. The analysis of domestic service in the United States frequently draws on an analytical scheme first employed by Lucy Salmon in 1897. She proposed three distinct historical phases: phase one started with English colonization and extended to the Revolutionary War, phase two began with the American Revolution and lasted to 1850, and phase three covered the period from 1850 to the 1900s.[3] Later analysts added a "modern" period, from World War I to the present. These phases are distinguished by the specific populations employed as domestics, they draw attention to the race, class, and gender dynamics operating in domestic service in the United States.

HISTORICAL OVERVIEW

The Colonial Period to the Civil War

In the colonial period, indentured servants were drawn from England's poor, the homeless, orphans, vagabonds, and criminals. Household laborers were hired for a wide range of household tasks including both agriculture and maintenance of the master's home and family. Remarking on the nature of servitude in colonial America, Soraya Coley observed that "little discrimination [was] made between the class of household servants and indentured servants, for household servants came under the same legal contracts and restrictions as did other indentures."[4] Consequently, the terms servant and slave were pretty much interchangeable. Masters frequently assumed total control over the behavior of their servants, including their leisure activities and marriages as well as their work duties. Indentured servants were distinguished from slaves in only one respect, "[following] their period of service, servants joined the ranks of the general population, with no legal distinction to be made between them and the freemen, although there were certain social distinctions."[5]

The racial stratification of domestic and personal services in the South resulted from the "peculiar institution," slavery. Summarizing census data from 1848, Charles Johnson reported that "slaves comprised 71 percent of all manual laborers, 36 percent of the skilled artisans, *98 percent of the domestic and personal service workers*, and 80 percent of the unskilled laborers" [emphasis added].[6] Ulrich B. Phillips described the situation as follows: "The repugnance of white laborers toward menial employment, furthermore, conspired with the traditional predilection of householders for Negroes in a lasting tenure for their intimate services and gave the slaves a virtual monopoly of this calling."[7]

Despite our images of slave gangs chopping cotton, domestic service was the major occupation for both men and women slaves, even though—unlike white indentured female servants in the north—black women did not work exclusively as house servants.[8] For example, the Charleston census of 1848 reported that "over one-third of the adult domestic workers were men. But while domestic work as a whole was not a sex-typed occupation for slaves, jobs within domestic service were commonly sex-typed."[9] The allocation of chores depended upon the owner's wealth and plantation size. Relatively large plantations with many slaves divided the workers into field hands and house servants. In contrast, middle-class and poor whites owned fewer slaves; therefore, the household worker "became the maid of all work, caring for the children, washing, ironing, cooking, cleaning and helping in the fields as well."[10] The relationship between slaves and masters varied according to the individual characteristics of the slave-owner. Slave narratives include accounts describing domestic service as being "like one of the family" as well as accounts depicting brutality and cruelty.[11] Elizabeth Fox-Genovese addressed the complexities of relationships between slaves and mistresses by pointing out that:

> The privileged roles and identities of slaveholding women depended upon the oppression of slave women, and the slave women knew it. Slaveholding and slave women shared a world of mutual antagonism and frayed tempers that frequently erupted in violence, cruelty, and even murder. They also shared a world of physical and emotional intimacy that is uncommon among women of antagonistic classes and different races.[12]

Female slaves frequently labored in white households throughout their lives and had to struggle to find time to care for their own families. Slaveowners' families demanded all the servant's time; she had time to be a "mammy" only to white children. The house servant was isolated from her family and from the community of other slaves. Carter Woodson depicted this dual function: ". . . she arose with the crowing of the fowl to sweat all but blood. On return home she had to tax her body further to clean a neglected hut, to prepare the meals and wash the clothes of her abandoned children." [13]

Judith Rollins characterized black slavery in America as "combining elements of feudalistic paternalism with the brutalities of chattel slavery, reflected what was perhaps the most anachronistic labor relationship that has existed in this country." [14] This situation continued long after Emancipation. A clear indication of racial stratification in domestic service can be seen in Southern poor whites' rejection of housework as "nigger work."

The fine words in the Declaration of Independence did not apply to black women laboring under the yoke of slavery. At the same time that black women were experiencing the most dehumanizing master-servant arrangement in the history of America, however, white native-born women were developing a more egalitarian employer-employee interaction. [15] Lucy Salmon described the circumstances in which white native-born women performed domestic labor as "a period chiefly characterized by social and industrial democracy, as the political system was also in its spirit democratic." [16]

Many writers argued that the relative positions of superior and inferior inherent in the master-servant relationship were not compatible with egalitarian thought. They suggested that, with the decline of unfree labor, both slave and indentured master-servant relationships would disappear. Alexis De Tocqueville is the premier example of one who believed that political democracy fundamentally altered the master-servant relationship. In his essay, "How Democracy Affects the Relations of Masters and Servants," he maintained that the relationship was fundamentally different because, under democratic capitalism, "classes are not always composed of the same individuals, still less of the same families." [17] In other words, class position is achieved rather than ascribed. The qualitative difference in the master-servant relationship under democracy is, therefore, the temporary nature of the servant's condition. De Tocqueville believed that:

> In democracies the condition of domestic service does not degrade the character of those who enter upon it, because it is freely chosen and adopted for a time only, because it is not stigmatized by public opinion and creates no permanent inequality between the servant and master. [18]

De Tocqueville further claimed that, because the structural conditions which created an ascribed servant class for the aristocracy had been eliminated, the social expectations of master and servant had also undergone a dramatic transformation. He fully expected service to lose its traditional functions—such as affirming and enhancing the master's status—and to become fully rational like other traditional trades modernized by capitalism: "masters require nothing of their servants but the faithful and rigorous performance of the covenant: they do not ask for marks of respect, they do not claim their love or developed attachment; it is enough that, as servants, they are exact and honest."[19]

The actual circumstances of domestic labor during the late eighteenth and early nineteenth centuries were far more complex than those suggested by De Tocqueville's theoretical analysis. Instead of withering economic classes and disappearing relations of domination and submission, we find the proliferation of master-servant relationships in which race, ethnicity, and gender replace class as immutable social structures dictating a person's place in the hierarchy. De Tocqueville's prediction that capitalism and democracy would make economic class distinctions less important was partially invalidated by the denial of social mobility to groups on the basis of gender or race. Channels of upward mobility were effectively barred to people of color, to women, and most especially to women of color. For some white women, domestic service was simply a stage of life or a bridge to better opportunities. For black and Asian women, for Mexican and immigrant women who were neither Anglo-Saxon nor English-speaking, domestic service was a trap—a situation of being dominated from which they could not rise and which they had to pass on to their daughters. Let us examine the situations encountered by different groups of women.

One group of domestic workers was composed of native-born young women who worked as hired girls for short periods of time to contribute to their families' incomes or to help a neighbor. Employee-employer relationships between native-born women and mistresses are perhaps best conceptualized as extensions of community patterns of mutual aid. Room and board were offered as partial compensation, blurring the distinction between paid and unpaid housework. Nancy Cott accounted for "helpers" in the eighteenth and early nineteenth centuries as "a function of age as much as economic need."[20] The peculiar status of native-born laborers was described by Faye Dudden as a relation of mutual aid grounded in a common community identity: "Although money changed hands, helping was not primarily a market transaction. . . . [T]he hired girl's treatment reflected her status as a member of another family, one whose independent standing in an economy of small producers was reinforced by republican ideology."[21]

The hired girl and the domestic represent unique working and living situations. Frequently, help was hired to see the family through an illness, harvest season, or temporary child care needs. Dudden distinguished "help" on the basis that the "work was organized more around task than time."[22] The experience of native born white women in domestic service was distinct enough for Dudden to argue that two different forms of nineteenth-century household service existed: help and domestics.

> Beginning in the 1820s and more noticeably in the 1830s, Americans began to hire more servants to work in an explicitly domestic sphere. Abandoning the language of help, they began to call them "domestic servants" or just "domestics." The difference was more than semantic; it reflected altered relationships, in many ways more burdensome to domestics and more problematic, yet more promising, for their employers than the helping relationship had been.[23]

As opportunities for public education and jobs in the mills expanded, native-born white women gained a measure of power and control over their work lives. As free laborers, white women who engaged in domestic work were able to shun any and all practices resembling indentured service or servant-master relationships. They frequently refused the use of livery, ate with the family, and participated in social events. Commenting on this distinction, Thomas Grettan wrote, "They satisfy themselves that they are *helps*, not servants,—that they are going to work with (not for) Mr. so and so, not going to service,—they call him and his wife their *employers*, not their master and mistress."[24] Hired girls were less likely to be subjected to the same indignities as slave and immigrant domestics. They were clearly hired to "assist" the homemaker in her daily chores.[25]

Unlike help, most domestics were not from the same racial or ethnic group as their masters or mistresses. Domestics frequently worked alone but not without supervision. They were expected to complete the demanding routines and labor-intensive tasks of housekeeping under the critical gaze of mistresses. Speedups, ceremonial cleanings and rituals of class deference were demanded of domestics. Affectionate personal relationships between mistress and help, like the "surviving letters to Harriet Beecher Stowe from the family's nurse" or "the Barclays' faithful domestic in *Home*,"[26] were not typically transferred to relationships with domestics from different ethnic backgrounds or with darker skin color.

In her description of the influx of immigrant women to domestic service, Lucy Salmon noted four events that changed the ethnic and racial composition found in domestic service: the Irish potato famine of 1845, the German Revolution of 1848, the establishment of treaty relations between the United States and China in 1844, and the abolition of slavery in the United States in 1863.[27] Irish immigration to the United States jumped from 20,000 to 51,752 in the year after the famine. Waves of Irish continued to immigrate at a rate of fifty to seventy thousand per year, at least through 1870.[28] While Irish men built railroads and dug mines, Irish women cooked and cleaned, competing with and displacing native-born American women in domestic service. German immigrant women, with a stereotyped reputation for order and cleanliness, were second only to the Irish

in their numbers in domestic service. Examining the 1900 census, David Katzman found that "among those employed, 60.5 percent of Irish-born women,
61.9 percent of Scandinavian-born women, and 42.6 percent of German-born
women worked as servants or laundresses."[29]

Throughout the first half of the nineteenth century, distinct regional patterns
developed. Geography influenced what were primarily racially based status assignments determining the composition of the occupation: Indian and mestizo
peons replaced Indian slaves in the Southwest, black slaves replaced indentured
white labor in the South, and native-born free laborers and immigrants replaced
Indians and indentured whites in the North. The situation was different on the
West Coast, where single male Chinese workers were imported to work the
mines and lay tracks. They left their women home, a fact that led to changes not
only in the racial composition of domestic service but in its gender composition
as well. David Katzman reported that "in 1880 California and Washington were
the only states in which a majority of domestic servants were men."[30]

As immigrant women entered domestic service in the North, class and racial
tensions heightened and native-born women began to avoid the occupation at all
costs.

> Whether from Ireland or Germany, the migrants represented a threat to native
> Americans. They were foreign and Catholic in an essentially Protestant Country.
> Moreover, they came at the time of initial industrial conflict. The sudden availa-
> bility of workers ready to take employment at lower than generally accepted
> wages. . . . fueled the opposition against them.[31]

Intense cultural, racial, religious, and class conflicts were played out in the
private sphere of the mistress's home. Racial and cultural differences between
employees and employers were so apparent that the "servant problem" became
synonymous with more general social conflicts over ethnicity, race, or religion.
Newspapers were full of recurring complaints about servants as "unskilled and
unstable foreigners who tended to drift in and out of employment."[32] Racial
stereotypes were reinforced when "the preference of mistresses for servants of a
given nationality or race became part of the folklore of household labor."[33]
Stereotypes of ethnic and minority women as "vulgar," "childlike," "ignorant,"
and Catholic in turn reinforced occupational stratification.[34] For instance, mistresses' attitudes that immigrant women were "unwashed, diseased, and ignorant
classes" led many to an obsession with cleanliness, which was manifested in
ritual handwashing and cleaning of everything the domestic touched.[35] Although
mistresses and domestics lived in the same house, the "barriers of ethnicity and
religion were added to the division of class in the United States and served to
keep servants and members of the employer's family apart." As Katzman pointed
out, the situation throughout the United States intertwined race relations and
domestic service.[36]

Black Women From Emancipation Through
the Depression

Emancipation cast large numbers of black women into the domestic work force, in direct competition with the first great waves of immigrants from Ireland and Northern Europe. Following the Civil War, Northern industries began actively to recruit Southern blacks.[37] Some families stayed in the South, making what must have been a socially difficult transition from slavery to the lower reaches of the working class. Others clearly preferred an unknown future in the North to the known fate of southern hospitality. Voting with their feet, freed slaves fled the plantations and small towns of the rural Confederacy and sought jobs and new lives in cities like Boston, Philadelphia, and New York.

In the South and North, however, job opportunities were distinctly limited for black women. Emancipation did nothing to free them from toiling in white women's kitchens and laundries. Freedom simply transformed black women from domestic slaves to low-wage servants. As Katzman noted, Southern communities considered domestic service to be "black women's work"; rarely did poor white women accept employment as domestics.[38] Moreover, the "racial etiquette" established under slavery continued regardless of African American household workers' manumitted status. Katzman described one particularly demeaning practice that has persisted in the South down to this very day.

> One peculiar and most degrading aspect of domestic service was the requisite of invisibility. The ideal servant as servant. . . . would be invisible and silent, responsive to demands but deaf to gossip, household chatter, and conflicts, attentive to the needs of mistress and master but blind to their faults, sensitive to the moods and whims of those around them but undemanding of family warmth, love, or security.[39]

After the Civil War, blacks deserted the South in droves. Former slaveowners complained of the labor shortage. Testifying before the United States Senate Committee on Education and Labor, white Southerners complained about the new servant problem. One former slaveowner, Mrs. Ward was shocked to discover that the servants "that we depended most upon and trusted and believed they would stay with us through it all. . . . were the first to go."[40] Katzman described an Alabama mill owner's lament that it was a "'difficult matter to get house servants at any price.' For his wife, the Civil War was most regrettable because of its effect on domestic labor: 'My wife says she would not have felt so bad about the results of the war if it had only left her negro servants.'"[41]

Despite their hope of avoiding oppressive social conditions and low wages, African American women who migrated to the North again found few job opportunities except for domestic work. Katzman noted that the recruitment of household workers was promoted even among the graduates of vocational- and industrial-training institutes. Specialized "household" employment agencies played an important role in importing domestics from the South.

> After the Civil War the Bureau of Refugees, Freedmen, and Abandoned Lands (the Freedmen's Bureau), motivated by a desire "to reduce the [Freedmen's] Bureau's relief roles" in the South, had its representatives in Boston in 1867 accept applications for "colored girl servants," and forward the requests to their Washington, D.C. headquarters. For white employers it promised to be advantageous. The Freedmen's Bureau paid the servants' transportation costs, and if the employee turned out to be unsatisfactory, subsidized the return fare.[42]

The conditions of domestic labor differed on either side of the Mason Dixon line. In the South, African American women were typically employed as day workers rather than as live-in maids. As day workers, they were able to place limits on the length of the working day and the amount of work done and thus retain more time and energy to interact with family, friends, and other members of the black community.[43] In the North, domestic workers were typically employed on a "live-in" basis. They had less control over the length of the working day and found it difficult to establish a private life, raise a family, or participate in community activities. Moreover, African American women seeking employment in the North were in direct competition with immigrant women, and racism placed black women at a disadvantage in obtaining the more lucrative placements.

The Southwest from the Mexican American War through World War I

The situation in the Southwest was different from those in the North and South. The black population was not a significant factor in the economy, but "Mexicans" occupied a similar position in the economy, including domestic service. There were two different Spanish-speaking communities in the Southwest after the region was annexed by the United States. Those born in the region had become American citizens by conquest and came to identify themselves as "Spanish Americans," "Hispanos," "Mexicans," "Mexican Americans," and later as "Chicanos." After the Mexican-American War and annexation, migration from Mexico continued and recent immigrants contributed to the growth of barrios and communities with greater "south of the border" identities. However, cultural distinctions within the Spanish speaking community were mostly invisible to the dominant Anglo population. Both native- and foreign-born workers of Mexican descent were identifiable by race, and both structural discrimination and overt racism resulted in dual wage systems and occupational stratification.[44]

Race-based occupational patterns dominated the economy throughout the region for more than a century after annexation, lumping together recent immigrants and U.S. citizens. The similarity in the experiences of Chicanas and Mexican nationals reflected not immigration status but discrimination grounded in physiotypical racial markers. In his book *Chicanos in a Changing Society*, Albert Camarillo summed up mobility patterns for Chicanos in southern California in the first third of the twentieth century: "Regardless of nativity and regardless of whether one was a second-generation descendant of Mexican-born parents or a first-generation descendant of one of the earliest Mexican settlers in California, the likelihood of upward mobility was almost nil." [45]

The development of occupational stratification in domestic service occurring after the Mexican American War was documented by Deena Gonzalez in her history of Mexicans in Santa Fe. She noted that in the two decades between 1860 and 1880, the proportion of women with Spanish surnames who were engaged in domestic service almost doubled, from twenty-five percent to forty-eight percent. The existence of a dual wage system is documented by the fact that in 1860 Mexican domestics earned one-third of the wage paid to white women in Santa Fe. White women laundresses or seamstresses earned twice as much as Mexicans. By 1880, Mexican domestics were paid forty-three percent of the wage paid white domestics. [46]

Preference for white workers—including foreign-born European women—relegated Mexicans to lower-paying positions within the occupation. For example, Lucy Salmon cited a turn-of-the-century advertisement in the *Fort Worth Gazette* that read: "Wanted—A white woman (German or Swede preferred) as cook in a private family." [47] Preference for white labor was not confined to Texas. [48] Victor Clark, an inspector for the Bureau of Labor, wrote an influential report on "Mexican Labor." His 1908 report argued that in some communities Mexicans were not hired as domestics because employers preferred white employees and considered even native born Mexican Americans to be foreigners and immigrants. Preferences for white employees were frequently couched in terms of competency: "Immigrant women have so little conception of domestic arrangement in the United States that the task of training them would be too heavy for American housewives." [49]

Although Anglo employers typically did not distinguish between Mexican Americans and Mexican immigrants, Americanization programs emerged throughout the Southwest in response to Mexican immigration to the United States. [50] Homemaking and other remnants of the cult of domesticity contributed content to Americanization campaigns aimed at Mexican women. Many Americanization activities identified domestic service as the ideal occupation for Mexican women and attempted to limit their labor to the drudgery of household work. These activities were spurred on by the growing industrialization along the western frontier.

The great coal fields of southern Colorado and northern New Mexico presented a specific case illustrating the development of domestic service as a "ghetto occupation" for Mexican American women. Thousands of foreign- and native-born Mexican miners were employed, but job opportunities for Mexican women were scarce. The miners relied heavily on women's work to support the family by taking in boarders and maintaining gardens for produce to sell. The largest and most paternalistic of the mining companies, the Colorado Fuel and Iron Company (CF&I), built the company town of Segundo, Colorado in 1901, in an area originally settled in the 1860s by Hispanos from Mora County, New Mexico.

CF&I maintained a "Sociological Department" to Americanize its immigrant work force. Adult education courses offered to miners' wives centered around cooking, hygiene, and other domestic skills. In school, miners' daughters were taught weaving, domestic science, and basketry. Dr. Corwin, the director of the Sociological Department, developed the curriculum because he believed that most of the children were destined to become miners or the wives of manual laborers. According to Howard Lee Scamehorn, the historian of CF&I, "girls were taught to maintain neat homes and prepare savory meals" because Corwin believed that by developing their domestic skills women would reduce drunkenness, which he defined as the major social problem in the coal camps.[51]

Of course, other benefits flowed from Americanizing and teaching domestic skills to the wives and daughters of Mexican American miners. The program created a domestic labor force ready to serve Anglo housewives in the nearby city of Trinidad. But there was a more important function. Like agriculture, coal mining was intermittent and seasonal; strikes and layoffs were frequent, but miners' daughters and wives found few employment options. Training them to take in laundry, cook, and clean to "American standards" meant that, during layoffs, the women's wages could support the family, thus keeping CF&I's trained work force from leaving to seek work elsewhere.

Relationships between white mistresses and Mexican domestic workers occurred within the employer's domain and, firmly on their home ground, some white middle-class Protestant mistresses took on the role of "missionaries," striving to recreate Mexican women in their own image. Combining the racial and religious prejudices of their communities with that model of benevolent maternalism called the cult of domesticity, these mistresses viewed Mexican domestics as ideal candidates for their crusades. They proselytized their imagery of motherhood and womanhood, campaigned to save the souls of papists, and tried to Americanize "foreigners" (even though Anglos were actually the foreigners in the Southwest).

The "cult of domesticity" advocated sex roles that were not really applicable to working-class Mexican Americans whose economic circumstances did not allow the maintenance of gender-specific spheres of activity—that is, women in the private sphere of the home and men in the public sphere of production and

Class misunderstanding

trade. Not understanding that it was necessary for Chicana wives to supplement the low wages available to Chicano males, middle-class women sometimes criticized them for working outside the home. Sarah Deutsch noted that Anglo women viewed Chicanas as having too few household duties and voiced the need to increase household labor.[52] Recognizing their own self-interest, however, most Anglo women advocated domestic service as the appropriate wage labor for Mexican women.

Almost twenty years after Clark's 1908 study, Emory S. Bogardus described similar attitudes in Los Angeles. Again, employers expressed the view that Mexican domestics lacked "knowledge and training" and were "handicapped because of this lack of knowledge of American household methods."[53] During the depression, Paul Taylor encountered similar discrimination in Colorado. One Mexican American recalled an employer in northern Colorado who refused to hire her saying, "People of your nationality are just terrible; I can't stand them, they're so crude, lazy, and so uncultured."[54]

In the Southwest, when Mexican immigrants and Chicanas successfully competed with immigrant white women for the higher-paying and higher-status domestic jobs, native-born white women moved on to clerical, sales, and teaching jobs. Although many Chicanas worked in the fields and in kitchens, domestic work still dominated their field of possibilities. One New Mexican woman, recalling her work schedule in the 1920s, said that she "topped" sugar beets in December and cleaned houses for the rest of the winter.[55] Wages varied, but they were universally low. During the 1920s, Mexican women working either as laundresses or domestics frequently made less than $200 a year. In Denver, Chicana domestic workers were paid between ten and twelve dollars a week.[56] Maria Chavez, a former domestic worker, remembered being paid fifty cents a day for housecleaning in Wyoming.[57] Josephine Turrietta recalled similarly low wages working as a domestic in New Mexico, "I went to work for fifty cents a day, doing housework."[58] Deutsch reported that "prospective employers continued to greet them [Chicanas] with both distrust and the expectation that they would work for a lower wage than other domestic servants."[59]

World War I through World War II

Nationally, there was very little change in the domestic-labor market until World War I, when job opportunities for African Americans in the North increased because of wartime labor shortages and restrictive immigration laws. African American women gained employment in a larger portion of Northern households as fewer immigrant women entered the service and their daughters moved on to employment in other occupations. Coley noted that between 1914 and 1915, "the number of immigrants who listed private household as their occupation declined. . . . from 144,409 to 39,774."[60] This shift was confirmed by Katzman's findings that the percentage of African American women in domestic service increased from 42.1 percent in 1910 to 50.2 percent in 1920. The proportion of African American women employed in northern households increased from 9 percent in 1910 to 19 percent in 1920, while immigrant women in household service decreased from 45.9 percent to 35.8 percent.[61]

After the turn of the century, more women began to find work in factories and there was a general decline in the number entering domestic service. Whereas in 1870 nearly half of all women in the United States had worked as servants and washerwomen, only twenty percent reported having done so in 1920. However, much higher percentages were reported for African Americans and Chicanas. In the North, between 1900 and 1920, native-born women servants dominated the occupation in small urban cities and rural areas while foreign-born women dominated in large cities. Katzman described the racial shift as follows: "Between 1890 and 1920 the number of white female servants declined by one-third, while black female domestics increased in number by 43 percent. In 1920, black women comprised 40 percent of all domestic servants."[62] By 1930, African American women dominated the service in many Northern cities.[63]

Similar conditions existed for Mexican women in the Southwest. As recently as 1930, forty-five percent of all employed Mexican women were domestics, and in some areas this percentage was much higher.[64] Mario Garcia, in his research on Mexican immigrants to El Paso, found that in 1920 Mexican women constituted over seventy-five percent of domestics and more than ninety percent of laundresses in the city.[65] Deutsch documented a similar phenomenon in Albuquerque and Denver, where the majority of employed Mexican Americans were domestics: "Sixty-five percent of unmarried Chicanas between the ages of fifteen and nineteen worked outside the home both in suburban Albuquerque and in Denver, almost two-thirds of them in low-paying housework or cleaning. Even in the villages it became increasingly common for a daughter and mother to do housework for wages."[66]

The meaning of these statistics is obvious, as Katzman concluded: "Domestic service drew less from women who chose service and more from those who due to race, ethnicity, lack of education, or marital condition had no choice."[67]

During the post-World War I period, middle-class white Americanizers continued to view Chicanas and Mexican immigrant women as dependent, inferior females who would be improved by exposure to "American" standards of housekeeping and parenting. These viewpoints appeared in the press, for example in Dorothy Overstreet's 1917 article on "Problems and Progress Among Mexicans of Our Own Southwest": "*When trained* there is no better servant than the gentle, quiet Mexican girl" [emphasis added].[68] Deutsch summarized the overriding ideology: "What better way to train Chicanas in 'American' mothering than by encouraging them to meet the demand for domestic servants?"[69] Self-righteous mistresses actually justified paying low wages on the basis that domestic service would teach skills for social mobility and provide moral benefits to Mexican servants.

Attitudes such as these reinforced the dual labor force practice of hiring Chicanas or Mexican immigrants for household tasks and cooking, while using only foreign-born white immigrant women as nannies. Chicanas and Mexican immigrant women were considered too inferior to care for children. One employer openly declared her prejudice, voicing an attitude—common even today—that Chicanas' bilingual and bicultural abilities handicapped their capability to care for children:

> And if the child learns from them nothing worse, he may learn manners and speech which are not up to the standards his parents and teachers set for him. He has to be untaught these constantly. Often also this maid of good character has a narrow outlook, religious doctrines confusing to a child and no depth—honest and warm-hearted through she may be.[70]

Mistresses were not alone in their efforts to domesticate Chicanas and create a servant class for upper- and middle-class whites. Domestic vocational training for Mexican students dominated the thinking of educators. Throughout the Southwest, schools with high Mexican enrollments offered vocational and industrial education to prepare female students to enter domestic service. In an article from 1929 entitled "Homemaking with the 'Other Half' along Our International Border," Grace Farrell argued for the benefits of submitting Mexican girls to "a practical course in homemaking." Offering a course that included "any part of homemaking from morals and manners to cleaning and cooking" was presented as a strategy to bridge the gap between Mexican parents and Anglo teachers as well as to facilitate the exclusive use of English.[71]

During the late 1920s, many books and teaching manuals aimed at the Americanization of Mexicans through domestic service were published. Kimball Young's book *Mental Differences in Certain Immigrant Groups* urged Mexican schools to develop a curriculum that prepared children for the job market. Similarly, Merton Hill advanced domestic vocational training. In his book *The Development of an Americanization Program*, he proposed that: "Girls should be trained to become domestic servants, and to do various kinds of hand work for which they can be paid adequately after they leave school."[72] Pearl I. Ellis, the author of *Americanization Through Homemaking*, argued that Americanization programs for Mexicans would raise their standard of living and their morals as well as teach skills such as housekeeping and sewing. Ellis's thesis was consistent with the popular myth of the time that promised upward mobility through domestic service. The emphasis on home economics for Mexican girls was frequently rationalized on the basis that many were likely to be employed as house servants.[73]

In his study of El Paso, Mario Garcia found that the city's school board maintained a segregated school system that tracked Mexican girls into a home economics curriculum to enable them to acquire the skills needed to work as domestics: "School officials argued that because of the need for Mexican children to work at an early age, the Mexican schools should direct their attention to manual and domestic education that would best assist the students to find jobs."[74] The Women's Civic Improvement League of El Paso similarly urged schools to teach housekeeping, cooking, and sewing to Mexican girls in order to provide better trained "house-girls" for American families. Deutsch reported similar occurrences in Colorado. In Denver, the president of Fairview School emphasized a curriculum of homecraft, domestic science, and care of the home for Mexican girls. Schools prepared Chicanas for three options: homemaking in their parents' homes, in their own homes, or in their mistresses' homes.[75]

Schools were aided by social scientists and government bureaucrats in their crusade to maintain a Mexican servant class in the Southwest. During the New Deal, several federal programs actively channeled Chicanas into domestic service.[76] In 1934, Emory Bogardus revealed the concerted effort of social welfare agencies to: "secure places in homes in the United States for Mexican girls and women as employees . . . It requires patience to be sure, but there are large numbers of Mexicans who can fill the household gap if the proper connections are made."[77]

New Deal programs trained Chicano men in technical and industrial skills, but the programs available to women were generally limited to instruction in traditional female skills and placement in marginal occupations. Chicanas were unlikely to earn more than fifty cents a week as domestics in the city, yet the WPA awarded several household training projects to urban areas.[78] One WPA school was established for Mexican girls. Florence Kerr reported that the WPA training program, supervised by home economists, had successfully trained 22,000 women and placed 18,000.[79] However, the trainees were less convinced, expressing "considerable questioning of household employment as an occupation."[80]

The National Youth Administration in Colorado and New Mexico followed the WPA's lead, training young Chicana women to make quilts and mattresses and to do housework and other domestic chores.[81] George Bickel, Assistant State Director of the WPA for Colorado, supported this training with the claim that a Mexican girl "must have her chance at a training program for motherhood and housewife. She must have opportunity to learn and work in a program of sewing, budget management, commodity usage, and personal hygiene."[82] These rationalizations notwithstanding, the Denver Occupational Adjustment Service reported that between 1939 and 1940, only 141 of the 984 Chicanos seeking employment were hired. Moreover, the majority of the 141 positions were jobs either on public relief projects or in domestic service.[83]

THE MODERN PERIOD

As a result of World War II and postwar prosperity, the American middle class expanded; they moved into smaller homes, and the use of labor-saving household technology became more popular. Families hired less help. New kinds of job opportunities were opened to more women, and the number of household workers began to decline. Commenting on the situation of household workers in Washington, D.C., Mary Waggamon reported a 20 percent decrease in the number of workers coupled with a sharp increase in wages and improved working conditions. Of course, race continued to describe and circumscribe women's chances in the market. Fewer opportunities opened up for African American women or Chicanas, and they remained overrepresented in domestic service. Thus, by 1950, 41.4 percent of employed African American women—ten times the number of whites—worked as household workers.[84]

Employment figures do not tell the whole story. Racial and ethnic differences continued to be reflected in the wages and general working conditions surrounding domestic service. Where African American women competed with white women for jobs, dual-wage scales were frequently maintained. Changes in the use of appliances, the length of the workday, pay, and benefits lagged by a decade or more in regions with high percentages of nonwhite domestic labor. For instance, the Interracial Committee of the YWCA on domestic workers in Washington, D.C., conducted a study in 1940 and found that the work week for full-time domestics ranged from 42 to 105 hours. Domestics averaged 11 to 12 hours a day and took home a weekly pay of about $8.10 or about $350 a year. The Committee concluded that "wages bore no fixed relation to hours or nature of work, to type of employer's household, to length of service, nor to the education or special training for the employees. They depended upon the capacity of the employer to pay and upon the need of the employee for work at a given moment."[85]

Five years later, Mary Waggamon analyzed the situation more deeply. She found that wages in Washington, D.C., ranged from $3.50 to $18.75 a week but that the average earning for white women was $9.35, whereas black women averaged only $8.85.[86] Susan Tucker reported similar findings in the South: "Rural-born [African American] women remembered being paid. . . . wages as low as $3.00 to $3.50 a week during the 1940s. In the city they could make as much as $10.00 or more per week."[87]

In the last few decades, immigrant women from various Third World countries have joined the ranks of domestics alongside native-born ethnic minority women. The composition of the domestic labor force has shifted from native- to foreign-born women of color. As one example, Elizabeth Petras found that 29 percent of Jamaican women in New York were employed in cleaning and maintenance, including domestic service.[88] Thus, while the proportion of native-born

African American women in domestic service steadily declined—from 36 percent in 1960 to 18 percent in 1970[89] to only 5 percent in 1980—women of color are still overrepresented among private household workers.[90] As immigration patterns have shifted away from Europe toward third-world countries, large numbers of immigrant women have been imported for domestic service.

Many of the attitudes and practices found in today's employment of Third World women in domestic service draw upon Americanization efforts applied to Mexican Americans and Mexican nationals in the Southwest. At this point, having broadly sketched the history of domestic labor as it impacted women of color in the United States, I want to examine the experiences of Chicanas and Mexican immigrant household workers in more detail. These women make an important case study; they are women of color who come from a community that is unique in sharing characteristics of both native-born and immigrant workers. The following section identifies attitudes and policies of past generations that concretized domestic service as "Mexican" and, later, "Latina" women's work in the Southwest. In the last few decades, Central and South American immigrant women have joined Mexican women in domestic service. Amazingly, nearly half of the 120,000 visas granted to Latin American women in 1968 were for prospective live-in maids.[9] Latinas' experiences in domestic service have important similarities with those of Chicanas and Mexican immigrant women.

Mexican Immigrant and Chicana Domestic Workers in the Modern Period

Attitudes and practices developed in the Americanization programs of the 1920s and 1930s continued to be incorporated as part of the racial etiquette between Mexican domestic workers and their Anglo employers. An analysis of the 1959 publication entitled *Your Maid from Mexico* offers valuable insight into race relations between employees and employers in domestic service. Written as a practical handbook for Anglo housewives on how to supervise servants, it is also filled with suggestions and advice for the employees. Perhaps some employers gave a copy to the maid to read, more probably however, employee suggestions were a literary strategy for developing the role expectations of the housewife employer. Thus, when a maid is advised to let her employer search her purse, we should probably read this as affirming and enhancing Anglo employers' "rights" as supervisors and the kind of deference that they should expect from their Mexican maids. In a similar vein, the following statement, although addressed to maids, actually suggests a strategy for employers: "Always try to remember that the man or lady of the house is probably trying to help you—not criticize you."[92]

From a sociological perspective, the book *Your Maid from Mexico* is a rich source of data on the folkways, mores, norms, values, and racial etiquette governing domestic service in the Southwest. Dos and don'ts provide insight into how racial and gender hierarchies are reproduced in the employer's home. Under the heading "Obligations of the Employer," for instance, the authors caution against common practices that may cause employee-employer problems: keeping workers beyond the agreed upon time, rearranging work schedules, changing days off, promising to raise salaries, training maids in the presence of the family or guests, and accusing maids of stealing. The authors' solutions to these issues are similarly informative. Rather than suggest that employers keep promises to raise salaries, the authors advise them to "explain why you do not or cannot do so."[93] Although the book acknowledges that public reprimands and training of the maid are humiliating, the reason offered for avoiding these tactics is that children are likely to replicate such behavior, reducing the maid's effectiveness as a babysitter.[94] Employees are warned against taking even the smallest item, such as a bobby pin, in order to maintain trust and avoid "misunderstandings." Furthermore, employees are urged to forego privacy by showing employers the contents of their bags when they leave for their day off.[95]

Gender construction is revealed in a section entitled "The Man of the House." Maids are clearly expected to maintain and support patriarchy. The maid is informed that "the man of the house" pays the bills and her salary. He is the "king" of the house and, presumably following the housewife's lead, the maid should do everything to make him feel that way. She is expected to serve dinner when the man wants to eat, regardless of any imposition on her or the rest of the family. She is even warned to expect his occasional escapades at cooking and instructed to "smile, and clean up after him willingly."[96]

Not unlike mistresses at the turn of century, employers hiring Mexican domestics in the 1950s and 1960s expected to purchase broadly defined labor power rather than specific labor services: "Remember that your employer pays you for your time, and though you may consider a task unnecessary, it may be important to her."[97] The job was therefore defined to include any task or personal service the employer or her family required: shampoo and set employer's hair, give permanents, sew dresses for children, give manicures, shine all the family shoes, wash the family car, etc. General housecleaning also encompassed ritual cleaning: "In many households, one day each week is set aside for the cleaning of silver, brass, copper, chandeliers, etc."[98]

Elements of the cult of domesticity resurface throughout *Your Maid from Mexico*. All aspects of the occupation were represented as opportunities for the maid's self-enhancement and fulfillment. Domestic service was packaged as the most rewarding occupation for Mexican women and the ideal training ground for learning middle-class ideas of motherhood and womanhood:

> You girls who work in homes can soon become more valuable to your employers than girls who work in offices, stores, or factories, because our homes and families are the closest to our hearts.

Remember, as you learn new skills day by day, you are not only learning how to become a better wife and mother yourself, but you are learning to support yourself and your family in a worthwhile career in case you must be the breadwinner.[99]

The authors adopted language that reinforced racial and ethnic hierarchies. Employers are referred to as women or ladies, employees are "girls." The section on "how to act on the job" illustrates how racial domination in the employer's home is maintained on a daily basis. Mexican household workers are instructed to act out the "non-person" role that Erving Goffman described: "The classic type of non-person in our society. . . is defined by both performers and audience as someone who isn't there."[100] Thus, Mexican maids are instructed to be invisible: "Give them privacy with one another and with their friends, but be available when they call you."[101] "Be considerate by not playing the radio or television loud when people are talking or reading. Run the noisy appliances when no one is around to be disturbed."[102] The role expectations for Mexican household workers are identical to the "requisite of invisibility" Katzman described as a common feature of domestic service in the South.[103] The most condescending and racist section in the book is one called "how to look on the job," subtitled "cleanliness":

if you stay clean, you will not only look better, but feel better. Your employer will show you where she wants you to bathe. She will want you to take a bath or shower regularly, and wash your hands with soap. You will be furnished a washcloth and towel for your own use.[104]

The manual specifies the occasions when the maid should wash her hands: "after you use the toilet," "after you use your handkerchief," "before you handle dishes, food, or other utensils in the kitchen," "after handling pets," "before you pick up the baby," and "before you handle the baby's clothes or things."[105] The maid is informed that she should provide her own toilet articles, particularly deodorant, however, sanitary napkins will be provided by the "lady of the house."[106] No explanation is given for this curious division of toiletries. Perhaps the employer can use Kotex to keep track of her employee's menstrual cycle and dismiss her if she becomes pregnant.

Your Maid from Mexico is a distillation of a century of management techniques used by Anglo housewives to manipulate Mexican domestic workers. Employers are taught to maneuver employees into doing more work through gifts, tips, and symbolic generosity: "Deeds of loyalty and sympathy are so much more important than words. You will always be rewarded, and you will find that they will help you as well when *you* need help."[107] The employee is assured that the employer "will probably give you many things *she wants you to have* [emphasis added]."[108] Domestics are told to expect extra work and "to do small favors for house-guests, such as light laundry or pressing or even serving coffee in the bedroom in the morning."[109] In payment for the extra work, they may be given a gift or money.

The maid's rights as a worker are never addressed. The discussion on extra work, which includes caring for special guests and the sick, does not advocate additional pay. Instead, the worker is told to ingratiate herself in hopes of tips or emotional rewards. Of course, the section on "the man of the house" makes no reference to sexual harassment, a common problem particularly among live-in domestics. This is a major omission in a manual about an occupation plagued with sexual stereotypes of the worker "as sexual initiator for the young males in the family," and "as object of the fantasies of the more mature males."[110] The section covering "accident prevention at home" discusses safety in the home but makes no mention of health insurance for the worker.

Your Maid from Mexico is not a historical artifact. Two recent publications aimed at Anglo homemakers hiring Spanish-speaking maids have been widely circulated throughout the Southwest. Apron Pocket Press sold 100,000 copies of *Home Maid Spanish*, which instructed monolingual English speaking employers how to train their Mexican maids. The manual consists of introductory phrases for informing the worker where the local Catholic church is, a list of her days off, and detailed instructions on how to do the work. Instructions to the maid include thirteen different sets of instructions for the bedroom and guidelines for child care that entail picking up after the children. Tasks include polishing the silver and doing the marketing. In the 1980s, Linda Wolf published a similar book, entitled *Tell-A-Maid*, aimed at Los Angeles area employers and an estimated 100,000 Spanish-speaking household workers. The phrase book was regarded a hit with homemakers. *Tell-A-Maid* consists of twenty-eight pages of Spanish and English clip-out phrases that can be left throughout the employer's home as a method of communication.

Given the level of servitude expressed in *Your Maid from Mexico*, it is not surprising to discover that Chicanas leave the occupation as soon as other job opportunities became available. Chicanas seek industry and office jobs because domestic service lacks any opportunity for advancement and because the work is monotonous and has long and irregular hours. More importantly, even though Chicanas and Mexican immigrants are usually hired for low-level and unskilled factory jobs, employers outside domestic service do not demand the same level of deference and servility. Even low-paid service positions do not carry the stigma found in domestic service. As Katzman explained: "Others held it in low regard because of those who performed the work—immigrants in cities, blacks in the South, women everywhere. Many women considered it degrading because it was women's work, done by unskilled poorly educated women who couldn't find other work."[111]

In Southwestern communities, as native-born Chicanas found other employment, Mexican immigrant women filled positions in domestic service. But working conditions experienced by Chicana and Mexican immigrant domestics tend to be quite different. Since the 1940s, the trend in domestic service has been toward day work; however, live-in conditions are still common among immigrant women.[112] Moreover, Mexican immigrants have not entirely replaced Chicanas in domestic service because limited job opportunities have locked many Chicanas into the occupation.

Tensions occurred in communities that attempted to maintain a dual wage system by hiring Chicana and Mexican immigrant domestics at different pay levels. In 1953, El Paso housewives organized the "The Association for Legalized Domestics." They wanted to hire maids from Mexico in order to pay lower wages and proposed a program that included screening potential immigrants for age, health problems, and criminal records. A minimum wage was set at fifteen dollars a week, employers were obligated to provide room and board, and domestics were allowed a day and a half off on weekends. The Chicana maids in El Paso objected to hiring Mexican maids from Juarez, when local domestic help was available. Fortunately, the Department of Justice rejected the Association's proposal.[113]

Today, Mexican immigrant women tend to predominate in larger cities, particularly along the border. Researchers estimate that anywhere from 18,000 to 26,000 domestics are employed in private residences in El Paso.[114] In El Paso and other areas near the border, labor is so cheap that most middle class families have at least one servant, and some also employ a laundress, nursemaid and yardman.[115] Although average wages for undocumented workers in all positions are well below the minimum wage, domestic workers are paid the least. Sasha Lewis reported that in the 1970's the highest-paid underground jobs were found in the construction industry, where undocumented men workers made an average of $2.98 per hour. Undocumented women domestic workers earned an average of $1.63 per hour.[116]

Household workers in El Paso's suburbs include both commuter maids with green cards and undocumented Mexicanas who dodge *la Migra* (the Border Patrol and the INS agents) as they cross the border. The extent of economic interdependency was demonstrated in March of 1979, when Mexican nationals blockaded the bridge between Mexico and the United States to protest *la Migra's* deportation of some 140 maids. Lewis described the incident as the "strongest border protest against the U.S. in recent memory."[117] She commented on the dual economy of border cities: "Some of the Mexican border towns seem to have only one reason for being where they are: to supply the U.S. with cheap temporary workers. They supply the maids for Juarez, who earn enough money in El Paso to support their families."[118]

In 1983, the *El Paso Herald-Post* published a special report called "The Border," which included an article on domestics entitled "Mexican Maids: El Paso's Worst-Kept Secret." Journalists Michael Quintanilla and Peter Copeland interviewed maids, housewives, government officials, academic experts, and social workers on both sides of the border in an attempt to uncover the plight of domestics in El Paso: "While no figures are available on how many maids work in El Paso, there may well be more maids per home in the city than anywhere else in the nation. The reason is the low wages and shortage of jobs in Juarez. At $40 plus room and board a week, many El Pasoans can afford them, not just the rich." [119]

A measure of the extent of underground economy is found in the fact that the 1980 census reported only 1,063 private household workers in El Paso. The director of the El Paso Planning, Research, and Development Department made the modest estimate of 13,400 domestics on the basis of only 10 percent of the households in El Paso employing domestics. However, a more accurate estimate comes from the city bus drivers, who claim that "If they [INS] ever cracked down on domestic help, especially illegals, we would lose our ridership." Half of the 28,300 daily trips taken on the city buses are maids. [120]

Maids in El Paso receive little, if any, vacation and no workmen's compensation, health benefits or retirement pension. Live-in domestics are usually paid no more than forty dollars a week. Day workers rarely receive minimum wage. Employers commonly threaten to deport undocumented domestics if they refuse to do more work, reject sexual advances, or attempt to return home. Isabel Garcia-Medina recalled an employer who threatened to call the immigration when she refused "to clean her house and iron two big plastic bags full of clothes—do everything for $5." She responded by pulling out her resident alien card and telling the employer to call whom ever she wanted. However, the fear of deportation serves to silence many undocumented workers. [121]

Immigrants almost universally receive lower wages than native-born workers and housewives rarely obey the law or pay even minimum wage; and the dual wage system thus established functions to depress wages for both foreign- and native-born people of color. Neither the INS nor the Department of Labor has been vigilant in regulating abuses involved in the indentured contracts often made to cover travel and immigration proceedings. Undocumented domestics are particularly vulnerable to exploitation, often being paid at far less than minimum wage. Native-born domestic workers are unable to raise wages or improve working conditions as long as employers have access to a virtually inexhaustible reserve army of undocumented women.

The effect of this competition can be easily seen. Across the board, the income of domestic workers is below the federal poverty level. Thus, in 1978, the wages for a sample of 583,000 African American household workers averaged $2,729, slightly below the poverty level of $2,884. Moreover, these wages did not include social security, health insurance, or other benefits. [122] Altogether, 54 percent of women reported incomes below the poverty level, a majority were heads of household. [123] Sherrie Rossoudji and Susan Rainey reported that Mexican immigrants employed as household workers earned less than ten dollars a day.[124] Other researchers reported somewhat higher wages and suggest a wider range of salaries and working conditions. In her study of Mexican immigrant women in California, Pierrette Hondagneu-Sotelo found that domestics were paid between minimum wage and fifteen dollars an hour.[125] Judith Ann Warners and Helen K. Henderson's survey of 522 legal temporary and permanent residents in Laredo, Texas, identified 200 Mexican immigrant women employed as private household workers. Almost 79 percent of the women reported salaries below the minimum wage level.[126] Leslie Salzinger found the hourly wage to fluctuate between five and ten dollars an hour for day work and one and three thousand dollars a month for live-in domestic work among Central American immigrant women employed through cooperatives in the Bay area.[127]

DISCUSSION

The sociological depiction of domestic service as a (gradually disappearing) vestige of feudalism, the social psychological perspective of "personalism and asymmetry," and the various "bridging" and acculturation theories ignore the brute social fact that domestic workers are disproportionately women of color. Domestic service cannot be separated from America's history and the capitalism that produced and continues to maintain a gender stratified and racially hierarchical labor market.

Feudal relations between master and servant no longer exist. We live in a relentlessly capitalist society, and while paternalism and maternalism may resemble feudalistic relationships, this level of analysis serves only to conceal real sources of exploitation. Capitalism transformed all social relationships, rooting out the community that maintained the master-servant dyad. Like all workers under capitalism, private household workers exchange their labor for wages, and even when the employee-employer relationship is masked by notions of the employee being "one of the family," employers take no responsibility for protecting or caring for them. As capitalists middle-class employers—like factory owners—own the means of production and the product of the labor; they constantly rationalize the work and control the labor process. Servitude and paternalism in the mistress-maid relationship are not a vestige of feudalistic relationships but are exploitative characteristics used within the capitalistic mode of production. Domestic service must be analyzed as a sphere of capitalist production in which race and gender domination are played out.

As the term is used here, racism is inescapably personal and institutional. It means that physical traits and cultural identity have been used by the majority to prescribe and ordain the life chances in the market for a minority. In the capitalist development of the United States, slavery was a form of racist exploitation unique to Blacks. Jim Crow laws and Klan violence, along with a host of less violent practices, maintained this racism long after emancipation. In a calculated fashion, former slaves and all of their descendants down to this very day have been discriminated against, allowed access to only the lowest-paid, lowest-status positions. The Chicano people of the Southwest experienced a different but likewise situation. They became Americans by conquest and owned valuable land and resources coveted by others. Their communities were attacked, their culture slandered, their religion devalued, and their land expropriated. These two communities of color were consigned to the lower class.

Across the board, women have similarly been denied access to channels of upward mobility on the basis of physical characteristics. Their life chances have been defined by sexism, but all women do not suffer sexism equally. They have shared, albeit at a lower level, the fortunes of their race. Sexism multiplies the effects of racism; the burden falls disproportionately on women of color. The history of domestic service reveals how middle-class homemakers' struggles to escape the drudgery of housework have been intertwined with racial politics.

Discriminatory institutional practices relegated women of color to the lowest status and lowest paying jobs in society. The educational system assisted in establishing and reproducing the most rigid occupational stratification. In her analysis of the role of educational systems in domestic service in South Africa, Jacklyn Cock identified two functions: "the allocation of occupational roles" and "the elaboration of appropriate ideologies to reinforce such roles."[128] Both functions worked against women of color in the United States. Educational programs for future white middle class homemakers aimed at self-development and fulfillment, whereas African American and Chicana students were limited to vocational training. Home economics socialized minority and immigrant women to domestic roles in their own homes and in the homes of white middle-class families. Thus, in the Southwest, vocational training functioned to maintain a segmented labor force. Denied equal access to education, Chicanas and Mexican immigrant women were locked into low paying, low status jobs.

Racist domination is particularly apparent when the experiences of white and nonwhite women in domestic service are compared. Comparisons of the mobility experiences of native-born white women with those immigrant and minority women demonstrate the importance of race and culture in the development of social class in the United States. Native-born white women employed in domestic service were not subjected to the negative aspects of the racial hierarchy. White women working as "help" reaped the benefits of egalitarian thought and obtained favorable working conditions, they sold labor *services*, not just time, to employers. As capitalism provided additional opportunities, white women's positions in the racial hierarchy helped them leave domestic work and obtain better-paying jobs. As the number of white women workers declined, domestic service came to reflect not only sexual domination but racial domination. As

James Bossard reminded us in his discussion of "Domestic Servants and Child Development," "the nature of the job has much to do with the relationship developed between servant and family."[129] In the case of women of color, "the employer-employee relationship is reinforced by considerations of racial attitudes and minority group status."[130] So, a dual system is maintained in the occupation. When white women do domestic work they are usually employed as nannies rather than as maids-of-all work and they receive higher wages.

Certainly women of different racial, cultural and class backgrounds have been relegated to homemaking activity and thus are all victims of sexism, but class interests and race have kept women from establishing similar interests based on gender. This historical overview has demonstrated several instances when middle-class Anglo women advocated gender issues but acted out of class interests. The "Americanization-through-homemaking" movement promoted domestic service as a "bridging occupation" for Mexican women. The Women's Civic Improvement League of El Paso supported vocational training in domestic science for Mexican girls. The Association for Legalized Domestics was a consortium of middle-class women's organizations joining forces to change immigration policy so they could cut the price of domestic workers. Each of these examples shows that gender issues were not paramount; the issues were defined by class interests and formed by racial privileges. Instead of challenging the sexual division of labor, white middle-class homemakers sought refuge in strategies that reduced the negative aspects of sexism by exploiting women of color. As the authors of *Your Maid from Mexico* explained to Mexican workers: "By taking our place in the home and doing many of our jobs, you can give us free hours to do the things we enjoy—playing golf, sewing, playing the piano, attending club meetings, or working at a job we like."[131]

In fact, the white middle-class women's homemaking movement actually furthered poor working conditions for women of color employed as household workers. In conjunction with management tools such as "domestic science," the movement created harsh working conditions for domestics and kept wages far below those of other occupations. Expanding domestic work to include ritual cleaning and modern "standards" added to the physical labor. By giving themselves the roles of supervisors and organizing the work around time rather than tasks, white middle-class homemakers defined women domestic workers of color as unskilled and ignorant. Extending the principles of the scientific and social homemaking movements to domestic service did not benefit workers but rather cheapened their labor service to labor power. In doing these things, white middle-class homemakers enhanced their own class and racial status and contributed to the oppression of other women and to the maintenance of an occupationally stratified work force.

Chapter 5

BONDS OF SISTERHOOD—
BONDS OF OPPRESSION

In the 1960s and 1970s feminists defined household labor as central to women's oppression, regardless of class, race, or ethnicity. Ann Oakley, Selma James, and others argued that shared experiences in the housewife role united *all* women.[1] The burden of housework was, for many feminists, the first obstacle to "liberation." Women's progress toward self-actualization involved freedom from the isolation and drudgery of housework. However, this stage in the feminist movement was not a universal experience. It appeared universal only when the theoretical and political concerns of housework were limited to women as unpaid housewives. Robert Coles's interview with an African American domestic captured distinct differences in women's experiences and the irony of this aspect of middle-class "women's liberation":

> The "missus" urged that women affirm themselves outside their home; to do so herself, she had to bring someone into her own home—thereby taking that person away from a home hardly with the resources to welcome and sustain a person known as a "maid." The husband went along with his wife, urged her to move from charitable work on a part-time basis to full-time employment, whereby one becomes "fulfilled" and "committed." To enable that shift, Helen [the domestic] had to work longer, stay over sometimes. . . . The "missus" constantly thanked something abstract for her "liberation"—a movement, which had "raised" her "consciousness." But the maid had an occasional thought that such a development, such a movement, wasn't so far doing much for her.[2]

Domestic service reveals the contradiction in a feminism that pushed for women's involvement outside the home, yet failed to make men take responsibility for household labor. Employed middle- and upper-middle class women escaped the double day syndrome by hiring poor women of color to perform housework and child care,[3] and this was characterized as progress. Some feminists defined domestic service as progressive because traditional women's work moved into the labor market and became paid work. However, this definition neglects the inescapable fact that when women hire other women at low wages to do housework, both employees and employers remain women. As employers, women continued to accept responsibility for housework even if they supervised domestics who performed the actual labor. If we accept domestic service as central to women's oppression, the contradiction, as Linda Martin and Kerry Segrave have pointed out, is that "every time the housewife or working woman buys freedom for herself with a domestic, that very same freedom is denied to the domestic, for the maid must go home and do her own housework."[4]

Although the system of gender domination places the burden of housework on women, middle class women have financial resources to escape the drudgery of housework by paying someone else to do her work. Village Voice columnist Viva illustrates the extraordinary degree of complacency with which contemporary American women accept domestic service as a solution to the burden of being a "superwoman."

> Should it occur to you that nursing a baby, supporting one or two more other children, continuing your career, shopping, cooking, cleaning, and otherwise single-handedly maintaining a family are incompatible activities, I will save you hours of anguish by saying definitively that a cleaning woman is the first form of help with which to start.[5]

Domestic service presents another challenge to the feminist notion of "sisterhood." Viva cautioned against hiring unionized maids through the yellow pages, which will "liberate your savings account"; instead, "hire an illegal alien from either Mexico, Central America or the Caribbean." In other words, hire a woman of color and pay her as little as possible to fulfill your housework duties and responsibilities. The most exploitative form of domestic service is maintained through systems of gender, class and racial domination. Thus, middle-class American women aim to "liberate" themselves by exploiting women of color—particularly immigrants—in the underground economy, for long hours at relatively low wages, with no benefits.[6]

Those in favor of hiring domestics argue that the source of the problem is a vestigial "master-servant" relation held over and perpetuated in the housewife-domestic relationship. As one Montreal journalist put it: "The problem relates to the whole question of how we relate to domestics. Women in particular say this is crap work, and the government accepts that. It comes down to women exploiting other women."[7] To a large degree, women employers govern the type of employee-employer relationship that is established.[8] Under the influence of community norms and values, middle-class women employers negotiate an informal labor contract with working class women in the privacy of their own homes. The hardships, isolation and degradation experienced by women household workers are thus directly controlled by women employers. There is an enormous latitude in the contract. In *Las Mujeres*, Ida Gutierrez recounted the ways in which women employers determined her working conditions:

> Some of the ladies pay Social Security, but some of them don't. It all depends. If you're lucky, you find a woman that is real nice to you. If you get to meet one of those ladies, you got it made—they pay for your gas, or they give you money. But not all people are the same. I've worked for rich ladies who thought they'd go broke if they gave me a Coca-Cola. And they make you work real hard for your money, too—clean the walls, get down on your knees and scrub the floor.[9]

The present chapter draws upon my research with Chicana domestic workers as well as studies of African American, West Indian, Japanese American, and Central American immigrant women. Interviews with domestic workers describe interactions between white middle-class women employers and working class women of color that take place outside the public eye. The accounts describe working conditions and work relations and provide insight into the function of gender in shaping interclass and interracial social relationships. Investigating daily rituals and practices involving employer and employee provides a microperspective on the process whereby systems of gender, class, and race domination are reproduced in domestic service.

WHY DO WOMEN HIRE OTHER WOMEN

Why do white middle class employers hire working-class women of color as domestics? The question is twofold: Who is being hired, and for what purpose? At first glance, the answers are obvious; that is, white middle-class women hire persons available in the local market to relieve them of their household work. They seek to hire the cheapest labor available, and in this society, that is the labor of women of color. However, the situation is far more complex.

Students of the history of domestic work maintain that in the past, employers hired domestics not only to labor in their homes by doing household chores but also to provide personal services and status.[10] Thus, Lewis Coser referred to the employer's family as a "greedy organization" that devoured the personality of the worker, demanding complete loyalty, including time, energy, and personal

commitment.[11] Yet, Coser described the occupation as undergoing modernization, moving toward a contractual basis in which workers were hired for specific
housecleaning tasks, not personal services. A magazine article published around
the time of Coser's book, however, confirms his original appraisal of domestic
service. Entitled "Liberated Women Liberating Domestics," the article described
the reasons homemakers reported for hiring domestics:

> Maids are cost efficient; they assist single parents; maids free women to relax or
> pursue personal interests; they help the working person; maids are essential to
> make up for skills a housewife might be deficient in, such as sewing; *maids give a
> household status*; domestic work provides jobs for those who might otherwise be
> unemployed [emphasis added].

Let us overlook, for now, the illusion common among white middle-class
women that hiring a woman of color to clean their toilets is a form of social
benefit, reducing the unemployment rate. It is clear that African American, West
Indian, Chicana, and Japanese American domestics describe working arrangements that challenge the thesis that personal service and status are vanishing
needs no longer fulfilled in the occupation. They report a broad range of tasks
including personal service and emotional labor, suggesting that servitude and
traditional demeanor are still expected by some employers. Examining the details of physical and emotional labor found in domestic service will provide
insight into contemporary answers to the question of why women hire other
women.

Physical Labor

On the surface, the idea of hiring another person to perform the housewife's
physical labor appears fairly straightforward. However, it is complicated by the
fact that employers hire persons to replace labor at once considered demeaning
and closely identified with family roles of mothers and wives. As employers,
housewives decide what aspects of their physical labor they no longer want to
perform, and in doing so they determine the employee's work. The needs fulfilled through domestics' physical labor structure the work: thus some employers
choose to include tasks that they feel are demeaning, others add new tasks and
methods of housekeeping that they themselves never engage in, and still others
are more interested in having their status affirmed and enhanced than in having
their floors scrubbed. The following section analyzes housework to discover the
complex set of needs fulfilled by the labor of domestic workers.

Detailed descriptions of actual housework performed by domestics indicate
that, while some women hire women to replace their own labor, others hire
women to do much more demanding household labor. The list of physical labor
reported by household workers included housecleaning, laundry, sewing, gar-

dening, babysitting, and cooking. In her study on domestic service, Elaine Kaplan described a varied inventory of work tasks, such as that reported by Ella Mae Robinson:

> I dust all the rooms, vacuum, mop the kitchen, den, clean the bathrooms, cabinets, put dishes in the washer, and do some ironing. Many times I have to take the clothes to the cleaners, feed the cat, wash the woodwork, and pick up the clothes off the floor and off the chairs.[12]

In their efforts to escape the diffuse duties of their housewife roles, employers do not acknowledge work boundaries. Even when the worker's tasks were agreed upon in a verbal contract, employees frequently reported that employers requested additional duties. For instance, household workers commonly complained that employers did not differentiate between housework and child care. In her interviews with women hired to do child care in New York City, Kathy Dobie found that "many of the women are hired as nannies and then asked if they wouldn't mind straightening up a bit. They are asked if they wouldn't clean, then shop, then do the laundry, then, etc." One child care worker told Dobie:

> I give her coffee. I take care of Stephen. I do the laundry. I go out and do the shopping. I buy her birth control tablets. I couldn't believe that. . . . Even the light bulbs in the ceiling, I change. Even her panties, I pick them up when she drops them on the floor.[13]

Soraya Moore Coley reported similar findings in her study on African American private household workers. Mrs. Green described how her job description changed:

> When she hired me, she told me I was to only take care of the children. Then, the woman starts leaving the house and asking me if I would do this or that. Before you know it, I'm taking care of the baby and doing the work. I enjoy the children and I guess I stayed because they become so attached to me—but the woman probably knew when she hired me, she wanted me to do other work.[14]

A closer look at the cultural meaning attached to certain tasks indicates the broad range of needs fulfilled through domestics' physical labor. Symbolic meanings are apparent in domestics' complaints about specific aspects of the work, for instance the task of "picking up." While some employers assisted the domestic by picking up toys and clothes from the floor and by placing dishes in the sink, others defined these activities as part of the job. Two West Indian women employed in New York City described to Shellee Colen how their employers structured the work to include picking up as an aspect of the work:

They had hampers and stuff like that, but when they undressed, they took [off] their clothes, they just walked out of them and left them on the bathroom floor.[15]

She throw everything on the floor. She leave all the cabinets open, you bump your head everytime of the day. She leave all the drawers out.[16]

However, the tasks of picking up clothes, books, papers, and other items do not have to be part of the domestic's physical labor. As one of the household workers noted, the solution to getting clothes picked up is "don't throw it on the floor. Put it in the hamper."[17] Mrs. Salazar distinguished between tasks that involved "serving" or "waiting" on others because these tasks made the work demeaning. (I suspect some women employers feel the same way about picking up after their children and husband.) In her account of an employer who assumed that picking up was part of the job, Mrs. Salazar pointed to the cultural meaning attached to picking up and the different needs fulfilled by the physical labor.

She kinda expected me to pick up after her children, like if they left underwear thrown, I was to put them into the hamper, and I've never done that. You leave underwear thrown, I either tack it to your door and let you see how disgusting it is or I throw it on your bed or something. But I don't run it to the hamper for you, that's your job. That's why I say, I don't do personal stuff.

Colen's account of a West Indian domestic's conflict with an employer over picking up clothes from the bathroom floor reveals that social needs are fulfilled when employers insist on retaining the degrading and demeaning work structure under which they previously labored as housewives. The employer refused to eliminate that aspect of the work, saying, "Well this is what the job requires and if you're going to hold the job, it's part." The employer argued "that she always picked up after her husband that's the way he is and she accepted him like that."[18] The employer's rationale exposes her implicit acceptance of a sexist structure of housework. She was apparently unwilling to confront her husband about his behavior, but eliminating "picking up" from the domestic's work would shift the burden of sexism back to herself. The employer not only wanted to escape the drudgery of doing the picking up but she sought to escape sexism by shifting the burden of her husband's behavior to the domestic. Employers' insistence on maintaining sexist practices in the division of household labor while not being the direct recipient of sexism is addressed in Rosanna Hertz's study of dual-career marriages: "Some women worry about emasculating their husbands by asking them to do more around the house, even if they employ full-time employees."[19]

Not all housewives structured the work to relieve themselves of the burden of housework. Workers encountered employers who disregarded their years of experience and treated them as unskilled labor that required detailed instruction and supervision. Instead of turning the housework over to domestics and engaging in other activities, these housewives spent their time following the worker throughout the house, specifying the order of the tasks, giving advice about cleaning techniques, and selecting all the cleaning materials. Mrs. Portillo recalled one employer who arranged the work to require her presence as a supervisor: "I used to have one lady that used to work right along with me. I worked with her three years. I found it hard. I was taking orders." In her interview with Studs Terkel, Maggie Holmes described the demeaning and unnecessary nature of supervision:

> I don't like nobody checkin' behind me. When you go to work, they want to show you how to clean. I been doin' it all my life. They come and get the rag and show you how to do it. [Laughs.] I stand there, look at 'em. Lotta times I ask her, "you finished?" I say, "If there's anything you gotta go and do, I'd wish you'd go." I don't need nobody to show me how to clean.[20]

In Evelyn Glenn's study of Japanese American domestics, Sachiko Adair and Mrs. Fujitani recalled experiences with employers who supervised:

> They say do this, do this, how to do. I know already everything, but still people try to tell you different ways.[21]

> The lady [employer] was too particular and she's always watching you, following you, whatever you're doing.[22]

Some employers expanded the role of supervision beyond methods of cleaning by attempting to structure all the workers' behavior and interaction. Mrs. Lucero's account depicted the way in which one employer tried to restrict workers' interactions. She worked for an employer who hired another woman to do the laundry and to clean the kitchen.

> I was suppose to do the living room, you know dust and all that, and she [employer] didn't want us to talk. You know we were working there in the same house and everything and she didn't want us to talk. One time she came home and I was in the kitchen talking to the girl and she got mad. I quit. I told her I didn't want to go back. She called me and I said no and the other girl finally quit her too. I thought she was a slave driver. You know because we were in the same house and we wouldn't avoid each other and what she wanted was for us to be working, working. So I quit her.

As might be expected, unemployed full-time homemakers are most likely to engage in supervision. Working women were viewed as more likely to hire them to "do the job" rather than as an opportunity to play the role of supervisor.[23] Chicanas consider full-time homemakers, with their insistence in monitoring and supervising the work, to be the most difficult employers to please. Mrs. Salazar reflected the sentiment of most Chicanas that I interviewed:

> I think women that weren't working were the ones that always had something to complain about. The ones that did work were always satisfied. I've never come across a lady that works that has not been satisfied. Those that are home and have the time to do it themselves, and don't want to do it, they are the ones that are always complaining, you know, not satisfied, they always want more and more. You can't really satisfy them.

Maggie Holmes expressed a similar view: "the younger women, they don't pay you too much attention. Most of 'em work. The older women, they behind you, wiping."[24] May Lund classified employers in a similar manner in her interview with Rollins:

> Twenty years ago, most of the people you worked for were over forty and women were at home. Today, they're career women and a lot don't even have children. They just don't want to spend their time cleaning house; they want to give their time to their careers.

ask to do stuff employer wouldn't do

Requests made by employers indicated that many housewives defined the work of private household workers as different from their own housekeeping. For instance, in their own homes most housewives never considered moving furniture to vacuum beneath it, cleaning the refrigerator or oven every week, or scrubbing the floors on their hands and knees. However, when housework became another woman's paid work, the activity was redefined to include new definitions of tasks, methods of cleaning, work standards and even expectations of the time necessary to complete a task. One of the most common experiences reported by women of color in reference to different standards was the request to scrub floors on their hands and knees rather than simply mopping. Maggie Holmes summed up the feelings of most women of color: "They [white women employers] don't get on their knees, but they don't think nothin' about askin' a black woman."[25] Anne Ryder articulated her views on employers' requests to Rollins:

> They [employers] would tell me to get on my knees and scrub the floor and I didn't do it. I didn't mess up my knees. I told one lady, "My knees aren't for scrubbing. My knees are made to bend and walk on." I didn't have a lot of bumps and no black knees from scrubbing floors. I took care of myself.[26]

Ella Thomas expressed similar sentiments to Susan Tucker:

Now they used to have hardwood floors, and one place I worked the lady had a big old box of this here paste wax sitting on the table and a bunch of rags. I came to work that day, and I just run the buffer over the floor. She say, "I see you didn't put the wax down." I say, "How you intended me to put it down?" She said, "Well I put the rags up there." I said, "Well not for me because I only gets on my knees to pray." Is that right or wrong?[27]

Bonnie Dill related a similar account of an employer who told her new employee, "My girl always scrubs the floor." The domestic found the mop hidden in the basement and decided not to "scrub" the floor with the bucket, the brush, and the knee-pad provided by the employer. Later when the employer asked why the floor was not scrubbed, the domestic explained:

"Well, you said your girl cleans the floor, and I'm not your girl. . . . and I don't scrub floors on my hands and knees." "Well," she said, "tomorrow I'll go out and buy a mop." So, I got my coat on and I said, "Why don't you just let me go down in the basement and bring the mop up?"[28]

Emotional Labor

Arlie Hochschild conducted the germinal analysis of emotional labor in her book *The Managed Heart*, but she did not include private household workers. Domestics are hired not only for their physical labor but to do emotional labor. In the same way that flight attendants and other women service workers created exchange value from emotions, private household workers manipulate and manage their feelings to fulfill the psychological needs of their employers. Previous researchers have addressed emotional labor as maternalism and personalism. Even though the concept of emotional labor has not been used in studies on private household workers, researchers have described and analyzed this type of labor in detail. Within discussions of employee-employer interactions are embedded descriptions of domestics being expected to perform the emotional labor attached to mothering and other homemaking activities.

One clue to the importance emotional labor has for the employer can be found in accounts showing the lack of concern over the *amount* of housework completed. Glenn's example of an older Japanese American domestic who referred to her work as a "hobby" illustrates the significance of emotional labor. The woman went to the employer's home and visited all day because she was too old to do much work.[29] Coley reported a similar case in which a domestic was eventually told not to bother with the housework and only to provide emotional labor:

When I went there they told me, "We're not paying you to scrub floors, but paying you just to take care of the woman, be a companion-like"; but I would do it all. If she was sick, I would stay nights. In the summer *we* would rent a summer cottage and I went there for five years with her.[30]

In Rollins' interview with employer Susan Keplin, the importance of emotional labor in keeping her current employee was mentioned:

> If I were hiring her brand new, didn't know her, I wouldn't keep her. Coming late, not cleaning very well. But if she left, I'd have a hard time finding someone else. It's worth much more to me to have her loyalty and her trust. And know if I'm sick, she'll come and take care of me, know I can count on her being there. That's much more important than the cleaning.[31]

Employers interviewed in Susan Tucker's study on domestic service in the South also discussed emotional labor. For instance, Anne Robertson remembered past household workers for the emotional rather than the physical labor they had provided.

> Oh, they gave us so much courage, encouragement, support, and love! I mean, I always think of the maid as being the family therapist. You know, you could go to them and say anything, and they would say, "Oh, bless you, you've have such a hard day". . . . And if they happened to clean and cook a little, that was fine! Psychologically they were very supportive.[32]

Of course, most employers expected both physical and emotional labor. Although employers hired household workers to perform a variety of physical and emotional labor, they never considered paying the market value of each task. Consider for example, the statement made by employer Sophie Stewart:

> It got where what they [two domestics] could produce for $3.39 an hour wasn't worth it. I just couldn't afford to have a black—I called them my black psychiatrists. They were "my black people who came," and we chatted and had a good time. I couldn't afford to pay them for that.[33]

Hertz found a similar attitude among dual-career couples who expected household workers "to be satisfied with relatively low wages, as compared to the fees paid to other service providers (such as doctors, accountants, or lawyers) for equally critical services."[34]

Sometimes domestics are seen as "protomothers": they are expected to perform the emotional labor of "mothering" both the women employers and their families. Older Chicana domestics whom I interviewed reported that younger employers expected them to serve as surrogate mothers. Young brides delegated their housecleaning chores to the domestic and relied upon her "motherly advice" for handling daily household and family crises. Over a period of time, domestics were encouraged to develop close relationships and to provide love to their children. They were expected to "mother" the children as well as provide employers relief from child care duties. Bonnie Dill's interview with Opal Broadway illustrated the worker's awareness of the type of labor employers wanted: "You have people that want you to be a mother, philosopher, father, nanny, governess and everything else to their children."[35]

Employers felt it natural to expect domestics, as protomothers, to do the emotional work of nurturing. Ms. Kirk described to Coley how she was manipulated into this caring and nurturing role:

> I remember when I first took the job with the family. She brought the children home from the hospital, and put the babies in my arms and told me, "These are your two children; raise them." And I saw their first step, first tooth for both children. I had a bedroom where I could stay with the children. And since me and my employers were all young and around the same age at the time, we kinda grew up together. Sometimes she would go away and leave the children with me.[36]

The calculated strategy that employers use to place domestics into nurturing and caring roles is evident in the following advice for keeping a maid offered in *Ladies' Home Journal*:

> If you are so fortunate as to find a maid you love with your whole heart, you might try binding her to you by having a child or two born during her tenure. Not high wages or Christmas gifts of blue-chip stock or every weekend off will prove so much a lure as children to whom she has grown attached.[37]

Dual-career couples in Chicago identified "women under twenty-five, older women, and recent (legal and illegal) female immigrants" as ideal child care workers on the basis of their economic vulnerability and limited job opportunities in the labor market. Consequently, such women would not be likely to demand higher wages but would more probably put up with unexpected "overtime."[38]

Companionship was another form of emotional labor commonly reported by household workers employed by the aged. Domestics expressed concern about older employers' welfare and sometimes continued working despite personal and economic sacrifices. One Chicana I interviewed explained why she continued working for a seventy-eight-year-old employer who lived a long distance from her, regardless of the low wages: "I guess you can say she needs companionship. I feel sorry for her, you know, she is one of my farthest ones [employers]. I go once a month to her house. I like to go early so I can sit and talk to her."

Domestics almost invariably found themselves counseling and consoling their employers. Mrs. Okamura described the following work situation to Glenn:

> I'd been working for a lady for two hours a week for a long time, but she didn't even give me a chance to work. Upon my arrival, she kept talking and going on

and on. For me, housework was much easier because even though I didn't understand English well, I still had to say, "Is that so?" "no" and "yes". . . . They just wanted to complain about their son or their son's wife.[39]

Although confidential information to which domestics become privy in these relationships may appear to make mistresses vulnerable to domestics, this is not generally the case. Working-class women of color are safe confidantes because they do not have access to the same social world. Jane Louis made this point in her interview with Rollins:

> Most employers like to talk to the people who work for them because you're not in their circle, you're not going to tell anybody who's important to them. I've been like a confidante. . . . They talk to you anyplace. A white person will go up to a black stranger and tell them very private things—because they know it's not going to go.[40]

The relationship of emotional labor is in no way reciprocal. Employers expect to be consoled; the inherent power relation of employer-employee means that middle-class white housewives have little fear of rebuttal, retaliation, or disparagement. Elaine Kaplan illustrated this point when she wrote about her mother's response to a question about her relationship with employers: "I have to listen to them, but I don't talk. It's none of their business. When they ask me how I'm doing I say just fine. That's all I say. They want to know my business so that they can tell their friends."[41] Her mother's response was validated by other domestics she interviewed:

> Most likely she [mother] spends her whole day responding to her employer with head nods, or one-liners like, "Yes, I understand," or "No, I don't," or "how nice." If it's a personal issue, she says, "it's too bad." She makes all the appropriate responses—like a robot who is not expected to have feelings or ideas.[42]

Several Chicana domestics recalled employers who initiated conversations seemingly only to respond with condescending remarks. Even when employers initiated conversations at a peer level, domestics complained that they assumed hierarchical positions by giving unsolicited advice or even scolding them and treating them like children. A few Chicanas recounted their anger at employers who made statements implying that "Chicanos have too many children" and "Chicanos don't value education and lack ambition." Yet because of the power relationship that governed the exchange, anger could usually be expressed only in silence. Not surprisingly, domestics frequently experienced employers' interest in their private lives as a form of prying rather than the sincere interest of a friend.

Accepting acts of benevolent maternalism is another form of emotional labor

Relate to Spang.

requiring domestics to manipulate their feelings in order to fulfill employers' psychological needs. Rollins listed a variety of maternalistic rituals associated with domestic service: "giving of gifts, the loaning of money, explaining bills, demanding to meet and approve friends, making business calls for the employee, making travel arrangements for her, and (in the South) interceding on her behalf with the legal system."[43]

Gift-giving is domestic workers' almost universal experience and stands as the most obvious symbol of employers' maternalism. Structurally, gift-giving occupies an important place within the underground economy, whereby working-class women are often given presents by middle-class employers in lieu of higher wages and benefits. Chicanas reported that Christmas gifts to them or their children were more common than annual raises. Unlike gift-giving in other work settings, gifts frequently replace higher wages, raises, or other benefits. The following quote from a domestic describes conditions under which the gift occurs: "I'm trying to show you they would do something nice for you when they really felt you needed it. But they wouldn't pay you nothing but these menial wages. Nobody else paid more, and nobody wanted to break the standard."[44] Odette Harris described similar circumstances to Rollins:

> They gave you things like clothes and pieces of furniture. They always like to change things in their house so they give the old things to you. But you never think of how many hours of your days are being spent. She [the forty-five-year-old employer] felt if she gave me things, she wouldn't have to pay too much. . . . [45]

Gift-giving is also a form of benevolent maternalism used to "buy" and "bond" the domestic. This is illustrated in the following account given to Susan Tucker by employer Corinne Cooke: "Now my cousin passed away not too long ago. She left five hundred dollars to one [domestic] that had been working for her since she was sixteen years old. So you can say in your book those servants were well cared for."[46]

Employers in domestic service commonly redefine as gifts items that would have gone to the Salvation Army or the trash. Glenn found that old clothes and other discarded items were the most common gifts given to Japanese American domestics. I found a similar case among Chicana domestics. Judith Warner and Helen Henderson reported that sixty percent of the 200 Mexican immigrant women surveyed in Laredo received used clothes from their employers.[47] This practice of giving old clothes within a work setting is unique to domestic service. It is almost inconceivable that the same woman would consider offering her old linen jacket to her secretary.

In order for the employer to obtain full benefits from her acts of benevolent maternalism, the employee must acknowledge her generosity. The critical importance of gratitude is expressed by employer Jane Stafford's complaint about a domestic she had employed for over twenty-five years: "I would give her a present, and she wouldn't even say thank you."[48] Thus, what determines the interaction as benevolent maternalism is the mistress's privilege and enjoyment of having her feelings noticed and considered important. When domestics accept and thank employers for old clothes, particularly unwanted items, they are engaged in "shadow work" that is not acknowledged by employers. Instead of responding honestly and refusing the old clothes, or even expressing hurt from the insult of such a gift, the domestic must labor to disguise her true feelings. As one domestic confided:

> They like to give me their leftovers. She gave me sneakers so worn, I wouldn't give them to anyone. But I know their feelings are so delicate, I take it.[49]

In her analysis of the custom of giving away old clothes, Rollins argued that the type of object exchanged and the way in which the exchange occurred "communicates to the parties involved and to the larger social group who the giver and receiver are and what their relationship to one another and to the community is."[50] Unlike an exchange of clothes that might occur in other settings among friends and relatives, "the employer, in giving old clothes and furniture and leftover food, is transmitting to the servant the employer's perception of the servant as needy, unable to provide adequately for herself, and willing to accept others' devalued goods."[51] The practice in itself defines an unequal, unilateral relationship. In some areas, the practice appears to be prescribed by the local racial etiquette. Leila Parkerson, who worked as a domestic in the South, recalled the practice to Susan Tucker:

> Every white person, poor or rich, always thought they could give me something. This family even—they gave me an old blouse with stains under the arms, perspiration stains. I took it and dumped it in the nearest trash can on the way home.[52]

Both the nonreciprocal nature of the interaction and the type of gift convey the message that domestics are needy and reinforces class distinctions. At the same time, gift-giving strengthens the employer's perception of herself as kind, generous, and thoughtful. Kaplan's interview with one housewife illustrates the point:

> I certainly feel that I have more than enough food and clothing here, and she must need some of these things. I don't mind sharing them. We are so fortunate, you know, and these things are still good. I think it cheers her up.[53]

Dobie illustrated how one employer was able to retain her self-image as fair and generous by using the gift to avoid the confrontation that might reveal otherwise:

After every nonargument—Mrs. Lure wringing her hands and murmuring, Sharon [the domestic] mute and enraged—a present is left on her bed. Perfume samples, soap taken from a hotel in Paris where they brought the kids last summer, hand-me-downs for Sharon's six-year-old daughter.[54]

Psychological Reasons Why Women Hire Women

As in the past, contemporary housewives hire women on the basis of personality rather than of more objective criteria like work history. Soraya Coley's assessment that an employee is evaluated by "how well she 'fits' or 'adapts' to her employer's idiosyncrasies"[55] is consistent with the advice given to employers: "Hiring the perfect help is to merge your idiosyncrasies with another's. . . . Be realistic, put your idiosyncrasies up front, and observe the reaction."[56] The importance of personality is evident in the following advice column to potential employers:

> Then there is the nearly perfect helper, who may be of any sex, color, or age. One was Vivolyn, Maria Campbell's first Jamaican housekeeper. "She was wonderful. She was just like her name—vivacious, warm, and wonderful with my child."[57]

However, personality traits are not the only concern that employers have in their selection of household workers. Women of color are sometimes hired for their ability to fulfill psychological needs stemming from American race relations. Developing personal relationships with the women of color whom they employ functions, for some white middle-class women, to affirm their self-image as nonracist. Kathy Dobie suggests that absolution of racism is one psychological need fulfilled in the relationship with women of color:

> Barbara [employer] wants something from Bertha [employee] and sometimes it seems like it's love, and sometimes it seems like it's forgiveness. But perhaps for most white people, a black person's affection can never mean more than an act of absolution for historical and collective guilt, an affection desired not because of how one feels about that particular person but because that person is black. "When I first started there, we never got along. She raises her voice. I raise my voice. She cries. I cry. She just wants you to be satisfied with her all the time". . . . "She wants me to tell her I love her. I just can't."[58]

Susan Tucker's interview with a white employer shows how hiring women of color allows some employers to act upon stereotypes involving the physical and emotional strength or spirituality of women of color. "They [African American women] sensed things. If you weren't feeling well, they could just pick something up, a rag or something and touch you, and it felt better."[59] Coley's interview with a domestic named Ms. Calvin confirms this function of the employee's race and ethnicity:

> I should charge for being a psychiatrist. They [employers] tickle me; sometimes they come and ask me questions and talk to me about their problems like I'm a doctor. They tell me *I'm* the only one they can talk to. They even ask me to pray for them; they act like black folks' prayers are different or like I have a direct line to the Lord. They just don't understand how I seem to be doing all alright.[60]

The Chicanas whom I interviewed expressed discomfort with employers' interest in them "as Mexicans," feeling, perhaps, that they were being treated as cultural curiosities. Often, when white middle class employers discussed Mexican culture, they attempted to explain their different life experiences on the basis of culture rather than class. For instance, Mrs. Rivera recalled an employer who decorated her house with valuable *Santos* and expensive R. C. Gorman sculptures purchased on annual trips to New Mexico. The employer was surprised to discover that Mrs. Rivera did not own an antique wooden statue of her patron saint. Even when Chicanas responded to inquiries about Chicano culture, history, or social issues, in the interviews they expressed the tension they felt, explaining that they avoided such discussions as much as possible. Employers frequently inquired about Mexican food and many eventually asked the women they hired to make tortillas or chile. The Chicanas were similarly hesitant about sharing food and felt the request was inappropriate.

Purchasing Status by Hiring a Woman of Color

Rollins has written extensively on the significance of hiring women of different class and racial backgrounds in order to affirm employers' status. In her analysis of the interracial interpersonal relationship, she identified two functions employers fulfill by hiring women of color: "affording the employers the self-enhancing satisfactions that emanate from having the presence of an inferior and validating the employer's lifestyle, ideology, and social world, from their familial interrelations to the economically and racially stratified system in which they live."[61] Furthermore, "their presence makes the employers' status clear to neighbors because women of color function better as contrast figures for strengthening employers' egos and class and racial identities."[62]

Taking an innovative research tack of analyzing family photographs, Tucker observed the importance of race and ethnicity in affirming employers' class and racial status in their communities. In her analysis of employers' family albums, she observed that "an attractive, well-dressed black domestic signified the family's membership in 'the better class' in the community."[63] In subsequent interviews with domestics, Tucker asked about their inclusion in the employers' family portraits. These African American women confirmed that "whites 'liked to dress blacks up' and sought to show that they had 'good-looking servants.'"[64]

The physical appearances of household workers can be further manipulated to function as visible signs of the hierarchical status distinguishing domestics from employers. In the past, employers sometimes insisted that domestics wear attire to match the table cloth or styles ranging "from bright plaids and red dotted Swiss formal attire to a '1942 version of a beloved Southern Mammy's costume'".[65] Nowadays, employers simply expect the employees' inferior status to be apparent in their physical appearances. In her interview with Coley, Ms. Nelson listed the ways her physical appearance was manipulated to assure the employer of her superior status: "Well they [employers] thought I was too dressy. I couldn't even wear make-up. They wanted some haggard looking woman."[66] Kaplan notes that the old housedresses worn by domestics alleviated "the housewife's insecurity about her own position."[67] Ella Mae Robinson's description of her interaction with the employer, Mrs. C, illustrates Kaplan's point:

> "Honey, you could hear Mrs. C gettin' all excited and makin' a big deal over my clothes. I hate to have to answer her questions about why I'm looking 'extra pretty today.' She makes sure I get them clothes off before she moves one step."[68]

White uniforms are used to distinguish the maid from families and friends, particularly when employers fear that others might mistake the reason for her presence. Dobie commented on a common experience: "The maid puts on a uniform when there's company"; otherwise she is allowed to wear jeans.[69] Most private household workers report that employers request a uniform to be worn on particular occasions, such as serving a special dinner or party or when accompanying the family on vacation. Mrs. Nishi expressed her opinion of the employer's request to Glenn: "I had to dress up in the maid's outfit when they had dinner parties. It was all part of it about how phoney these people were that I worked for."[70] In her recollection of an employer's request that she wear a uniform while accompanying the family to Miami to take care of the children, Judith Thomas exposed the purpose of the request:

> She wanted me to wear the uniform. She was really prejudiced. She just wanted that the maid must be identified. . . . She used to go to the beach everyday with the children. So going to the beach in the sand and sun and she would have the kids eat ice cream and all that sort of thing. You know what a white dress would look like at the beach?[71]

Both Mrs. Nishi and Judith Thomas were aware of the uniform as a symbol signifying their employers' positions to family members and friends.

Purchasing Deference

Confirmation of the employer's status is not always accomplished by the mere physical presence of women of color or white uniforms; it frequently requires daily practices of deferential behavior that continually affirm and enhance the domestic's inferiority. Thus, Chicanas in Denver reported encounters with racist employers who defined their superior status on the basis that they were white and the domestics were not. This phenomenon explains the seeming contradiction of hiring Mexicans while disdaining them. In the following account, the household worker realized that her ethnicity was important to the employer, and she understood that deference was part of the job. Her refusal to engage in the necessary emotional labor cost her the job. Mrs. Duran recounted this experience:

> She [employer] would make me feel like I was nothing or like I was doing this [domestic service] because I was so poor or because I was a Mexican. One day she said that Mexican people are all very poor. They weren't educated. And that did it! I dropped what I was doing. I left it there and I said, "here take this and shove it. I don't have to take this abuse from you or from anybody. I'm Mexican, yes, but I'm proud of what I am and I'm working." I says, "Everybody has a job and I have this as my job and if you felt this way, you didn't have to hire me." I says, "You knew I was a Mexican when you hired me. Why did you hire me?" She didn't know what to say. I said, "I am not working to get abuse." I said, "I'm working because that's what I like to do." So I said, "Take your job. Pay me for what I did" and I said, "I'll get out of here and don't you ever dare call me again because I will not come work for you again."

Mrs. Garcia also recognized that her ethnicity played a role in the superior status assumed by employers. She expressed her pain and resentment toward employers who established their status by treating her as an inferior:

> Some of them were really hateful. They thought you know, you're just anybody there to clean their house and they really would take advantage of you. And I didn't enjoy it. . . . I don't know if it was just cause they thought you know, that you were Spanish and stuff, they would just sort of take advantage of me and I didn't like it.

Women employers rely heavily upon deference for the status previously denied them in their housewife role. As Katzman noted, "Employing a domestic offers them a position of power not otherwise available to housewives."[72] To ensure their positions of power, housewives seek an employee "to whom they can feel superior and dominating. . . . rather than seeking an intelligent, resourceful, and independent worker."[73] Rollins illustrated the employer's need to feel superior by citing an incident that occurred during her participant observation: "Although Ms. Caton and I had agreed at our interview that I would start working for her the following week, she called me the night before I was to begin and expressed hesitancy about hiring me because 'you seem so well educated.'"[74] Rollins was able to ease the employer's apprehensions about her "suitability for the job" by acting subservient. Similar experiences are reported by West Indian immigrants in New York City. Colen found that domestics acknowledged their employers' expectations (and requirement) of subservient behavior and referred to the need to learn to be "maidish."

Writings on the experience of women of color suggest that the deference created in employers' homes was not unlike that of previous generations. The inferior status of the nonwhite domestic and the superior status of the white employer were affirmed through daily rituals and practices involving the use of language and space. The classic example of linguistic deference in job settings is the use of "girl" in reference to women workers. However, the practice in domestic service has a long history tied to race relations between whites and African Americans. The practice is based not only on gender and class inequality but on racial inequality. In *Manchild in the Promised Land*, Claude Brown recounted a white employer's use of the term "girl":

"George, do you know where I might find some nice honest colored girl who could come in and help my wife clean up the house? . . . You saw the girl who was here. She was a very nice girl, and she's been with us a long time, for three or four years." Man you should've seen this girl. This girl was about sixty years old. Her hair was gray, but she was colored, so she was still a girl.[75]

In her interview with Rollins, Odette Harris analyzed the meaning behind the practice:

Why am I your "girl?" I didn't like it because it sounded like ownership. Like masters and slaves, talking about "my" . . . But you had to accept being called a "girl" and being called by your first name. You would prefer to be addressed as "Miss" but there wasn't anything you could do so you accepted it . . . They never referred to us as "ladies." They figures it's too nice for us. We're not "ladies."[76]

Maggie Holmes unmasked the racist meaning behind an employer saying "All you—you girls . . . She stop. I say, 'All you niggers, is that what you want to say?'"[77] Reference to household workers as "girls" by employers was so common in New York City that Maria Laurino reported that a training session teaching survival skills to workers included the following chant:

I AM NOT A MAID. I AM A HOUSEHOLD TECHNICIAN. I AM NOT YOUR GIRL. I AM A GROWN WOMAN. IF I WERE YOUR GIRL YOU WOULD

NOT LEAVE ME WITH YOUR CHILD OR YOUR MOTHER. I'M NOBODY'S
GIRL.[78]

Another common and almost universal practice was to address domestics by
their first names and employers by their last names. Employer Elinor Birney
revealed the significance of the practice to Susan Tucker when she expressed her
concern over her daughter's refusal to follow the custom: "The servant calls the
woman Mary and Mary calls the servant by her name. Now, I think your
employer-employee relationship sometimes could get very sticky if you don't
have some separation."[79] West Indian domestics reported that employers in New
York used their first names but expected to be addressed formally.[80] Laurino
remarked on the irony of the practice because a domestic was in the position of
knowing "the personal details of the employer's life, yet will most likely address
her as Miss or Mrs.—and in return, she'll be called by her first name."[81]
    Another practice of linguistic deference is the employers' refusal to use the
domestics' proper names. Tucker found that white employers in the South frequently called African American domestics "Mammy," "Aunt," and "Uncle."[82]
Bonnie Thornton Dill found that employers in New York and Philadelphia
changed the names of their African American employees. As one domestic recalled: "My name is Opal. Very simple, very Southern: Opal. When she would
talk to me, I was called everything but that . . ."[83]
    Several Chicana domestics similarly reported that employers refused to pro-
nounce their names correctly and eventually Anglicized them. On the basis of
the stereotype that all Mexican women are named Maria, white employers in the
Southwest frequently refer to all Latina domestics as "Maria."
    Other linguistic patterns used by the employer to establish her superior status
included: assuming familiarity toward domestics by inquiring about their personal lives, initiating discussions, selecting appropriate topics, and offering unsolicited advice about cleaning techniques, child-rearing practices, and the like.
Rollins found that some domestics, such as Nancy Clay, clearly understood employers' conversations as merely transparent attempts to reinforce inequality:

> They want to know all your business so they know just where you're coming from.
> They tell you some of their problems so that you'll tell them your business. It's
> knowledge for control they want. They're uneasy if they don't know enough about
> you, if they don't know what you're thinking.[84]

    Status is also established through spatial deference in the employer's home.
Generally, the kitchen is the only room in which the employee sits, and that
usually occurs only during lunch. If employers initiate a conversation elsewhere
in the house, domestics rarely sit to listen, certainly not without being requested
to do so. In her book *From Mammies to Militants*, Trudier Harris commented

on the importance of the kitchen in maintaining spatial segregation in the white woman's home and assuring her status:

> The most comfortable realm of the latter's [black woman's] existence is the kitchen; it becomes the black town, the nigger room, of the white house. The black woman cleans the living room or the dining room or the bedroom or the bathroom and retires to the kitchen. She sits in the kitchen when she has time for sitting and there requests that she go to other parts of the house come to her. . . . The kitchen is also the one room in the house where the white woman can give up spatial ownership without compromising herself. Kitchens have connotations of hard work and meniality—sweat, grime, broken fingernails, and other things from which the mistress wishes to dissociate herself. Passing *that particular* space on to the domestic is a royal decree of her subservience and inferiority.[85]

Although domestics are expected to create and to respect the private space of employers and their families, they themselves are denied privacy. This is particularly true for live-in domestics. Unlike employers at the turn of the century, middle-class employers today rarely own homes with maid's quarters. They make decisions about accommodations based not on a concern for the domestic's privacy but rather on convenience. Employers who allow the domestic to sleep in the extra bedroom do not always ensure privacy. If the room continues to function as a storage area, the employer and her family are likely to reserve the right to enter the room at any time rather than respect privacy absolutely. Employers who do not have an extra room or who are unwilling to reallocate the guest bedroom are most likely to provide sleeping arrangements that deny privacy. The combination of not having a bedroom and not having access to the rest of the house for resting or leisure activity continually affirms the worker's inferior status in the employer's home.

Traditionally, American homes were built with spatial deference in mind. This was accomplished by segregating areas of the house through the use of entrances, passageways, and rooms. Even though few homes today are built with servant's entrances, women of color report numerous practices used to separate their presence from the employer and her family. They move around the house, ignored as if they were invisible, their existence acknowledged only when their services are required. Rollins writes about incidents of invisibility while doing participant observation. She begins her discussion on invisibility in domestic service by sharing her field notes.

> Mrs. Thomas and I were both cleaning in her large kitchen when her sixteen-year-old came in to make a sandwich for lunch. They talked openly as if I weren't there . . . I said nothing because I felt that was what was expected of me. This situation was the most peculiar feeling of the day: being there and not being there. Unlike a

third person who chose not to take part in a conversation, I knew I was not expected to take part. I wouldn't speak and was related to as if I wouldn't hear.[86]

The practice of ignoring household workers while they move about the same
space in which others are interacting is so common in domestic service that
Erving Goffman used the experience to illustrate his concept of the "nonperson."
He quotes Mrs. Trollope's *Domestic Manners of the Americans*:

> A Virginian gentleman told me that ever since he had married, he had been accus-
> tomed to have a Negro girl sleep in the same chamber with himself and his wife. I
> asked for what purpose this nocturnal attendance was necessary. "Good Heaven!"
> was the reply, "If I wanted a glass of water during the night, what would become
> of me."[87]

Although such extreme cases of the nonperson as cited by Goffman may be a
thing of the past, household workers are still expected to be invisible and to
move throughout the house cleaning, without interrupting the employer family's
routine. In their episodes of "invisibility," Chicanas pointed out the added difficulty the situation created. As day workers, employed once or twice a week for
five to seven hours, they resented employers who did not consider their presence
in planning family activities for that day or who did not bother to tell them about
planned activities that required a change in the work routine. Having to clean
houses while employers and their families ignored their activity involved rearranging the work around the families' daily activities. At times, this required
them to carry the vacuum cleaner and other cleaning materials up and down the
stairs two or three times, rather than complete an entire floor at one time. They
voiced their frustrations about having to vacuum and wash the floor while children and pets ran through the room.

Deferential behavior is also constructed through eating arrangements. Rarely
did domestics eat in the dining room or in the presence of mistresses' husbands.
Mrs. Garcia remembered an employer who told her: "If you brought your lunch
you wait out in your car or in the patio or out in the street or where ever." West
Indians in New York City employed as live-in workers faced the archetypal
situation of the domestic eating alone in the kitchen. As one woman described,
"I couldn't eat with them at the table. . . . I have to eat after they finish eating. . . . And then I eat in the kitchen."[88] Aware of the status hierarchy produced
from acts of deference, the woman quoted above also commented that "there are
people who do that because they want us to know that we are not equal."[89]
Another West Indian woman described the purpose of deferential eating arrangements as a way to create symbols of her inferiority: "The first day I got there
[the employer] took out a fork and a plate and told me that this was mine to
always use. They gave me the impression that I wasn't clean enough."[90]

Deference is achieved not only through eating arrangements but also through the allocation of food. In her interview with Mary Yelling, Aletha Vaughn recalled an employer who marked an "X" on all the food that she was not to eat. She was left with peanut butter, jelly, bologna, and other cold food. Colen described a variety of ways in which employers distributed food within their households to maintain superior-inferior relationships:

> Some employers left food for the worker to prepare for the children but none for the worker herself, though she might work an eight-to-twelve-hour shift. One worker was accused of consuming "too much" of a particular food, milk, which she never drank. When one woman on a live-in job ate some pork chops which had been in the refrigerator for several days while her wealthy corporate executive employers dined out, she was informed that several pork chops were "missing" and that she should "find" them. With her own money, the worker replaced what she ate, and no comment was made.[91]

Domestics reported that some employers offered them garbage to eat. Ms. Douglas recounted the following account to Soraya Coley: "The woman I worked for was a crank-pot. She would buy meat and have me cook it and then for dinner she'd cut off the part with the meat and give me the fat."[92]

Glenn presented a similar incident in her study of Japanese American domestics: "Mrs. Takagi recalls being offered a lunch consisting of asparagus stalks whose tips had been eaten off by the employer's son."[93] Aletha Vaughn remembered another employer offering her a sandwich consisting of bread, mayonnaise and bananas. When she refused the sandwich, the employer "just raked it on in the garbage."[94] Frequently, employers considered the meal as part of the domestic's pay. Yet clearly some of the food offered as a meal would otherwise have been thrown away.

The accounts given by women of color employed as household workers not only provide details about the type of labor they perform for their employers but reveal a variety of social functions their labor fulfills. A closer look at the interaction between employee and employer illustrates the ways in which the work structure shapes their relationship.

RELATIONSHIPS BETWEEN WOMEN

Domestic service is a unique social setting in which to explore relationships between women. Rarely in our society do women (or men) from different social-economic, racial, and ethnic backgrounds interact in an informal and intimate setting. The employer's home, in which domestics and employers interact brings several important factors to bear simultaneously: shared gender, interracial and interclass oppression, and location within women's primary unrecognized work-place—the household. It is within this context that white middle-class women negotiate informal labor arrangements with women of color to do physical and emotional labor. In their own homes middle-class white women make decisions that transform sisterhood into a means either to extract emotional and physical labor or, conversely, to improve working conditions and to increase pay and benefits for women of color employed to do their housework.

Household-labor negotiations frequently occur within the underground economy; they involve few government regulations. Consequently, employers have enormous leeway to determine the working conditions by setting wages, establishing job descriptions, and determining the work structure.[95] Recent studies report household workers describing a wide variation in wages and working conditions. Employers decide whether to give raises, and they usually decide whether social security or benefits are obtained. Domestics have little influence over working conditions outside the choice to accept a job or to quit. Given the power that employers exert over working conditions, domestics—more than other workers—feel dependent on and at the mercy of their employers. Since the majority of household workers are not unionized, the struggle to improve working conditions remains an individual struggle.

For these reasons, in domestic service personal relationships between employers and employees play a major role in determining working conditions. Zelda Green explained her working conditions as a domestic to Tucker: "It's not so much the work—it's the people you're working for. That's what makes the difference."[96] For many household workers, the only avenue available to improve material circumstances is through personal relationships with employers. Linda Barron experienced that reality as the daughter of a domestic. In an interview with Tucker, she said, "Some people now still aren't getting W–2 forms, aren't getting paid vacation, aren't getting Social Security. I knew my mother she had to depend on the whites [employers] for loans for us and things."[97]

The Promise and the Gift Revisited

Pie-in-the-sky promises that domestics will gain access to some material privileges carry much weight in an occupation that pays poorly and offers few if any benefits. Coley's study revealed numerous promises employers held out to their employees: "Stay because I have left you in my will"; "Lucy, we never want you to leave"; "We'll do anything to make it easier for you"; "If you stay another ten years, we'll get you a mink coat".[98]

The other side of the paternalistic practice of giving "gifts" in lieu of higher wages and benefits is to establish a sense of obligation, thus placing the worker into debt. Glenn explained that "a sense of mutual obligation" "transcend[s] purely economic or instrumental considerations."[99] Employers' rewards and inducements bind the worker in an emotional and economic trap. Simply the promise or expectation that the employer might pay more, provide gifts, or help the employee get a green card obligates the worker beyond the boundaries of the contractual work arrangement. In her article on women of color employed as domestics in New York City, Maria Laurino described an incident that exemplifies the way employers can bend closeness and emotional attachment to their own personal interests. "One woman recalled trying to leave a live-in job once she had gotten a green card. The employer would break down crying, begging her to stay, telling her it was unfair to leave after all they had done for her." [100] Coley referred to the obligation as a form of "blackmail."

> They [the employers] always thought they could do anything with money. Whenever I get angry about something, she would say, "here's a new dress," or if I raised some other concern—like not having taken a vacation, she'd say—"go anywhere and we'll pay for it." But the point is, you just get tired.
>   You have got to stay for the children's sake; they need you. You are the only one who can handle them [the children]. [101]

The relationship between the gift and obligation is a common feature of domestic service. Most workers realize that the promise of higher wages and benefits is exchanged for the domestics' loyalty, commitment, and obligation to employers—and they resent it. One domestic repeated the caution she received from her father in an interview with Coley: "As my father use (sic) to say those people always giving you something, means that they want you to feel indebted and one day they're going to call in that debt." [102] In recalling an employer's offer to assist her financially, Clelia Daly expressed a similar concern to Mary Yelling:

> She told me when I first went out there that she was as close as the telephone and that she did have a bank account of her own and if I ever needed anything, she could always let me have it. But I don't care where I work, I ain't going to get no money from them white folks. See, a lot of people just be in so much debt with them that they really have to love 'em. They have to come when they say come. No, I'd do without till I could get the money myself. [103]

Odette Harris expressed her feelings about the sense of obligation:

> After a while, I began to resent what they [employers] were doing. They have a way of making you feel a sense of guilt by being over kind to you. But, you see, they were doing so much for me to keep me. And I resented it after a while. [104]

Hertz notes that dual-career couples prefer private household workers over institutional child care services because of the potential flexibility in working late and requesting dinner parties on short notice.[105] Last minute requests are more likely to be fulfilled when employees can be manipulated.

The Chicana domestics whom I interviewed were not immune to the friendship exhibited by employers but they expressed ambivalence about it. For instance, Mrs. Portillo questioned her employers' gestures of kindness. She cautioned that employers may be "very generous," but they "use their generosity to pressure." Domestics understood that the gift distorted the employee-employer relationship and placed the domestic under obligation to be loyal and committed. The obligation was paid not only in emotional labor but usually included additional physical labor.

In this day and age, unlike feudalistic arrangements between masters and servants, the relationship between employee and employer takes place under capitalism and is wage labor. Under capitalism, employers' gifts or promises of a reward for employees' loyalty are not the same as the obligation a master had to care for his servants. The employees' involvement in the interpersonal relationships is a gamble. In her critique of employers' references to the family analogy, Ms. Harvey exposed the gamble she was unwilling to take:

> I say, if I am one of the family, then why am I doing all this work. Some [employers] even talk about leaving you in their will, but who says I'm going to outlive them. Give me my benefits now.[106]

In her interview with Mary Yelling, Voncille Sherard shared an incident in which she gambled and lost:

> And she [the employer] always said she would pay me extra but that she was saving my extra money back for me because she knew I wanted to go to college. But when the time came to go to college, the only extra I got was two skirts from the Spiegel catalog.[107]

Willie Mae Fitzgerald recounted to Tucker her inability to obtain higher wages even though her employers expressed a great deal of warmth. She realized that she did not control the outcome. Employers' rewarding twenty-odd years of service became a matter of luck or "blessing":

> I met a lady in the hospital the other day, and she was saying that the people she worked for she helped them raise their children, and they liked her and they showed it and they would raise her salary. She didn't have to ask for a raise, and they retired her. They told her she had worked hard, and they helped her get on retirement. I told her—I said, "Well, you're blessed." I say, "I worked at a place—the last place I worked at twenty-odd years—and they didn't raise my salary." Oh yeah, I thought they was crazy about me. I did. They loved my cooking. They were crazy about my dinners.[108]

The family analogy in domestic service calls forth images of the master-servant and mistress-maid legacies that depicted the faithful old servant taken care of in old age or the young, single, and attractive domestic marrying into the employer's family. The images convey the "rags-to-riches" stories that are part of the folklore in domestic service. Even though such soap opera romances and inheritances are unlikely occurrences in the United States, the myth remains.

For the overwhelming majority of domestics, the material gains obtained through personal relationships with employers were left-over food, cast-off clothing, and discarded furniture. Kaplan pointed to the irony in such "material gains" in the description of employers' "useless items, like decorative bowls" in her own home when growing up. "Our very small apartment was filled with expensive sheets, blankets, dresses, and shoes. Each item cost more than the $50-a-month rent." [109]

The system of gifts and obligations in domestic service tends to shape the personalism in the employee-employer relationship into a strategy of oppression. Redefining work obligations as family or friendship obligations assures employers access to both the emotional and the physical labor of their employees. Personalism camouflages work conditions which become distorted and unintelligible within the context of the interpersonal relationships between domestics and employers. Employers' refusal to relate to domestics' concerns as workers' rights distorts the real conditions of their interaction.

Just Like One of the Family

Alice Childress testified to the way that personal relationships distort working conditions in her essay on the family analogy in *Like One of the Family: Conversations From a Domestic's Life*.[110] The domestic's view of the employer's attempt to redefine her as "one of the family" rather than as a domestic was presented in an exchange between the two. Mildred, the domestic, overheard the employer tell a friend:

> "We just love her! She's *like* one of the family and she *just adores* our little Carol! We don't know *what* we'd do without her! We don't think of her as a servant!" [111]

Mildred responded later to the employer's characterization by listing the ways her interaction with the family distinguished her as a nonmember, an outsider with inferior status.

> The family eats in the dining room and I eat in the kitchen. Your mama borrows your lace table cloth for her company and your son entertains his friends in your parlor, your daughter takes her afternoon nap on the living room couch and the puppy sleeps on your satin spread . . . and whenever your husband gets tired of

something you are talkin' about he says, "Oh, for Pete's sake, forget it. . . ." So
you can see I am not *just* like the family.

Now for another thing, I do not *just* adore your little Carol. I think she is a
likeable child, but she is also fresh and sassy. I know you call it 'uninhibited' and
that is the way you want your child to be, but *luckily* my mother taught me some
inhibitions or else I would smack little Carol once in awhile when she's talkin' to
you like you're a dog, but as it is I just laugh it off the way you do because she is
your child and I am *not* like one of the family.[112]

Mildred was quite aware that she was an employee and had to act like one and
that she was not eligible for the privileges and benefits of being a member of her
employer's white middle-class family. She listed her activities in the employer's
home:

After I have worked myself into a sweat cleaning the bathroom and the kitchen
. . . making the beds . . . cooking the lunch . . . washing the dishes and ironing
Carol's pinafores . . . I do not feel like no weekend house guest. I feel like a
servant . . ."[113]

Mildred stripped the emotional meanings that the employer had attached to
her work and exposed her activity as the hard labor that it was. Furthermore,
she emphasized that the employer's home was not her home but her workplace.
Many household workers reject the employer's use of the popular phrase "one
of the family." Their objections to the analogy are related to employer's distor-
tion of the real basis of their relationship which results in the extraction of unpaid physical and emotional labor. Ms. Pratt's response to Coley's question
about feeling like family addressed this concern:

I don't think you can feel like one of the family. I'm not white, or Jewish; I'm not
adopted. We are friends. And I don't expect her to say do something without
pay.[114]

Although the phrase "one of the family" represents "the epitome of the personalized employer-employee association,"[115] domestics' use of the family analogy points to aspects of the emotional labor that some workers are willing to
accept and those that they reject. On the one hand, this analogy suggests that
domestics are engaged in the emotional labor involved in nurturing and caring;
on the other hand, it suggests that domestics are treated with respect and are not
forced into doing the emotional labor required to create deference.

In their accounts of emotional labor, domestics expressed an awareness that
deferential behavior was the result of their employers' desire for status. Employers could simply have asked domestics to engage in deferential behavior, how-

ever in almost all cases they manipulated appearances and structured the interaction, which introduced a great deal of tension into the relationship when
employees resisted accepting an inferior status. Issues of status and deference
are regularly underscored in domestics' depictions of their relationships with
employers, listen as Mrs. Lucero describes the way in which her employers
structured the interaction:

> Most of them treat me like I was of the family, except for one, one of them that
> their kids are very strange. Like they think that they're really uppity and they're
> really not. They're [employer] the least well to do, I think. Yet they are very
> unsociable. Kind of avoid me . . . but the others [employers] treat me almost like
> if I was family. If I'm ever around them and they have a family gathering, they
> make me really feel good like I'm really important in their lives.

Mrs. Lucero classified relationships according to whether employers inter-
acted with her as peers or as superiors. She contrasted the two types as a dichotomy of extremes: treatment as a "nonperson" versus treatment as a "family
member." Ms. Smith made the dichotomy even more succinct in her interview
with Coley:

> I guess I felt like one of the family on this job. . . . They didn't treat me like a
> piece of furniture, either.

Again, the family analogy exemplifies the drastically different interaction that
results when employers seek status by establishing the domestics' inferiority and
their own superiority. Domestics, particularly women of color, may be more
vulnerable to employers' definition of their relationship as "one of the family"
because they seek respect, a rare quality in the employee-employer relationship.

Some domestics willingly exchange certain types of emotional labor for respect, status, and influence, for instance by manipulating traditional "feminine"
qualities attached to housework. By being "motherly," they support and enhance
the well-being of others while eliminating many negative and harsh attacks on
their self-esteem.[116] The search for respect and dignity in domestic service leads
most household workers to trade additional physical and emotional labor for
psychological benefits. Researchers report various incidents indicating that domestics willingly and consciously make the exchange. Glenn quoted Mrs. How-
ell to illustrate the importance of "emotional succor" received from elderly employers:

> Old people look like my grandmother. . . . I'm so comfortable because these
> people can give me love: I can give love. I enjoy every four hours that I'm work-
> ing. . . . I like old people. I can depend on them: I can trust them.[117]

Coley found that when the domestic workers defined a "one-of-the-family" relationship, it identified their feelings of rewards (emotional and otherwise) above and beyond the standard contractual relationship.[118] In her interview with Rollins, Ms. Harris explained the psychological benefits that she received from working as a domestic:

> But at the time, I didn't have a good relationship with [the relatives I was living with] so I thought it was better to work for them since I was getting a little bit of love there. It did give me a sense of belonging. And I needed that.[119]

Not all domestics consider the added obligations of the personal relationships with their employers to be unpaid labor. For instance, in the description of an interpersonal relationship that Mrs. Lopez related to me, she did not treat the additional labor performed as burdensome or oppressive.

> I considered her [the employer] my friend. I started out cleaning for her like anybody else but we got to be really super close, like, you know, she'd have to go shopping or she had to work while I was going to be there, she'd ask me to babysit the kids or she have a load of laundry she really had to take care of before the day was over, she needed something that was in the laundry she'd ask me to do it. She'd call me and say "So and so is going to come to work in the house to do this" and she'd say, "Would you stay a little extra until he gets there and make sure that the house is locked" and stuff. We got to be pretty close. And we still talk and stuff. I really got to be close with her.

Although the description of her personal relationship with the employer was dominated by a list of the additional physical labor she does, Mrs. Lopez did not feel exploited. She considered the psychological rewards she obtained sufficient. Tensions only arise in these interpersonal relationships when domestics feel that the monetary payment or psychological rewards fall short of the full value of their physical and emotional labor.

The Businesslike Relationship

The alternative to the affective interpersonal domestic-employer relationship is the instrumental relationship usually referred to as businesslike. Household workers who portray their relationships with employers as businesslike describe the work as "spelled-out," consistent, and limited to housecleaning tasks. Frequently, verbal exchanges are limited to short discussions, phone calls, or notewriting. Other than brief morning and afternoon greetings, employer-employee interaction centers around the labor: schedules, tasks to be done, the need for materials, or changes in plans. Workers characterize this interaction as contractual.

Establishing and maintaining a businesslike relationship is difficult in many respects. Virtually all contemporary jobs are structured to include breaks. However, regular morning and afternoon breaks are aspects of work culture absent from domestic service. During her participant observation, Judith Rollins elicited a negative reaction from an employer for taking a break after working nonstop from 9:00 A.M. to 12:30 P.M.[120] Coley also reports breaks to be uncommon in the occupation. As Ms. Kirk explained:

> One of the biggest problems with household work is that the employers work you too hard. They want you to do everything in one day. They aren't sensitive to you even taking a half hour lunch break.[121]

Structuring breaks and time off is a particularly serious problem for live-in domestics because the hours, tasks and obligations of the job are constantly redefined. Furthermore, live-in workers even find it difficult to guarantee their days off. Coley used Ms. Calvin's account to describe the problem for live-in workers:

> Thursday was my day off. But every Thursday morning, she would get up as she did every other morning and give me something to do. And usually she would say you can leave after you do so and so. Well, often by the time I finished the task, or giving the children lunch it was usually after 2 o'clock and I had no real day off.[122]

Rights that are assumed in other work settings are absent in most employers' homes. Instead of responding as professional employers to employee requests for proper equipment to do the job, domestics' employers view such requests as unreasonable or at best silly. Even among women who have come to respect the general rights of workers for equipment that is in good working order, adequate supplies to complete the job, and even extras such as a comfortable break or lunch period, these rights are often treated as gifts or favors. In the popular media, domestics' requests are frequently presented as ridiculous. Viva's *Village Voice* article again illustrates such ridicule as she belittles her domestics' requests for work tools, cleaning materials and other items:

> She [the domestic] made only one demand: You had to have the following cleaning ingredients on hand: Windex, 409, Spic and Span, sponge mop, Easy-Off, Draino, Comet, Vanish, rubber gloves, broom and dustpan, dust mop, several clean rags, plastic brillo, Joy, Cascade, All furniture polish, and Beacon wax. This initial investment was an absolute must. Were you a stringsaver, the type who would suggest say, vinegar and water instead of Windex, or more Comet instead of 409, your Guatemalan refugee would give you a look guaranteed to inspire a trip to your local Safeway. . . . Make sure all appliances are in perfect working order. This

includes a vacuum cleaner, VCR, Juicer, and blender (she may want to mix herself a health drink).[123]

Like other employers who hire workers in the underground economy, middle-class housewives seldom structure a regular routine for raises. The Chicanas who were interviewed in Denver rarely found employers who offered raises annually or on any regular basis. Domestics generally feel that domestic service is like any other type of job and that employers should thus understand that raises are part of hiring workers. However, domestics understand that employers will try to cheat them of extra wages as long as they can. Instead, employees achieve raises only by threatening to quit. Mrs. Rodriquez and Mrs. Salas described their experiences as follows:

> I remember getting paid like fifteen dollars a week or something like that and I didn't know any better to ask—I mean for a raise because one time I told them that I was going to quit. I said, "Well, you never gave me a raise." And they said, "Well, you never asked for one." I said to myself, they should of offered me one, you know. They should never wait until you ask. I know if I had money and somebody was working for me and I could afford it I'd—I would give them a raise.

> Most of them [employers] realize that I should of gotten a raise but they don't offer. They think—they figure that she don't ask for a raise I won't pay her more. But if I do ask they're usually pretty good and the ones that sort of look at me sort of—I usually just say, "I'll give you some time," I says, "to think about it and if you think that is good," I says, "you can find somebody else to work for you because I need more money than what you are giving me."

In their accounts of requesting raises, some domestics expressed a need to force employers to recognize that domestic service is "real work." Instead of approaching employers on the basis that they deserved or earned a raise, some approached them as peers and drew comparisons to their material circumstances. Willie Mae Fitzgerald recounted to Tucker one unsuccessful attempt to get a raise:

> So one day I say to her, I say, "Miz Brown," I said, "things is high now." I say, "And what you pay for meat and bread," I say, "that's what I have to pay, too." I say, "I been working here for a long time." I say, "I'd like a raise."[124]

In response to her employer's offer to raise her daily pay from twenty-five to twenty-six dollars after two years of service, Mrs. Lujan shamed her employer into acknowledging that she was denying another worker the same rights that she expected as a worker. She drew her employer's attention to the broader issue, which the latter failed to consider applicable to domestic service. Mrs. Lujan said, "I know you get more than a dollar raise where you work and you would feel cheated and insulted if you were offered one dollar."

Wages are the tip of the iceberg. Benefits assumed in other working environments: overtime, vacation, sick pay, a health care plan, and any procedures for redress of grievances, are rarely if ever found in domestic service. At the same time, negative sanctions against employees are common, domestics report that employers expect breakage costs to be borne by the workers. Consider the following account by one of the Chicanas whom I interviewed. After waxing the kitchen floor, Mrs. Tafoya left an open can of floor wax on the dining room table. While she was upstairs vacuuming, her employer opened the sliding doors next to the dining room table to let a breeze in. The curtains flew up, tipped the can, and spilled floor wax onto the table. Mrs. Tafoya was held financially responsible for half of the cost of the repair. In another account, Mrs. Garcia was charged the cost of a glass tabletop that she broke while cleaning. Although the breakage costs did not involve the direct exchange of cash, employers collected by withholding wages for a certain amount of time. Inquiries about breakage revealed that employers who did not charge domestics were the exception. Mrs. Salazar explained:

> Most of them have been very nice about it. We have dealt with it—either I have worked an extra day for them or some of them have said "leave it up to experience" and like saying "don't do it again" or "be more careful" but I never have gotten fired for that.

DISCUSSION

Descriptive accounts offered by women of color challenge many perceptions about the function of domestic service in American society today. Even though employers state that they hire domestics to escape the drudgery of housework and to gain freedom to engage in other activities, descriptions of working conditions reveal a more complex set of needs. Interviews with employers and employees alike indicate that domestic service still performs important functions in enhancing the status of middle-class housewives and their families. Moreover, the analysis of the structure of paid housework reveals that the work includes both physical and emotional labor, much of it as shadow work and unpaid labor.

The daily rituals and practices of domestic service reproduce the systems of gender, class, and race domination. All of the gender-specific aspects of unpaid housework—identified in the housewife experience—are also present in domestic service. Even though domestics are paid workers, they do not escape the sexism attached to housework but rather carry the burden for their middle-class women employers. The never-ending job described by housewives is transferred to workers employed by women who treat domestic service as an opportunity to "hire a wife." Employers frequently disregard the contractual or informal labor arrangement made with employees, constantly increasing the work load and incorporating more of their own homemaking duties and obligations. Household workers are faced with tasks that both exceed their job descriptions and are as emotionally and physically burdensome as those completed by housewives. The most common violation of the original labor agreement is the practice of adding child care to general housecleaning instead of keeping the two jobs separate.

As women employed to do "women's work" in the home, domestics are "protomothers": their labor is assumed to incorporate both skill as a worker and affection for the employer's family. Because they are women, they are expected to be caring and nurturing, acting in many instances as surrogate mothers to the employer and her children. The emotional dimensions of the work, such as child care, are frequently manipulated to expand the worker's obligation beyond instrumental and economic considerations. Employers' references to domestics as "one of the family" concretizes these gender-specific characteristics, equating the work with homemaking.

The battle that housewives have in convincing males and children that housework is real work is replayed in the conflict between domestics and housewives. Housewives typically clean house once or twice a week and assume that the domestic's experience is comparable. However, the domestic's routine is repeated every day for a different employer (and increasingly for two and three employers a day): carrying vacuum cleaners up and down stairs, vacuuming behind sofas, washing and waxing floors, scrubbing ovens, sinks, tubs, and toilets, and on and on. Backaches from scrubbing and picking up toys, papers, and clothes are common. Like housewives and unlike other workers, domestics face the additional stress of having their work treated as nonwork. Domestics recounted occasions when employer's children or guests spilled drinks on the floor or messed up a room, expecting the "maid" simply to redo her work. Although domestics are paid for housework, the job is treated in a manner no different from that of the housework done by housewives.

Housewives who become employers fail to recognize that once a domestic is hired to do housework, their homes become an employee's workplace and that the domestic is a worker rather than an extension of the housewife. The use of the family analogy by employers distorts and masks this fact. Interviews with domestics reveal that universal working conditions found in other jobs, are uncommon in domestic service. Employers resist the implementation of modern work culture in their homes.

Personal relationships between employee and employer blur the distinctions between paid and unpaid housework and weaken workers' ability to maintain contractual agreements. When employers grant favors, make promises, and give gifts, the employee becomes ensnared in a web of debt and obligation that masks considerations of the employee's rights. Yet, although researchers have depicted the interpersonal relationship between domestics and their women employers as preindustrial and rooted in the feudalistic master-servant tradition, this is not an appropriate model. The cycle of gift-giving and obligation may resemble rituals previously practiced in domestic service, but today the domestic-employer relationship must be analyzed within the context of capitalism. Gift-giving is simply another employer tactic for keeping wages low and for extracting additional unpaid labor for the employee.

Paid housework that is structured to replicate the unpaid domestic work of the housewife includes practices affirming women's inferiority. The sexist division of labor that exists in employers' homes, assigning mothers and wives the duty of waiting on and serving their husbands and children, is passed on to the domestics. Middle-class women employers who expect women household workers to "pick up" after their husbands and children reproduce the demeaning and sexist aspects of housework. Rejection of such sexist practices is reflected throughout the service sector when workers refuse to "pick up" after others by saying, "I am not your mother." In the same vein, domestics resist practices that structure paid housework to affirm sexist cultural values by requiring the employer to confront her children and husband about leaving their clothes and wet towels on the floor, leaving dishes and glasses throughout the house, and not throwing trash into the garbage. However, many women employers simply perpetuate the sexist division of labor by passing on the most devalued work in their lives to another woman—generally a woman of color. Thus, white middle class women escape the stigma of "women's work" by laying the burden on working-class women of color.

The way in which employers structure the physical labor of housework demonstrates the importance of status enhancement among white middle-class women employers. Many employers want more than just a clean house; they want their psychological needs to be fulfilled and their self-esteem and well-being to be enhanced. In some cases, they achieve this goal by supervising and monitoring paid housework, thus elevating their feelings of power and authority and relegating employees to mindless activity. Another strategy occurs when employers redefine their housework for other women. Upgrading standards, imposing specific cleaning methods, and adding ritual cleaning make the work more demeaning and increase its physical demands. This finding is consistent with Betty Freidan's and Ann Oakley's descriptions of the attempts of full-time homemakers to establish housework as a vocation in an effort to elevate their self-esteem.

In her discussion on the differential treatment of female and male workers, Hochschild explained the different standards of feelings that influence the treatment of others. Summarizing H. E. Dale's concept of the "doctrine of feelings," she stated that "high-status people tend to enjoy the privilege of having their feelings noticed and considered. The lower one's status, the more one's feelings are not noticed or treated as inconsequential." [125] The corollary of the doctrine of feelings, according to Hochschild, is this: "A person of lower status has a weaker claim to the right to define what is going on; less trust is placed in her judgments; and less respect is accorded to what she feels." [126] This devaluation is accomplished by discounting the lower status person's feelings "by considering them rational but unimportant or by considering them irrational and hence dismissable." [127] "Given this relation between status and the treatment of feeling," Hochschild concludes "that persons in low status categories . . . lack a status shield against poorer treatment of their feelings. This simple fact has the power to utterly transform the content of a job."

Hochschild's analysis of status and feeling explains the treatment of women of color in domestic service. The doctrine of feelings situates the feelings of women of color below those of other workers employed in domestic service, thereby providing white middle class women with even more "privilege in having their feelings noticed and considered important." Women of color employed as domestics are less likely than their white counterparts to have respect given to their feelings. Thus, negative reactions to racial jokes are taken to indicate that the employee is "too sensitive," her refusal to scrub the floor on hands and knees indicates that she is "too lazy" or "too uppity." The doctrine of feelings explains how employers' personal preferences for particular housecleaning methods and detergents become claims of expertise, whereas, the knowledge and skill that domestics have acquired from years of experience are disregarded or treated as inconsequential. The deference that is generally expected from ethnic minority women places them in a weaker position than other workers in negotiating wages and raises and in maintaining informal labor contracts.

The emotional labor required to create the deference that affirms and enhances the employer's status is not only dependent upon the class background of employees but includes their racial and ethnic backgrounds. The deferential behavior described in the daily interaction between white middle class employers and working class women of color reflects the degree to which domestic service functions to establish status. The process that affirms the status of white middle class women employers involves deferential interaction that treats nonwhite working-class domestics as inferior. Domestic service invokes and draws upon traditional racial stereotypes, which in the United States include a powerful image of African American women as "mammies," and associates darker skinned women with strength and spiritual power.

Employing white women or college students as household workers does not establish the same power differential as does hiring ethnic minority women and Third World immigrant women. In fact, domestic service is not the same job for a woman of color as it is for a white woman or a man. A day's accumulation of

they very well could be there class about them

the employer's abuse differs for a woman of color from that for a white woman or man. White women are not subjected to racial slurs, condescending comments about their families or patronizing remarks about their culture. White middle-class women are unlikely to ask white women or men they employ to use separate dishes and silverware, to graciously accept useless discarded items, to wear old housedresses, or to act "maidish." The additional assaults upon their *could be* personhood forces women of color to do more emotional labor than white women or men in order to keep their jobs.

The experiences of women of color identify those structures that support cultural systems of gender, class, and racial domination. As Zenobia King so earnestly pointed out to Dill: "I don't think domestic work is demeaning work. It's what people make it—like you have to use the back elevators, and can't eat the same food. . . . It's not demeaning work to do."[128] In other words, the nature of housework is not intrinsically degrading or demeaning, nor is it intrinsically sexist. Accounts given by household workers indicate that conflict exists when employers attempt to structure the work to include demeaning and degrading aspects.

The following chapter continues to explore the structure of paid housework and the social relationships surrounding domestic service by analyzing the labor process. Just as relationships among industrial employers and employees are characterized by the struggle for control over the work process, housewives and domestics engage in the same battle. On the basis of my research on Chicana domestics, I will show how employees attempt to control the work process, minimize personalism, and thereby create better working conditions.

Chapter 6

THE STRUGGLE TO
TRANSFORM DOMESTIC LABOR

In free time @ beech,
Flor learns English — how
far away from usual
work do? is this
actually?

Domestics never passively accept the working conditions established by employ-ers, they develop proactive strategies as well as techniques of resistance to bur-densome working conditions and social relationships. Conflicts between em-ployee and employer arise from various sources, including such familiar workers' issues as wages, work load, work pace, raises, breaks, and benefits. A major source of tension unique to domestic work is the daily rituals and practices of deferential behavior. In the interviews, private household workers demon-strated an acute awareness of the cultural meaning attached to requests for uni-forms, special eating arrangements, or linguistic and spatial deference. They also described resistance to the emotional labor that affirms and enhances the employer's status, particularly when the labor involved acting inferior.

Past analyses of domestics' struggles concentrated almost exclusively on in-terpersonal relationships between women of color domestic workers and their white women employers. Analysis was dictated by a social psychological frame-work that limited the discussion to coping strategies or other muted forms of rebellion. The structure of housework was ignored and treated as an extension of the hierarchical relationship between women from different racial back-grounds. However, the relationship is best conceptualized as an employee-employer relationship and an instance of class struggle. Like so many other employee-employer relationships under capitalism, control over the work pro-cess is not cooperative. Worker and employer define their interests in opposition and struggle for control. My research on Chicana household workers describes the active struggle for control of the work process. Only by gaining a measure of control can the employees restructure the work to eliminate demeaning and degrading practices. This chapter presents a detailed investigation of domestics' struggles for better working conditions. Beginning with an overview of previous research, I turn to the experiences of Chicana household workers to analyze their struggle to change the occupation.

INTERPRETATIONS OF DOMESTIC CONFLICT AND DOMESTIC HARMONY

Social Psychological Approaches

The social psychological approach used in recent studies of women of color analyzed workers' struggles as strategies to maintain dignity and self-worth. Domestic service was treated as an occupation whose practices were vestigial remnants of its feudalistic origins. The interpersonal relationship between employee and employer became the locus for struggles which were depicted as coping strategies and forms of resistance. For instance, Bonnie Thornton Dill maintained that domestic service is "shaped by an ideology that excluded consideration of basic principles of labor and management . . . [b]oth employers and employees ultimately focused their attention on personal traits: the employee's manner of speech or dress, her attitude and appearance, or the employer's kindness and generosity."[1]

In interpersonal relations with poor and working-class women of color, employers use feminine characteristics to establish the relationship of benevolent maternalism that preserves racial and class status differences. Within this framework, domestics' struggles are viewed as reactive strategies to minimize subjugation and familiarity. Even though they recognize that the emotional closeness domestics experience in their relationships with employers results in the extraction of unpaid labor, the researchers' central concern remained the dialectic of intimacy and domination in the interpersonal relationship. The most systematic and thorough analysis of the dialectic of intimacy and domination was presented in Judith Rollins's book *Between Women*. She described the hierarchical systems created and maintained through interpersonal rituals that reinforce inequality between domestics and their employers—for instance, degradation rituals of deference and maternalism whose function is to confirm the domestic's inferiority and the employer's superiority.

Susan Tucker similarly relied on dialectical concepts of domination drawn from Hegel and Fanon to discuss the psychology of the relationship between domestics and employers. In her book *Telling Memories*, Tucker portrayed African American domestics as victims, but she used the concept of "existential impasse" to argue that Southern white women were victims as well:

> The oppressed provide recognition and validation to the oppressor, to his or her superiority. But according to the whole reasoning of oppression—with one group of people said to be superior—this validation is ultimately worth little, since it comes from someone defined as inferior. Thus, the oppressor becomes weaker and lazy, feels no need to excel, and lacks the will and wish to change.[2]

Providing yet one more practical demonstration of the fallacy of using Hegel's idealistic concept of the dialectic of master and slave to analyze any real situation, Tucker concluded that conditions of domestic service reflect the "hierarchy of customs and responses that exploit all women." Applying concepts of shared gender, women's culture, and gender bonding, she went so far as to claim that both African American women and white women "do not think that domestic work, particularly child-rearing, is a job that should be compensated by more than the minimum wage."[3]

The framework of interpersonal relationships of domination limits domestics' struggles to coping strategies aimed at maintaining dignity and self-esteem. For instance, Rollins claimed that, unlike other victims of domination, domestics do not cope with powerlessness by identifying with the oppressor—the employer. Rollins argued that domestics maintain a sense of self-worth because the strength of their moral system is built on

> their intimate knowledge of the realities of employers' lives, their understanding of the meaning of class and race in this country, and their value system, which measures an individual's worth less by material success than by "the kind of person you are," by the quality of one's interpersonal relationships and by one's standing in the community.[4]

Following Rollins, Tucker argued that African American domestics in the South are able "to ward off the problem of accepting the perceptions whites had" because "they compared themselves favorably with their white employers."[5]

Just as Rollins discussed membership in the African American community as essential in protecting household workers from the stigma of domestic service, Dill and Colen described community as an important means to retain self-esteem. Dill argued that the African American community provides resources to enhance self-image and offers domestics nonstigmatized roles. Belonging to a community permits African American domestics to develop a collective consciousness that affirms "the knowledge of social inequalities that unjustly consigned Black women and their daughters to this low-status, low-paid, and dirtiest of women's jobs."[6] Whereas Dill claimed that "community resources" were brought into play as day work came to replace live-in conditions, Colen countered that West Indians employed as live-in domestics were able to "maintain their own identities deriving from their own systems of respect operative in their home countries and in their communities in New York."[7] Nevertheless, researchers agreed that domestics are able to maintain psychological and material independence by defining themselves not by the occupation but in terms of family, church, organizations and community.

Within a framework of relationships of domination, employed women of color were treated as powerless to change their working conditions in domestic service. Rollins maintained that "domestics' ways of coping with employers' degrading treatment have been effective, then, in protecting them from the psychological damage risked by accepting employers' belief system but have not been effective in changing the behaviors themselves."[8] Instead they have little choice but to "pretend to be unintelligent, subservient, and content with their positions" or "they know the position could be lost."[9] Applying Max Scheler's concept of *ressentiment* to the feeling domestics have toward their employers, Rollins explained, "it is a long-term, seething, deep-rooted negative feeling toward those whom one feels unjustly have power or an advantage over one's life."[10]

Unlike Rollins, Dill did not find that domestics were limited by their "employers' definition of the situation" but rather "played their parts with a skill and acumen that often redefined the employers' notion of the relationship."[11] In her study on African American domestics in Philadelphia and New York, Dill identified some strategies that workers used "to achieve some kind of parity within the confines of a relationship of domination." Termed "stories of resistance," the strategies included confrontation, chicanery, or cajolery. Her analysis showed how these tactics are used "to establish limits for themselves within a particular household," "to define very carefully what they would and would not give to their employers in the way of time, commitment, and personal involvement."[12] Tucker discussed similar tactics among African American domestics in the South. "One way black domestics dealt with such feelings of powerlessness was by tricking whites [employers]—by manipulating the situations in which they were perceived as childlike, lazy, or inferior."[13] "Their [domestics] knowledge of whites also helped them to fool whites [employers]—to play the part expected of them."[14]

The analysis of domestics' struggles within the framework of interpersonal relationships of domination suggested that strategies were based on the worker's individual characteristics rather than on structural opportunities. For instance, Dill explained "stories of resistance" within the context of personal management skills. In her study on West Indians in New York City, Shellee Colen also leaned toward an explanation of struggles as individual attributes. Similarly to Rollins and Dill's work, Colen credited the domestic's abilities to cope and survive to personal characteristics. "The women in this study are strong, determined, secure and confident."[15] Drawing "on their strength, determination, and networks of support," West Indian immigrant domestics "cope with and resist the exploitation they confront on the job."[16]

Social psychological approaches describe strategies that Jacklyn Cock refers to as "muted rituals of rebellion." Consisting primarily of silence and mockery of employers, Cock characterized the rituals as "a crucial mode of adaptation, a line of resistance that enables the servant to maintain her personality and integrity intact."[17] A mode of adaptation similar to that reported in research on women of color in the United States is described in Cock's study of domestics in South Africa: "the domestic workers' main mode of adaptation is the adoption of a mask of deference as a protective disguise."[18]

It is necessary to shift our analysis away from interpersonal relationships and idealistic "dialectics" of intimacy and domination to an examination of the labor process itself. Domestic work is no vanishing historical artifact. As more women enter the labor force, questions of the race, ethnicity, and gender of those engaged in paid reproductive labor become even more important. Since women of color will likely retain their "dominance" of the occupation for some years to come, researchers must examine under what conditions their reproductive labor for pay takes place. Only by examining domestic work as a specific instance of labor struggles can we arrive at a possibility for action and change to destigmatize housework and win for domestics the respect and rights due them as workers.

Toward a Structural Analysis of the Dialectics of Domestic Work

Historically, the major change in domestic service that led to improved working conditions was the move toward day work. Studies by David Katzman and Elizabeth Clark-Lewis have documented the shift from live-in to live-out.[19] Evelyn Glenn described nonresidential jobs as contributing to the modernization of domestic work by bringing it closer to industrialized wage work: "Work and nonwork life are clearly separated, and the basis for employment is more clearly contractual—that is, the worker sells a given amount of labor time for an agreed-upon wage."[20] For some private household workers, particularly immigrant women, live-in employment persists; the struggle to change the work structure by shifting to day work continues. Thus, in her study on African American domestics in New York City and the surrounding suburban area, Soraya Coley included moving out of the employer's home in a list of techniques "used to enhance or safeguard their personal dignity or to protect their physical and emotional well-being."[21] Only women unable to find day work continued to live in, and they maintained a rented room elsewhere which enabled them "to act independently and resist the potential ill-treatment of the employer."[22]

The shift to day work gives workers more autonomy because they can have several employers at one time. As Glenn noted, "domestics working for several families were less dependent on one employer. Work hours could be adjusted to fit in with the workers' other interests and responsibilities."[23] Furthermore, day work also provides independence to quit employers and seek new ones. In her study of Mexican immigrant women, Pierrette Hondagneu-Sotelo describes domestic workers with numerous employers as being able to negotiate better working conditions.[24] However, like other workers, domestics quit jobs only as a "last resort." Leaving an employer involves a loss of pay and offers no guarantee that a new employer will be any better. Domestics are also reluctant to face the adjustment to another employer's idiosyncrasies and the resulting emotional roller coaster ride.[25] Coley and Glenn also noted that domestics expressed a sense of defeat in quitting because they were unable to endure or change the situation.[26]

Glenn argued that "the conflict took its most concrete form in a struggle between employer and employee over control of the work process."[27] Employers want the work done in a specific way; they monitor employees closely to ensure that the worker will not "loaf or cut corners."[28] Struggle over control is also apparent in disputes about the amount and pace of the work; employers try to lengthen the workday and increase the work load while employees seek to do the opposite. Glenn characterized Japanese American domestics as using their resources to resist employers' control over the work. Strategies mentioned included shifting from live-in to day work, working simultaneously for several employers, quitting employers who stay home to supervise, and defining the job by task rather than by time.

Although Glenn centered her analysis on the work structure, she viewed the relationship between domestics and employers as premodern, feudalistic, and a dialectic of personalism and asymmetry.[29] She claimed that "although the totalism of the traditional servant-master relationship has been reduced under conditions of day work, relations between white employers and Japanese domestics retain two essential and interrelated characteristics of the earlier period—personalism and asymmetry.[30] Glenn further stated that "a sense of mutual obligation, a carryover from feudal values, also colors the ties between employer and employee. . . . The commitments are often lifelong and continue even when the terms of the original 'contract' can no longer be fulfilled—for example, the domestic no longer perform the same duties, or the employer can no longer afford to pay adequately."[31]

Coley also considered structural factors in her analysis of strategies used by union and nonunion members of the National Committee of Household Employment (NCHE). She found that union members exhibited an occupational identity and felt they had "achieved control over their work," whereas, nonunion members considered the work as "merely a means to an end" and expressed a powerless resignation.[32] Although many of these tactics appear similar to the "management skills" described by Dill, Coley used the frequency with which certain tactics were employed to analyze both circumstances and long term efficacy. She found that both union and nonunion domestics retaliate against poor working conditions and degrading treatment by direct confrontation, trickery, and quitting. Trickery and confrontation are especially successful in resisting employers' attempts to increase the work load and help to maintain the boundaries of tasks. Even though craftiness and trickery are considered more desirable because of the minimized risk and economic hardship involved, confrontation was the most frequently cited form of resistance.[33] Coley concluded that "confrontation was often the more expedient mode of establishing a clear understanding between the employee and employer on one's expectations."

Even though other researchers have centered their analysis on the interpersonal relationship between the domestic and employer rather than the work process, they have uncovered ways in which workers attempt to control the work structure. Dill and Tucker discussed a strategy that domestics use to control wages and benefits by carefully selecting wealthy employers. Dill referred to the strategy as "building a career," explaining that domestics find wealthy employers who can provide high wages and benefits which increase the domestic's social position and feelings of self-worth. Coley noted a similar technique among unionized members who created upward mobility for themselves by assessing the occupational structure and selecting the job description that conferred more money and status.[34]

Discussion

This overview of previous research suggests that while some domestics resign themselves to a powerless position, others do not accept or endure the work structure imposed by employers. Some domestics do actively struggle to improve their working conditions by changing the work.[35] The work histories of the Chicana domestics whom I interviewed directed my attention to the calculated choices workers make even when their choices are limited. Faced with limited job opportunities, Chicanas described why they chose domestic service over other low-paying, low status jobs and how they made the most of their options. Although they recognized the importance of relationships with employers and their families, the work structure remained the main focus of their struggle. Descriptions of their experiences expand Glenn's analysis of the struggle over the work process, drawing our attention to the direction of changes in the occupation. My findings also suggest a broader range of relationships co-existing in the occupation.

The research on Chicana household workers supports many of the findings on working conditions detailed in studies of women of color in domestic service. Employers maintain a benevolent attitude toward "their" domestics, demanding loyalty and deference. Employers treat employees with the type of kindness reserved for domestic animals or pets and children or treat employees at times even as "nonperson." Even with the change to hourly work, the employee-employer relationship retains characteristics of the mistress-maid and master-servant relationship. However, I disagree with Coser, Glenn, and others, who treat aspects of this relationship as premodern or preindustrial and suggest that they are outside the nature of capitalism. The lifelong commitments between Japanese American domestics and employers cannot be attributed simply to individual conditions of an employee and employer: "The domestic can no longer perform the same duties, or the employer can no longer afford to pay adequately." The problem with this type of assertion is that the interpersonal relationship is not a premodern feudalistic remnant but a social relationship existing within a capitalist economy. Regardless of the level of personalism, it remains an employee-employer relationship and exemplifies the class struggle. When personalism results in "a sense of mutual obligation," the interpersonal nature of the relationship reflects the competitive nature of capitalism, according to which the employer seeks to maximize the amount of unpaid labor. Asymmetry not only exists in the power relationships between employee and employer but is exaggerated and accentuated by the sexual and racial systems of domination. Within the structure of advanced capitalism, racism and sexism cannot be considered personal relationships but are part of the structure of exploitation.

Focusing on the work structure rather than on the social psychological aspects of personalism, asymmetry or domination, I analyze the content of the interpersonal exchanges between employee and employer as part of the labor process. This process includes the emotional labor involved in nurturing, caring, and enhancing the employer's status. As I pointed out in the previous chapter, employers do hire domestics for emotional labor. Emotional labor is a commodity. Sometimes emotional labor is paid labor and may even be more important than physical labor; however, when employers refuse to acknowledge the emotional work, the labor becomes shadow work, as unpaid labor extracted by the employer, it becomes unpaid labor. Conflict and tension arise over the exchange value of the labor, particularly in the case of unpaid labor extracted through the manipulation of gifts or under the disguise of family and friendship obligations.

The struggle to maintain dignity and self-worth is also the struggle against doing the emotional labor that affirms and enhances the employer's status as superior and that emphasizes the domestic's inferior status. In the accounts of their work experience in domestic service, Chicanas outline their options and carefully make choices aimed at controlling the work process. "Making the most of their options" means an active struggle to structure the work so as to increase the exchange value of the labor and to eliminate any shadow work and emotional work involving the enhancement of status.

CHICANA DOMESTICS AND EMPOWERMENT

Early in the study, I was made aware of the stigma attached to domestic service. Potential interviewees were reluctant to admit that they were employed as private household workers. During the interviews, some of the women appeared quite defensive about their jobs and others emphasized the temporary status of their current employment. The women I interviewed expressed embarrassment at doing degrading work, and yet they continued in the occupation because they earned more than in other low-status jobs they had held; moreover, it offered autonomy. Faced with limited job opportunities, their challenge was to manage the dilemma of the occupation in everyday life and to maximize the advantages domestic service has to offer. In twenty-five work histories, each recounted how they weighed their options and made choices based on the work situation that offered maximum advantage. Chicanas apeared to be taking active steps to transform and improve the occupation by eliminating the vestiges of servitude. Chicana domestics resisted personalized and asymmetrical relationships with employers and attempted to establish a businesslike environment.

Choosing Domestic Work

The importance of analyzing the selection of domestic work as a strategy to improve working conditions is captured by Leslie Salzinger: "If we look at these women outside the context of the local economy, their occupational strategies are opaque. It is only if we pay attention to what they are choosing *between* that their strategies become comprehensible."[36] The majority of the Chicanas whom I interviewed had been employed in a variety of jobs over their lifetimes, including farm workers, waitresses, factory workers, sales clerks, cooks, laundresses, fast-food workers, receptionists, school aides, babysitters, dishwashers, nurse's aides, cashiers, non-union factory workers, and various types of line workers in poultry farms and car washes. In general, these were jobs with no benefits or jobs in which workers are subject to frequent layoffs and little chance for promotion.

Most of the women reported that they began day work when they were unable to find other employment or that they began working in domestic service as a temporary job to be held until they were ready to look for full-time employment.

Five of the women joined the ranks as a response to a relative's need for a replacement during an illness, vacation, or family obligation.[37] Unlike other jobs that these Chicanas had sought, domestic service was one job that was always available to them, and they had no difficulty finding day work. Inquiries into their search for employers revealed the process that initially moved these Chicanas into domestic service.

To acquire most of these jobs, the women relied upon word of mouth. Information on job openings was obtained from husbands, sisters, cousins, friends, and neighbors.[38] All but four of the women reported that a relative or friend assisted in obtaining employment as a domestic. Only two women reported a cleaning agency as an entry into the occupation. However, they quickly abandoned the agency and preferred to work independently where they obtained a higher wage. The other two women were contacted by the parish priests. Networks drawing women into the occupation usually consisted of family members and were almost always confined to the local Chicano community. For instance, the women who began domestic work replacements for a relative who was sick or going on a vacation were similarly linked to the network. Mrs. Salazar recalled working in the beet fields with her family when the employer approached her husband with the offer to do housework. New employers were added in the same way, including the assistance of current employers who recommended their employees to friends, neighbors, and relatives. A strong preference for informality and job leads obtained from the informal network of family and friends provided a sense of security when entering a new employer's home.

In many ways these Chicanas demonstrated employment patterns similar to those of other working women in traditionally female occupations. Movement in and out of the labor market coincided with stages of family life: the birth of a child and children's entrance into school. Husbands' unemployment, underemployment, or financial crises were the major reasons for reentry into the labor force. However, their ability to obtain immediate employment may distinguish these Chicanas from other women who seek employment during times of financial crisis. These Chicana workers were unique in that they could always find employment as domestics. Their challenge was to find a job *outside* domestic service.[39]

Although the women I interviewed preferred factory positions because of the pay and benefits, many found themselves hired during the peak season and subsequently laid off. Most of the jobs that the women had held that paid more than minimum wage or offered benefits were usually related to the war on poverty programs, such as cook in a head start program, aide in a bilingual educational program, and secretary for a community-based organization. These jobs became available only when employment opportunities for the Chicano community increased. Only after retirement or periods of unemployment did these women again return to day work to supplement the family income. The women who experienced social mobility did so when their networks, which were based in Chicano communities, were broadened to include more job opportunities. The use of informal networks as a method of job searching has likewise been documented for various other workers, including professionals.[40] However, the resources within the network are limited. Glenn observed that while community resources provide Japanese American women with immediate employment as domestics, the residential and social segregation also "tend to insulate members from information about other occupations."[41] The variety of jobs depicted in Chicanas work histories suggests that the network was not quite as insulating, however, resources for women were usually limited to low paying, low status jobs.[42]

In analyzing their work histories, in particular the reasons given for leaving or returning to domestic service, I was struck by the way in which Chicanas make the most of their options.[43] The reasons given for continuing employment in domestic service or returning to the occupation after a period of unemployment demonstrate that workers assess their possibilities and make calculated decisions. In comparing domestic service with other available work options, all of the women identified certain advantages. For instance, Mrs. Garcia's decision to continue working as a domestic after she had tried working in a laundry and a nursing home was based on a comparison of working conditions in each. She states the negative aspects of the jobs at the laundry and nursing home: "I was allergic to the lint or something in the laundry and was sick all the time I worked there"; "I get depressed being around such sick people that have no hope of getting better." Mrs. Garcia compares the advantages domestic service offers:

> I like being free to do the work the way I like it and I like doing housework. . . .
> They're [employers] not fussy about having to punch a clock like you do when
> you're working [at another job] that you have to punch a clock and always have to
> be worried about being there at the same time and have to think I'm going to lose
> my job.

Most of the women considered the flexible schedule as the major advantage of domestic service over other jobs they had held. Mrs. Mondragon recalls that her decision to return to domestic service after her youngest child entered school was related to the flexible schedule. She was unable to find another job that allowed her to arrange a work schedule around her child's school day.[44] Several working mothers with small children also wanted the flexibility of taking their children to work with them.[45]

Independence and autonomy are other characteristics that Chicanas cite as advantages of domestic service over their previous jobs. Mrs. Rivera states:

You're not under no supervision. Once the person (employer) learns that you're
going to do the job, they just totally leave you to your own. It's like your own
home. That's what I like.

Mrs. Rojas continues to work as a domestic after her job in a hospital because
of the independence the job offers:

When you work like in a hospital or something, you're under somebody. They're
telling you what to do or this is not right. But housecleaning is different. You're
free. You're not under no pressure, especially if you find a person who really trusts
you all the way. You have no problems.

Mrs. Salas describes the independence she experiences doing day work:

I like it because you can choose your hours. You can quit whenever you want to if
you don't like the people or if you don't like what you're doing you can quit.

For Mrs. Salas, day work allows her more freedom to change her working conditions than other jobs.

The importance of independence in domestic service is alluded to in Richard
Sennett's and Jonathan Cobb's assessment of workers' ranking of certain occupations. They conclude that workers rank occupations lower than others when
the job makes them "more dependent on and more at the mercy of others."[46]
Domestic service is only one of several low-paying, low-status jobs the women
held during their lives. However, horizontal mobility can make significant differences in the quality of one's life. As Howard Becker explains:

All positions at one level of a work hierarchy, while theoretically identical, may
not be equally easy or rewarding places in which to work. Given this fact, people
tend to move in patterned ways among the possible positions, seeking that situation
which affords the most desirable setting in which to meet and grapple with the
basic problems of their work.[47]

For most of these Chicanas, the flexibility, autonomy and independence they
experienced as private household workers outweighed the stigma attached to the
occupation.

Although Chicanas consider flexibility, autonomy and independence the advantages of domestic service over other jobs, these characteristics are not inherent features. Domestics have to negotiate directly with employers to establish a
flexible work schedule and autonomy on the job.[48] An analysis of their work
histories in domestic service reveals that Chicana domestics actively negotiate
informal labor arrangements that include both strategies to eliminate the most
oppressive aspects of the occupation and to develop instrumental employer-

employee relationships aimed at professionalizing it. Unable to find employment offering job security, advancement, or benefits, Chicanas make calculated attempts to improve the occupation by minimizing employer control and personalism.

From Labor Power to Labor Services

Domestics use several strategies in their struggle for control: (1) increasing opportunities for job flexibility; (2) increasing pay and benefits; (3) establishing and maintaining an informal contract specifying tasks; (4) minimizing contact with employers; (5) defining themselves as professional housekeepers; and (6) creating a small-business-like environment. The critical locus of their struggle is to define the work on the basis of a contract—by the house or apartment—rather than as hourly work. Examination of the strategies reveals differences from the experience of other contemporary women of color employed as domestics. Unlike many of the black domestics studied in the East, the Chicanas in this group are not sole supporters of the family or union members; unlike the Japanese American women in Glenn's study, most of them are second or third generation, and they are much younger than the women studied by Glenn. As U.S. citizens, they are not as vulnerable as undocumented Latina immigrants. Many are also members of a dual-wage family, which lessens their vulnerability in the labor market. The Chicanas whom I interviewed have more formal education, and for the most part are not being replaced by newly arrived immigrants.[49] The most important difference is that Chicana domestics have attempted to restructure the work as a small business by transforming it from wage labor to an occupation involving labor services.

Job Flexibility

As live-out workers, Chicanas obtain more job flexibility than domestics who are employed on a live-in basis. Like other women employed in domestic service, Chicanas work for several employers. Having different employer every day allows domestics to be more independent and reduces the employer's control. In recent years, some of the women have begun to clean more than one house a day and thus have two or three employers in one day. This is particularly common among domestics whose employers live in condominiums or apartments. Having numerous employers at one time provides domestics with the leeway to quit because they can replace one employer with another without affecting the entire the work week.

Chicanas are able to use the job flexibility they gain as day workers employed by several employers to rearrange the workweek to fit their personal needs. For instance, many of the older women reduce their work week to three or four days, whereas the younger women who need more income are more likely to clean two apartments a day and work six days a week. A few women, like Mrs. Lovato, use the flexibility to work as part-time domestics during times of economic crisis:[50] "I worked for Coors (brewery) for about three years and I would still do housecleaning, sort of part-time in the morning."

Job flexibility can further be increased by the informal labor arrangement with employers. During negotiations with employers, Chicanas establish work hours that provide the flexibility lacking in other jobs. Although employers struggle to structure the work, Chicanas are insistent about arranging certain work hours and state hours as a condition of their employment. They try to establish a flexible schedule that includes occasional changes in the length of the working day. The personal arrangements and verbal contracts between employer and employee make it easy to negotiate a half day's work or to skip a day. As Mrs. Garcia, a fifty-four-year-old domestic, explains:

> You can change the dates if you can't go a certain day and if you have an appointment, you can go later, and work later, just as long as you get the work done . . .
> I try to be there at the same time, but if I don't get there for some reason or another, I don't have to think I'm going to lose my job or something.

Payment and Benefits

Pay and benefits in domestic service traditionally lag behind those of other occupations. However, domestic service paid more than the other jobs these Chicanas had held. Domestic service takes place in an underground economy in which workers choose whether to report their income. Older women recall earning $1.25 an hour in the early 1960s and $3.25 an hour in the 1970s; however, most of the women were averaging between $7 and $8 an hour in the mid–1980s—a lot more than with other jobs they had. For many women, the higher pay earned in domestic service reduces the financial need to work six days a week. Daily payment in cash is frequently cited as an important aspect of domestic work. As with so many working-class families—even those in which there is a working husband—many live from paycheck to paycheck, with little if any money left over for unplanned or extra expenses.

In all but two cases, employment in domestic service is not reported to the IRS, and these women express relief that income tax is not filed. This appears to be partially the result of their husbands' fears of raising the family into a higher tax bracket, but it is also the case that they do not know how to file income tax and feel uncomfortable in requesting employers to do so. However, three women expressed concern about social security and urged employers to submit the required paper work. Two of the oldest women interviewed are receiving social security benefits as a result of their long-term employers' concern about their welfare.[51]

One-third of the women receive benefits unknown to other domestics or other low-status workers. Nine Chicanas who have worked for employers over a long period of time report that they receive paid vacations—usually involving no more than one or two days paid per employer. Christmas bonuses are more common that annual raises. However, nine report annual raises, and three of the women increase their wages annually by requesting raises or quitting one employer and raising the cost for new employers.

Negotiating Specific Tasks

In the informal labor arrangement, domestic and employer must verbally negotiate working conditions, including tasks, timing, technique, the length of the working day, and payment. When starting with a new employer, the domestic works one day, and if the employer is satisfied with her work, the two agree upon a work schedule and the specific tasks to be accomplished. Mrs. Rodriguez describes the ideal situation: "Once the person learns that you're going to do the job they just totally leave you to your own. It's like it's your own home." This ideal is similar to the informal arrangements Glenn reports. However, half of the women I interviewed explain that the ideal situation is achieved after some supervision and negotiation. Such an experience is alluded to in Mrs. Portillo's explanation of why she left an employer: "I don't want somebody right behind me telling me what to do. I will not work like that and that's why I didn't stay any longer with this lady."

The priority of domestics in the informal labor arrangement is to negotiate a work structure that provides autonomy and independence. Autonomy on the job is created when the worker controls the planning and organization of the housework, as well as the work pace and method. Gaining autonomy also assures the worker that the parameters of the work are maintained. The ideal situation is to have the worker structuring the work, with the employer removed from direct supervision. Chicana domestics stated their desire for autonomy, using the common expression "being your own boss."

Fifteen of the Chicanas make a practice of carefully distinguishing specific tasks that are considered part of the agreement from other tasks that are undertaken only for additional pay. Although informal work arrangements frequently imply a set number of hours, the typical arrangement is referred to as "charging by the house."[52] Mrs. Salazar explains the verbal contract:

> When you say you're going to clean a house, after you find out how big it is, you tell them [the employer] "I'll clean it for say sixty dollars." You're not saying how

long you're going to be there. To me, that was just a contract between you and the customer and after awhile when you've been there awhile, you know how fast you can work and I was doing it in less than eight hours.

Mrs. Lopez expresses her preference for "charging by the house": "I never liked to work by the hour because if I would work by the hour the lady would just go crazy loading me up with work, with more work and more work to do."

Charging a flat rate also eliminates employers' attempts at speedup by adding more tasks and forcing the domestic to increase the work pace. Glenn also found that Japanese American domestics attempt to limit the amount of work by specifying tasks rather than time. Charging a flat rate is a significant change in the occupation, particularly in light of the broad range of physical and emotional labor domestics report. The list of tasks suggests that many employers purchase labor power rather than labor services; that is, workers are not hired simply to provide the labor service of cleaning the house but their labor is purchased for a certain amount of hours to do a variety of unspecified tasks. "Charging by the house" involves specifying the specific tasks and, thus, placing boundaries on the job description.

All but one of the women interviewed attempt to control the work load and establish a concrete verbal contract outlining the specific tasks. Mrs. Gallegos is the only woman I interviewed who voiced a different strategy for controlling the amount of tasks given by the employer.

When you work by the hour, they're [employers] not going to line up any work. And once you start using a system, you can do it . . . take your time, you know. I see a lot of ladies—they [employees] want too much when they [employers] do pay them so much but they [employees] ask too much. I won't go for that. I told them [employers] I work by the hour, I will not take a flat rate cause if it takes me five, six hours, I want to get paid and if it takes four hours that's my problem. I will not work flat rate.

Mrs. Gallegos argues that the hourly wage places a limit on the amount of work and assures the worker that she is paid for all of her labor.

Like the dialectic between employer and employee Glenn describes, there is an ongoing negotiation as the domestic attempts to maintain the agreement while the employer attempts to lengthen the work day or to add more tasks. For instance, Mrs. Tafoya recalls an incident in which an employer attempted to extract additional unpaid labor:

I guess the niece came home. I knew the record player was playing and she was kinda—but I thought she was just tapping like you would tap [indicates with her hand on the table], you know. She was dancing and I guess the wax wasn't dry. She made a mess. I said to Mrs. Johnson [employer], I says I'm not going to clean that again. You get your niece to clean that. I did it once and it was beautiful. And I did it because nobody was here and I know that it would dry right. So if you want it redone you have your niece do it. And she says but you're getting paid for it. I says yea, I got paid for it and I did it.

By refusing to wax the floor over again, Mrs. Tafoya maintained the original labor arrangement.

Mrs. Sanchez gave an account that illustrates her attempt to place limits on the amount of work done and her efforts to maintain the original verbal contract. Mrs. Sanchez described a current problem she was having with an employer who is attempting to add more work. Mimicking the high-pitched voice of her employer, she repeated the employer's question: "Would you mind doing this? Would you mind doing that?" Mrs. Sanchez confided that she wanted to respond by saying, "Yes I do mind and I won't do it" but instead she said "Well, I'll do it this time." She expressed the importance of pointing out to the employer that the task would be done this time but was not to be expected in the future.

Another strategy Chicanas use to limit the work and reduce employers' efforts to extract unpaid labor involves developing a routine for handling "extras." The women describe preparing a monthly or bimonthly schedule for rotating particular tasks, such as cleaning the stove or refrigerator, and thereby avoid many special requests. Another common practice is to establish an understanding with the employer that if one task is added, another is eliminated. If the employer does not identify the tasks to be eliminated, the employee simply selects one and later explains that there was not enough time for both. Mrs. Garcia recalls learning this strategy from her cousin:

My cousin said, "Do the same thing every time you come in, as far as changing the sheets, vacuum and dust, and window sills, pictures on the walls, and stuff like that unless they ask you to do something extra. Then, maybe don't clean the tile in the bathroom, or just do the windows that really need it, so you can have some time to do this other stuff that they wanted you to do extra." And she said, "Never do more than what they ask you to do, because if you do then you're not really getting paid for it."

The struggle over control of the work process is evident in the fear of employers that domestics are cheating on their time. Three women reported that previous employers insisted that they work until the very last second, leaving little if any paid time for putting away appliances and cleaning materials or ignoring the additional time required to complete a task. One domestic recalled employers bringing her lunch to her on the stairs or elsewhere so that she would not take a lunch break. However domestics, like Mrs. Sanchez argue that the work "averages out":

Suppose one day they [employers] may be out of town and that day you go to work. You won't have much work to do, but you'll get paid the same. And then maybe some other time they're going to have company and you end up working a little more and you still get paid the same. So it averages about the same, you know, throughout the month.

Glenn described a similar view among Japanese American domestics: "If they worked extra time, they did not want to be paid extra; if they accomplished the task in less time, they reserved the right to leave." [53]

Chicana domestics, not unlike African American and Japanese American domestics, did not necessarily find an affective relationship the ingredient for a satisfying working relationship. In fact, the opposite is the case, because affective relationships provide more opportunities for exploitation. Frequently, close friendships result in fictitious kinship references, such as a younger employer adopting the domestic as a surrogate mother. Redefining the work obligation as a "family" obligation places the domestic in a difficult position. As Mrs. Portillo explains, the personal nature of the relationship creates an atmosphere conducive to manipulation: "Some people use their generosity to pressure you." Maintaining the conditions of the contract also becomes difficult because extra requests are made as if from a friend rather than from an employer. When employers use personalism as a means to extract additional labor, many domestics are able to increase their pay by threatening to quit. However, when they no longer feel in control, many choose to quit and find another employer.

Minimizing Contact With Employers

Domestics commonly report conflict over the work process. In order to structure the work as a meaningful and nondegrading activity, domestics struggle to remove employers from control of decisions. When employers control the work process, domestics are reduced to unskilled labor and housecleaning becomes mindless hourly work. Furthermore, domestics strive to eliminate the rituals of deference and the stigma of servitude. Minimizing the contact with employers was the most successful strategy for gaining control over the work process.

Employers are reluctant to turn over the control of the process to the domestic. Instead they attempt to structure the work to be supervised and monitored. Chicanas report that some employers give detailed instructions on how to clean their homes; they specified washing the floor on hands and knees, using newspaper instead of paper towels on the windows, or even in which direction to scrub the wall. Mrs. Portillo, a retired domestic with thirty years of experience, expresses the frustration of working for an employer who retained control of the work process:

> I used to have one lady that used to work right along with me. I worked with her three years. I found it hard. I was taking orders. I'm not the type to want to take orders. I know what I'm going to do. I know what general housecleaning is.

Under supervised conditions, domestics find themselves simply taking orders, which reduces their work activity to quick, monotonous gestures.

Mrs. Sanchez voices the general consensus that the less interaction there is with employers, the better are the working conditions: "The conflicts have been mostly with people who stay at home and really just demand the impossible." Five domestics even commented that they selected employers on the basis of whether the employer worked outside the home.

Chicanas argue that working women are more appreciative of the housework done and are relieved to turn over the planning and execution of cleaning to the domestic. Unemployed women, on the other hand, are portrayed as "picky" and unwilling to relinquish control. Three domestics whom I interviewed suggested that unemployed women feel guilty because they are not doing the work themselves and thus retain control and responsibility for the housework. Mrs. Lucero's description represents the distinctions domestics make between working women and full-time homemakers:

> I think women that weren't working were the ones that always had something to complain about. The ones that did work were always satisfied. I've never come across a lady that works that has not been satisfied. Those that are home and have the time to do it themselves, and don't want to do it, they are the ones that are always complaining, you know, not satisfied, they always want more and more. You can't really satisfy them.

Working women tend to be ideal employers because they are rarely home and are unable to supervise.[54]

The selection of employers is essential in maximizing the advantages of domestic service over other available jobs. For instance, Mrs. Gallegos explains that she selects jobs on the basis of the type of work that she wants to avoid: "Well, if I can help it, I don't like to do ovens. I hardly do that anymore. . . . I don't like to work for people who are very dirty either." Four characteristics that the women most frequently mention as qualities of a good employer are trust, respect, the understanding that family responsibilities come before work, and the ability to maintain a system for housecleaning. Only employers who trust their employees will allow the worker to structure the housework. Such respect indicates that employers are not trying to affirm and enhance their status by establishing the domestic's inferior status. Most of the women felt that family obligations, such as a sick child, superseded the work obligation. Therefore, they sought employers who were willing to accommodate occasional changes in the schedule and did not threaten to fire the worker. Domestics prefer to work for employers who maintain the house between cleanings and are not "dirty." Bad employers are characterized as "constantly looking over their shoulder," expecting the domestic to pick up after the children, leaving too many notes, and adding extra tasks. Domestics control their work environments to a large degree by replacing undesirable employers with more compatible ones.

A high turnover rate has always been characteristic of contemporary domestic service. Nevertheless, if a good working arrangement is established, domestics continue with an employer for some time. Over half of the women in this study worked for the same employer for at least two-thirds of their work histories as domestics. The women with the most extensive domestic experience have very impressive records. For instance, Mrs. Portillo, a sixty-eight-year-old retired domestic, had the same employers for the entire thirty years of her employment. Another woman, Mrs. Rivas, a fifty-three-year-old domestic with thirty-two years of experience had the same employer for twenty years. Two younger women, Mrs. Montoya, age thirty-three, and Mrs. Rivera, age thirty-two, both have twelve years of experience and have worked for the same employer for eleven years.

Half of the women stated that they consider the first couple of days with a new employer a time to decide whether to keep the employer. For instance, Mrs. Fernandez bases her decision to stay with a new employer on watching for signs of supervision and monitoring and unreasonable expectations.

> You can tell if they're [employers] going to trust you or not. If they're not over-looking—see, you know—over you all the time. If they start looking or saying "I don't want this moved or I don't want this done or be careful with this"—well, you know, you can be so careful but there's accidents happen. So if they start being picky I won't stay.

Mrs. Lopez classifies the type of employer by the attitude they expose in the first few minutes of their first encounter:

> I have had ladies that have said "I know you know what to do so I'll leave it to you" or they pull out their cleaning stuff and tell you "This is for this and this is for that" and I say "I know I've done this before." "Oh, ok, I'll let you do it."

Supervision and monitoring of workers not only function to control the work process but remind the worker of her subordinate position in society. Offering unsolicited advice about cleaning techniques—such as scrubbing floors on hands and knees rather than with a mop, or the safest way to bend while picking up the vacuum cleaner and moving heavy furniture—symbolizes a level of servitude. Asking a domestic to scrub floors on hands and knees—not a common practice of housewives today—is experienced as demeaning. The inferior status of the domestic is also evident in the employer's instructions on how to bend without themselves offering assistance.

Becoming an Expert

Another strategy used by Chicanas in the struggle to transform domestic service is to define themselves as expert cleaners or housekeepers. It is a unique strategy not reported among the African Americans studied by Rollins, Coley, or Dill or the Japanese Americans in Glenn's study.[55] This strategy attempts to transform the employee-employer relationship, creating an ideal situation in which employers turn over responsibility for the housework to the domestic. Establishing themselves as expert housecleaners involved defining a routine set of housework tasks and eliminating personal services such as babysitting, laundry, or ironing. Older Chicanas recalled babysitting, ironing, cooking and doing laundry, but in recent years they rarely do such tasks. Even younger Chicanas in their thirties, some with twelve years' experience, do ironing or laundry only for employers they started with ten years ago.

The importance of redefining social relationships in domestic service is most apparent in the women's distinctions between the work they do and maid's work. Mrs. Fernandez, a thirty-five-year-old domestic, indicates the distinction in the following account:

> They [the employer's children] started to introduce me to their friends as their maid. "This is our maid Angela." I would say "I'm not your maid. I've come to clean your house and a maid is someone who takes care of you and lives here or comes in everyday and I come once a week and it is to take care of what you have messed up. I'm not your maid. I'm your housekeeper."

These Chicanas define their work as different from maid's work. Mrs. Montoya's statement illustrates the equation of personal services with maid's work:

> I figure I'm not there to be their personal maid. I'm there to do their housecleaning—their upkeep of the house. Most of the women I work for are professionals and so they feel it's not my job to run around behind them. Just to keep their house maintenance clean and that's all they ask.

Mrs. Rojas, a thirty-three-year-old domestic with twelve years of experience, equates deferential behavior with being a maid.

One or two [employers] that I work for now have children that are snotty, you know they thought that I was their maid or they would treat me like a maid you know instead of a cleaning lady.

These workers resisted attempts by employers and their families to structure the work around rituals of deference and avoided doing the emotional labor attached to personal services.

The Chicanas interviewed consider themselves experts. They are aware of the broad range of knowledge that they have acquired from cleaning a variety of homes. This includes the removal of stains on various surfaces, tips for reorganizing the home, and the pros and cons of certain brands of appliances. A source of pride among the women was the fact that they had introduced a labor-saving device or tactic into the employer's home. Mrs. Garcia's experience in removing stains illustrates the assistance domestics give employers:

They [employers] just wipe their stoves and then complain "this doesn't come off anymore." They never took a SOS pad or a scrub brush to scrub it off. They expect it just to come off because they wiped. . . . Their kitchen floors would have Kool-Aid stains or they would have it on the counters, so I would just pour Clorox on it and the Clorox would just bring it right up and they would say "But you'll ruin it!" "No it will be alright." "Are you sure?" I never ruined anything from helping them out.

Mrs. Cortez's habit of providing cleaning hints points to some employers' willingness to accept the expertise of the domestic.

I cut out pieces of cleaning [information] that tell you how to do this an easy way . . . I'll take them and paste them on like their pantry doors and I'll put them there and then when they go to open [the pantry door] they say "Oh, that's a good idea." So then they start doing it that way.

As expert cleaners, the women take responsibility for all decisions regarding the structure of the work process, the pace of the housework, and the selection of work materials. Ideally the domestic enters the employer's home, decides where to begin, and arranges the appliances and cleaning products accordingly. She paces herself to finish in a certain number of hours. If she needs to leave early, she can speed up and not take a break; in other cases, a more leisurely pace is indicated. This situation differs from the speedups that Glenn describes in her study: "If the worker accomplished the agreed-upon task within the designated period, the employer added more tasks, forcing the worker to do everything faster."[56]

Half of the women recalled offering employers advice on the care of appliances and the best detergent or cleaning utensil for a particular surface. For instance, Mrs. Montoya describes the type of advice some employers requested:

> They'll [employers] ask you how to clean the tile up in the bathroom or they ask me—like one of them even asked me how I did her bed so nice—the corners— because she couldn't do it, you know, so she asked me how I did it and to teach her how to do the corners in her bed. Some of them even ask me how to change a vacuum bag or how to put a belt in the vacuum because they had never done it before and they happen to use at a time that it broke so they asked me how to fix it. So they'll ask me how to do things like that which are really funny.

Household workers also attempt to routinize and rationalize the housework by reorganizing family practices and introducing new methods, perhaps cleaning neglected areas of the house to create additional space or rearranging the furniture. Mrs. Rodriquez describes her approach as follows:

> I would take one room and give it a full general cleaning which was walls, windows, everything, and from there I would do the rest light housework. Then the next week, I would take another room and give that a general cleaning and go to the rest lightly until I had all the house done real good and after that it was just a matter of keeping it up.

Taking responsibility frequently includes finding replacements during their absence.[57]

> I worked for my mother-in-law sometimes and if she was sick or if she was going out of town, I'd do some of the houses that she does every week and she really couldn't leave without somebody going to do something because it would be really a mess when she came back and it would be more work on her. So I would go and fill in for her.

Only one domestic referred to her relationship with employers as "one of the family." All the other women retained a separation between tasks completed for their employers and "work of love" given to their families. The household workers attempted to enforce a new set of norms that transform the domestic-mistress relationship into a customer-vendor relationship. In their struggle to change the occupation, the Chicanas altered the employer's role to that of client or customer. They attempted to create businesslike relationships similar to those established by male workers employed to shampoo carpets, paint, and do repairs. The new definition of the relationship stressed a professionalism and lessened the opportunity for psychological exploitation and the extraction of emotional labor. Chicanas aimed to eliminate tasks that diffuse roles and add emotional labor, particularly unpaid shadow work. For instance, cooking Mexican food for employers was a request refused by all but two of the women. Their reasons for refusing the request suggest that they make a division between paid tasks and "work of love" and take precautions against selling their personhood: "I only cook for my family." "I didn't want to share my culture with them [employers]." The workers' struggle against the personalization of the employee-employer relationship involves a struggle against the personalization of the work. Domestics attempted to standardize housework and improve the occupation by defining housework as skilled labor.

In order to convince employers to accept the new working relationship, private household workers have to present the advantages. One strategy used to convince the employer that she does not want to be a supervisor is to create a situation for the employer that demands more detailed supervision. This includes such tactics as doing only the tasks requested and nothing else, not bothering to inform the employer that the worker has used the last vacuum bag or has used up the cleaning materials and refusing to offer the employer assistance in fixing a simple mechanical problem in an appliance. Consequently, employers who refuse to shift control and responsibility are confronted with domestics who take no interest in or responsibility for completing the housework.

To redefine their work as skilled labor, Chicanas capitalize on the fact that working women are no longer interested in supervising the labor of the private household worker. Women hiring domestics to escape the double day syndrome cannot reap the benefits of the work if they supervise the work of a "menial laborer." Acknowledging housework as skilled labor affirms the worth of the housewives' housework. In shifting housecleaning to "expert housekeepers," the housewife fulfills her responsibility to the family by obtaining skilled services; and in doing so, she defines the work as difficult, time consuming, and requiring skilled labor.

Creating a Businesslike Environment

As in other female-dominated occupations—such as nursing and teaching—private household workers lack authority and must therefore rely on the employers' cooperation to change the structure of the work and social relationships.[58] Mrs. Rojas describes one woman she worked for who accepted her obligation as an employer and maintained the agreement to hire Mrs. Rojas every Wednesday.

> I use to work for her on Wednesday and she would be going on a trip away with her husband and stuff because he did a lot of out-of-state work and she would go with him and being that I was going to be there on Wednesday and she wasn't she'd pay me anyway so I got paid from her whether I went [to work] or not as

long as it was her who was going to be gone and not an excuse from me or some-thing. She is about the only one that ever did that.

This employer is unique because most employers in domestic service expect the domestic to keep a work schedule to clean their houses on a regular basis but do not accept the responsibility of providing the work they promised.

In another account about an employer's daughter expecting her to be subor-dinate, Mrs. Rojas illustrates the role some employers play in eliminating ser-vitude aspects of the occupation.

> I told a young lady something about leaving her underclothes thrown around, and she asked me what was I there for? I went straight in, called her mother and told her the situation. Her mother came home from work and let the young lady have it. She [the mother] was thoroughly upset. I was not there to be her [the daughter's] personal maid and she was told that in no uncertain terms.

Analysis of the informal networks used by both employers and employees points to a key role in establishing a businesslike environment. The informal network between employers and employees socializes both to the value of mod-ernizing trends in the occupation. Chicana work histories revealed that, partic-ularly for younger workers, the introduction to domestic service involved an informal apprenticeship program. Like the domestics interviewed in Coley's study, the new recruit accompanied a relative to work for several days or weeks until the new recruit decided she was ready to work alone.[59] Mrs. Rodriquez describes the introduction and "training" into domestic service she received from her sister:

> She would go look it over and see if I missed anything or like in the bathroom you have to polish all the chrome and I didn't know that so I cleaned it and it was clean but she's the one that gave me all these tips on polishing up the chrome and stuff.

While assisting her sister, Mrs. Garcia pointed out the advantages of charging a "flat rate" rather than by the hour:

> When I was working with my sister, I told her she shouldn't be cleaning by the hour because it's not worth it to be cleaning by the hour. You are there too many hours and you don't make much money that way.

Although the Chicanas identified these training sessions as providing experi-ence in cleaning, learning about new products or appliances, and discovering the pros and cons of structuring the work in particular ways, the most important function may have been the socialization of new recruits to expect certain work-ing conditions and wages and to learn ways to negotiate with employers.[60]

Employers are similarly tied to the network. Employers ask domestics for the names of interested persons to work for neighbors, while domestics ask employers for the names of their friends interested in hiring housekeepers. Domestics are often very careful in their recommendations:

> They'll [friends] call and see if I know anybody that needs help but I have to know the person, and if I don't think the person is going to do the job, I will not send them . . . I'm very careful who I send—who I recommend.

In assisting friends and neighbors to find workers, employers inform other potential employers of existing conditions and thereby are instrumental in creating certain expectations. By obtaining new jobs through the network, Chicanas are reasonably assured that the new employers are socialized to appropriate expectations.

> I right away tell them what I do and what I expect to get paid and they already know because of their friends because they have already discussed my work.

Employers' involvement in improving the occupation may not be limited to exposing new employers to contemporary expectations. Two domestics report that employers actually apply pressure on other employers to upgrade working conditions. Both domestics work for employers who set standards of fairness and urge their friends and neighbors to conform—for instance, by complying with federal regulations by filing income tax and social security forms. Mrs. Salazar has such an employer:

> I don't ask for raises anymore. I have one woman who kind of sets the pace and she's given me a raise almost every year and then she hints around to some of the other ones that she knows that I work for and then they all bring it up to her standards.

The controlled environment created by the use of the informal network paves the avenue for Chicanas to establish their self-definition as professionals and their informal work arrangement as a business relationship.

CONCLUSION

Faced with limited job opportunities, Chicanas turn to domestic service and restructure the occupation to resemble a businesslike arrangement. Similarly to the union members in Coley's study, the Chicana household workers I interviewed define themselves as professional cleaners hired to do general housework. They urge their employers to turn over the planning along with the execution of the work. They consider themselves skilled laborers who are well able to schedule tasks, determine cleaning techniques, select the appropriate work materials, and set the work pace. Verbal agreements specifying tasks minimize supervision and increase the degree of autonomy. Eliminating the employer from a supervisory role also removes the worker from a subordinate position. Like the household worker's collective that Salzinger studied in the Bay area, Chicanas are "redefining domestic work as skilled labor, and on that basis struggling for increased pay and security and for autonomy and control over their work," and "they are in fact engaged in what in other contexts has been called a 'professionalization project.'"[61] Domestics' ability to select and change employers is the critical locus of autonomy and control in what would otherwise be a powerless, subservient position. Working for a different employer—and in many cases two to three employers—places Chicanas in a strong negotiating position.[62]

Like other full-time domestics, Chicanas employed as day workers in private households are moving away from "wage work" and from selling their "labor time" toward a "flat rate" in which a "job" is exchanged for a specified amount of money. In this situation, any efficiency realized by the worker saves her time and can sometimes be converted into profit that will accrue to her. Chicanas are attempting to transform domestic work in the direction of the petit-bourgeois relation of customer-vendor rather than the preindustrial relation of mistress-servant or even the wage worker-employer relation of capitalism. This arrangement is most successful with employed housewives who readily accept the skills of domestics. The strategy to transform domestic service by selling labor services rather than labor power is also useful in eliminating potentially exploitative aspects of the domestic-mistress relationship. Strategies described by Chicanas in the study are consistent with the emergence of cleaning agencies that advertise expert and skilled labor.

Although there is a long history of attempts to organize maid's unions,[63] most private household workers are isolated from each other and struggle for better working conditions on an individual basis. Nevertheless, the goals of individual struggle have similarities with issues of collective action: raising wages; providing benefits such as paid vacations, holidays, sick leave, and workers' unemployment compensation; changing attitudes toward the occupation; and creating public awareness about the value of the labor.[64]

Focusing on workers' strategies to restructure housework points to the wide range of variation in work tasks, wages, benefits, and social relations in the occupation. Household workers' ability to negotiate working conditions is not restricted to the degree of their vulnerability in the labor force. In her discussion of dual-career couples' decisions about the wages and working conditions of household workers, Hertz found that several factors affected the outcome, including the couples' attitudes toward live-in arrangements, the importance of flexible child care, "similarities in status or values of the workers," and the couples' ability to exploit a cheap labor pool.[65] Clearly, "dual-career couples have an indirect but material interest in maintaining an unstable, low-wage pool of labor."[66] However, dual-career couples are only one type of employer seeking private household workers. Salzinger identified a "bottom tier" of employers that consisted of elderly people, two-earner working-class families, and single mothers needing cheap child care. Although there is variation in working conditions between the upper and bottom tier of employers, domestic service is perhaps best described as a segmented market. The lack of state regulation and unionization results in dual markets that are maintained by employers taking advantage of the vulnerable status of women of color, particularly undocumented immigrants, in the labor force.

Chapter 7

THE HOUSEWORK DILEMMA

Throughout the course of researching *Maid in the U.S.A.*, I have often reflected on the chance meeting with the sixteen-year-old domestic in El Paso described in chapter one. Perhaps what is most remarkable about that encounter was the lack of communication between the young employee and her employer over the definition of the work situation. At the time I thought it rather peculiar that my colleague discussed domestic service in terms of charity and good works rather than as a work issue. I now realize that this was not at all uncommon. The same tension I experienced with my colleague in El Paso has repeated itself during question and answer sessions following presentations of this work in progress at conferences and universities. The majority of the questions raised by academic audiences seem consistently to have been formed and informed by the concerns of employers. That is, the comments of my colleagues and their critiques of my work have almost universally been made from the position of middle class men and women who hire poor women of color to clean their houses and care for their children. They have been very defensive about this relationship. Instead of their grappling with theoretical issues, again and again I have heard testimonies from academics that they have maids who are "just like one of the family." My colleagues insist either that their employees expect or are grateful for gifts of old clothes or that their housekeepers or domestics are benefiting in the classic sense of a bridging occupation.

These experiences have provided me with additional information on "the employer's side of the story," this time from college professors, administrators,

researchers, writers, and students. After making my presentation, while my colleagues described the modern version of the "servant problem," I have almost
always tried to relate their comments directly to the workers' account of the same
situation. However, engaging a discussion on the relationship between the two
perspectives has been hampered by employers' inability (or refusal) to see their
homes as a place of employment or to define the domestics they employ as
workers. Their economic positions and class interests seem to make them unable
to recognize the similarity between the domestics' needs as workers and the
benefits that academic employees enjoy in their own jobs: work breaks, vacations, sick leave, benefits, annual raises, and proper equipment to do the work.
Apparently, academics are more at ease about discussing race, class, and gender
from a macrolevel using large faceless data bases for analyzing stratification.
Clearly, an analysis of the interpersonal interactions between middle-class whites
and working class women of color in the intimate confines of the home creates
an enormous amount of discomfort in academic settings. From time to time it
has even provoked fairly dramatic outbursts of hostility.

The analysis of domestic service makes visible two painful failures of modern
feminism. First, despite the fact that both the first and second wave of feminism
in the West advocated women's involvement outside the home, the social movements failed to make men take equal responsibility for the household and children. Despite (sometimes bitter and painful) struggles within the family, husbands' and children's relation to housework typically continues to be one of
"contributions" rather than "responsibility." Second, feminist movements in the
United States have not been successful in establishing collective solutions to the
problem of household labor. The failure to socialize responsibility for reproductive labor is exemplified by the lack of funding for maternity leave and benefits,
family leave, day care, and home care. For the most part, public or collective
strategies for redistributing domestic labor are available only under special circumstances.

Still, the social processes that make the housework dilemma so acute continue
to accelerate: more women are entering the labor force, upward mobility and the
breaking down of sexist barriers mean that some women have established themselves in more responsible positions that make increased demands on their time
and energy; increased geographical mobility means that extended family members are likely to be dispersed throughout the city or the country and thus fewer
family members are available to share the burden of day-to-day domestic chores.
In the absence of societal responsibility for domestic labor and the isolation from
kinship groups and community, if women are to avoid the double day, those who
can afford it have little recourse but to purchase the labor and services of others.

Not surprisingly, then, many of the academic women who have criticized my
presentation of the domestics' viewpoints hold attitudes not different in kind
from those of the women employers described by Jane Addams in 1896, Mar-

garet Mead in 1976, and Susan Tucker in 1988. That is, when confronted by the perspective of domestic workers, their comments and questions exhibit high levels of cognitive dissonance, discomfort, guilt, and resentment. As feminists, they recognize one aspect of "sisterhood" in the brute fact that all women share the burden of housework. At the same time, they enjoy class privilege in their ability to shift that burden to another woman. In striking a balance between their own careers and the demands of housework by hiring a domestic worker, feminists find that domestic service challenges in practice the notions of sisterhood to which they adhere in theory. Academics with the most well-developed feminist ideology are faced with a peculiar dilemma in putting their beliefs into practice.

The demands of feminism and the situation in which both members of a couple work fall quite differently on the shoulders of working-class women. Hiring a domestic worker is, of course, rarely an option for poor and working-class families. They are left with only two options: either to accept the traditional division of domestic labor and continue the double day for working women, or to redistribute the male-female and the adult-child division of labor within the family. Efforts to redistribute domestic labor include couples choosing to work different shifts so that one will always be home to cover child care and increasing the contributions made by husbands and children. Given the difficulties that most middle-class working women have experienced in escaping the double day, it is not surprising that housework in working-class families remains women's work.

Upper- and middle-class women can avail themselves of a variety of strategies, most of which cost money, to escape both the worst aspects of the double day and the difficulty of shifting the responsibility for housework to other family members. They purchase goods and services including prepared meals and convenience food, domestic service, cleaning agencies, day care, and a variety of lessons and activities to occupy children while they work. Although cleaning agencies and day care centers throughout the country have been increasing in number, some women express a preference for personal services. These women choose to hire a responsible and trusted employee with her own key to their houses. This choice frees them from having to be home to unlock the door and gives them "a helper" to rely on for emergencies such as picking up a sick child from school. Similarly, working mothers prefer household workers as child care providers because they offer flexibility not available in day care programs. Women also voice discomfort with not having the same employee all the time. In addition, private household workers are usually less expensive, especially if employer and employee participate in the underground economy by avoiding taxes and social security payments.

For these reasons, and regardless of unresolved issues surrounding social class, sisterhood, and inequities in the sexual division of household labor, many feminists with the financial means to employ private household workers do so.

As employers, they face a variety of hiring decisions: Is it better to hire a woman or a man? If a woman, should they hire a white or nonwhite woman? Would it be better to hire an immigrant? a student? an au pair? Should they hire through an agency or in the underground economy? What benefits should they pay? How much wages should they offer? What tasks should they expect to be covered? In listening to students', administrators', and faculty's descriptions of their experiences as employers, I noticed several different strategies that employers use to hire and keep their private household workers, and I heard many of the rationalizations that explain their participation in what they clearly recognized was a less-than-perfect solution to the housework dilemma. On the basis of these encounters, I have categorized their comments into a typology that illustrates the wide range of views Americans hold about domestic service today.

1. *Bosses.* The first group are distinguished by their insistence that in hiring domestic service they were in effect no different from any other employer. The goal of their relationship with an employee was simply to get the highest level of service for the least amount of money. Although the "bosses" were not the majority, they made their comments loudly and with enough arrogance and anger that they were always heard. Although their characterizations and criticisms of domestic service were not always consistent, they shared a commitment to keeping the occupation unchanged, asserting their right as the boss to extract as much work as possible for the least amount of pay. Frequently they argued that the "going rate" for household workers was far beyond the skill and training the women brought to the job. Some even seemed to think that these "high" wages qualified the employees as members of the middle class. One sociology professor expressed disbelief that a domestic she employed had children who qualified for a low income college scholarship. Bosses expected to be able to specify any task. Incredible as it may seem, several people expressed resentment that household workers refuse to wash windows or do the laundry. Poor working conditions were excused on the basis that domestic service was a "bridging occupation" whereby rural immigrant women learned white middle-class skills and values and used the experience to get ahead in life. Many women expressed indignation over the discussion of "sisterhood" in the context of domestic service and argued that as employers woman should not be held to another set of criteria.

2. *Utopian Feminists.* This group, who presumably do not employ domestic workers, responded to my work by insisting that the occupation was inherently exploitative and had to be abolished. While the bosses argued on behalf of the status quo and the necessity of a traditional mistress-maid relationship, the utopian feminists held the opposite view. Spokespersons for this perspective argued that the oppressive and exploitative aspects of "cleaning up after others" or of dealing with "dirt" cannot be avoided and that the only solution is for everyone to clean up after themselves. This group rejected completely my analysis that the Chicanas I interviewed were adopting strategies to take control of the work

situation and "modernize" domestic work. Contending that housework is an inherently demeaning activity, they asserted that only persons regarded with contempt in society are assigned such work. In their analysis, attempts to improve employer-employee relationships or working conditions simply result in reinforcing class and race privilege and do nothing to change the circumstances that produced a mistress and maid (or a white middle-class woman employer and a working-class woman employee of color). Furthermore, they believe that changes such as control over the work process can never eliminate oppressive conditions but merely make the oppression more tolerable, a "behavioral valium." In an argument analogous to the radical perspective that the struggle of labor unions for wages and better working conditions propped up capitalism and hindered the revolution, they rejected any suggestion that working conditions could be improved.

Because advocating elimination of the occupation suggests that everyone, rich or poor, will begin doing his or her own dirty work, I would argue that such a position is not a realistic option. We do not live in an ideal world, reproductive labor must be performed, children must be cared for, and workers with more income than time will continue to buy the labor of others. Within the context of the local economy and political realities domestic work is still an important source of income for women of color struggling to support families. Moreover, it offers higher wages and a flexibility not found in other low-income, low-status jobs.

3. *Dodgers and Duckers.* Some feminists have developed what at first blush looks like the ideal solution to having their housework done without oppressing women; they hire a houseboy. Dodgers and duckers proudly announce their success in eliminating the racial and gender division of domestic labor by hiring white male college students as private household workers. Clearly recognizing that the systems of race, class, and gender domination manifest themselves in domestic service, dodgers and duckers understand that selecting vulnerable workers, particularly through the underground economy, allows employers to extract additional physical labor and keep wages low. They are uncomfortable with the issues of power and control apparent in the employee and employer relationship, particularly interracial dynamics. So they seek to remove themselves entirely from the present system of stratification and oppression, while still buying the labor of a private household worker. They seek to turn the situation on its head; hiring a man rather than a woman is celebrated as a victory over the sexist definition of housework as "woman's work." More significantly, hiring a male college student from one's own community is defined as an important strategy for equalizing an otherwise unequal relationship.

Occupying a position similar to that the of "help" found in New England during the early nineteenth century and described by Faye Dudden, male college students who work as household workers reflect their status as men from the middle class.[1] Interaction between employer and employee is conditioned by the fact that the worker is actually a college student training to become an accountant, a doctor, a lawyer—anything but a domestic. This approach, of course, has the effect of placing an additional burden on poor or working-class women. In what was once one of the few segments of the economy in which they had hegemony, they now have to compete for jobs with men from privileged backgrounds.

Race, class, and gender stratification in the United States relegates women of color to the bottom of the labor force while white men and women compete for the better jobs. For this reason, the decision to hire white middle-class male college students—or any other person outside the categories of the poor, the working class, immigrants or women of color—does nothing to improve the plight of women. As a personal strategy to avoid race, class, and gender stratification, it results in a dual wage system: the reward of high-paying jobs in nonsexist, nonracist environments to white college students or other white women or men, while women of color compete against one another for the lower-tier positions in domestic service. The implication—a version of blaming the victim—is that the absence of women of color frees the environment from sexism or racism. Just as employers can benefit from race and gender discrimination by hiring women of color for less, they can also decide to hire women of color for the more lucrative jobs in domestic service instead of discriminating against them.

4. *The Common Victim*. Many professional women define their own situation as one of being just as exploited as the women they employ. "What are we to do?" they argue: "As employers, professional women are victims of sexism because we compete in a man's world and still remain responsible for child care and housework." They are concerned about being able to hire affordable household workers while retaining the same standard of living as their male counterparts. An example of the victim's position appears in Mary Ann Mason's discussion of the unequal burden of household labor on professional women in relation to men in similar occupations. She bemoans the loss of "reliable domestic workers" and the appearance of "an unreliable procession of illegal immigrants and transient workers."[2] The common victim's gender analysis does not include paid housework, nor does it take into account the privileges and benefits gained from racial and class-based systems of inequality. When similarities between paid and unpaid housework are drawn, the victim denies that the burden of sexism has been shifted to another woman employed as a household worker because the labor is paid. In this view, the oppression of housework is tied to its unpaid status.

There is a critical flaw in the common victim analysis. Feminist analysis should consider not only the privilege and benefits that husbands obtain at the expense of their wives but also those that one group of women obtain at the expense of another. Certainly, as employees, professional women are sometimes victims of sexism, but they still make decisions that ultimately result in shifting the burden of sexism. Hiring household workers to take the place of wives or mothers maintains male privilege at home. As mothers and wives, employers deplore being treated like a "maid." The burden of sexism is shifted to the worker when employers pass on to her the same degrading treatment that they experience from their husbands and children who expect to be waited upon and served. Women employers in effect decide whether to structure paid housework to eliminate practices such as picking up after their husbands and children or to shift the burden of sexism to the workers by expecting them to do it instead.

Including race, class, and gender in the analysis of reproductive labor forces us to reassess the argument that housewives carry the burden for housework regardless of whether they do the work or not. The words of Sojourner Truth— "Ain't I a woman?"—make the inescapable point: legal or illegal, white or non-white, poor or middle-class, we are all women. A feminist agenda cannot succeed without including the plight of all women, not just the specific circumstances of professional and career women. Research on the double day or the second shift cannot continue to ignore the domestic by suggesting that the employer retains responsibility for housework when she in fact passes it on to a more vulnerable woman. The gender issues surrounding housework cannot be understood by allowing domestics to be visible only when they are perceived as part of the problem.

5. *Maternalists.* Maternalists define their position as that of "employers" but reject work or class analyses of their experiences as inappropriate. They focus entirely upon the interpersonal relationship. Even after I have read quotes from Alice Childress's essay "Like One of the Family," maternalists have argued that what Childress describes is not always the case and that "their" Mexican, African American, or West Indian maid *is* "just like one of the family." They are much more emotionally involved than any of the other types of employer in the worker' s personal life. Friendship and caring, particularly the employee's devotion and loyalty are identified as central features of the relationship. Descriptions of the relationship are dominated by a list of things the employer has done to improve the employee's life: encouraging her to go to college, giving pay advances to deal with emergencies, recommending top-notch dentists, physicians, and lawyers, helping get her children into school, and so on. These descriptions suggest that manipulation is a major component of the relationship and is used by both employee and employer. Interestingly enough, not all maternalists consider their employees to be good household workers, but since the personal relationship takes priority, poor work habits are not grounds for dismissal.

6. *Contractors.* Of all the employers, contractors appear most willing to accept the modern relationship that household workers are struggling to establish.

Instead of hiring the private household worker and unilaterally setting salary and working conditions, they negotiate with the worker both the cost of cleaning the house and exactly what the job entails. When they reach agreement, the contractor essentially accepts the verbal contract offered by the worker and purchases the service of housecleaning rather than a certain number of hours of labor. The critical aspect of the contract relationship is that the domestic assumes responsibility for the work process and can benefit directly by any economies and efficiencies that she introduces. Contractors do not pay by the hour but rather by the job, and this tends to work out to a level higher than the wages paid by other employers: an average of about 15 to 20 dollars an hour. Since contractors usually work full-time outside the home, they do not hire a worker for companionship, nor do they impose requirements for ceremonial cleaning or expect to be waited on and served. Contractors are not available to micromanage the work, allowing the employee to select her own cleaning materials. Such arrangements actually relieve the employer of more domestic labor; if they pick up newspapers, clothes and toys from the floor and collect the dishes, cups, and glasses and place them in the sink or dishwasher before the housekeeper arrives, they consider such tasks in preparing the house for cleaning analogous to preparing for painters, carpet cleaners or carpenters. Although they might have chosen to contract with a cleaning service, they prefer the privatization of domestic service because this arrangement offers flexibility and the stability of a trusted employee who takes responsibility and does not require supervision. Like other employers, they sometimes rely on workers to deal with unexpected work, such as a sick child, an unplanned dinner party, or guests.

While contractors frequently offer the most lucrative jobs available in domestic service, they do not necessarily include social security, vacation, or annual raises, and rarely do they offer sick leave, insurance, or job security. Like other employers who try to replace the mother or wife, contractors also sometimes attempt to add tasks and extend the workday.

The foregoing typology offers an overview of various attitudes and practices regarding domestic service found within feminist circles. Diverse individual reactions to the race, class, and gender issues surrounding domestic service reiterate decisions that other upper- and middle-class women employers make. And, like them, feminists cannot shy away from responsibility for creating or maintaining working conditions in domestic service that may make the job intolerable to workers with other options. They set wages and establish working conditions; they decide how much the work is worth and how much they are willing to pay, and they determine whom to hire. Employer decisions about salary and working conditions reflect their view of the domestic either as an experienced and skilled household worker hired to perform specific tasks or as an unskilled laborer replacing the wife and mother and requiring supervision. Their decisions determine whether emotional labor is to be part of the job. Thus, employer-employee relationships can be structured around racist and maternalistic norms or structured on the principles of equality and justice. In this way the structure of the work and of the social interactions either reinforces or weakens cultural values based on gender, race, and class domination.

Employers can go a long way toward improving the working conditions in domestic service. Attempting to do so may not be an ideal solution to the housework dilemma, because the sexual and racial division of labor remains. Nevertheless, hiring poor and working class women of color, improving the immediate working conditions, and increasing pay are important. Recognizing the rights of private household workers as no different from the rights of other workers is an important step toward transforming domestic service. Supporting the struggles of private household workers involves the transformation of paid housework to include higher wages, annual raises, social security, vacation, benefits, and job security.

This is not to argue that individual acts of resistance can eliminate demeaning working conditions from the occupation or that a few employers can raise the wages and benefits for all employees. Supporting and advocating the unionization efforts of household workers, child care workers and home care workers are essential to transforming paid domestic labor. Although household workers are difficult to organize because they work in isolation from each other, informal networks among workers and collectives serving immigrant women can function as ports of entry to unionization. Efforts at unionizing the bottom tier of workers in domestic service will eliminate the advantages employers gain by hiring poor and working class women of color, particularly undocumented immigrant women. Unions can take the concerns already identified by the workers to the local, state, and national levels.

Clearly, resolving the housework dilemma calls for more than the transformation of domestic service. As a society, we cannot continue to define reproductive labor as women's work. Cultural values and norms reinforcing equality must start at home with the simple act of picking up for ourselves. Beyond this, reproductive labor must be recognized as society's work, a responsibility that requires collective responses rather than private and individual solutions. The goal must be to develop strategies to allocate the social burden of necessary reproductive labor in such a way that it does not fall disproportionally on the shoulders of any group.

NOTES

Chapter 1

1. The conditions I observed in El Paso were not much different from those described by D. Thompson in her 1960 article, "Are Women Bad Employers of Other Women," *Ladies Home Journal*: "Quarters for domestic help are usually ill placed for quiet. Almost invariably they open from pantry or kitchen, so that if a member of the family goes to get a snack at night he wakes up the occupant. And the live-in maid has nowhere to receive a caller except in the kitchen or one those tiny rooms." "As a general rule anything was good enough for a maid's room. It became a catchall for furniture discarded from other parts of the house. One room was a cubicle too small for a regular-sized bed." Cited in Linda Martin and Kerry Segrave, *The Servant Problem Domestic Workers in North America*, p. 25.

2. David Katzman addresses the "servant problem" in his historical study of domestic service, *Seven Days a Week, Women and Domestic Service in Industrializing America*. Defined by middle-class housewives, the problem includes both the shortage of servants available and the competency of women willing to enter domestic service. Employers' attitudes about domestics have been well documented in women's magazines. Katzman described the topic as "the bread and butter of women's magazines between the Civil War and World War I"; moreover, Linda Martin and Kerry Segrave, *The Servant Problem*, illustrate the continuing presence of articles on the servant problem in women's magazines today.

3. Lillian Pettengill's account *Toilers of the Home: The Record of a College Woman's Experience as a Domestic Servant* is based on two years of employment in Philadelphia households.

4. Ruth Schwartz Cowan, *More Work for Mother: The Ironies of Household Technology from the Open Hearth to the Microwave*, p. 228.

5. Earning money as domestic workers to pay college expenses not covered by scholarships is not that uncommon among other women of color in the United States. Trudier Harris interviewed several African American women public school and university college teachers about their college

day experiences in domestic service. *From Mammies to Militants: Domestics in Black American Literature*, pp. 5–6.

6. Judith Rollins, *Between Women: Domestics and Their Employers*; Bonnie Thornton Dill, "Across the Boundaries of Race and Class: An Exploration of the Relationship Between Work and Family among Black Female Domestic Servants;" idemo. "'Making Your Job Good Yourself': Domestic Service and the Construction of Personal Dignity." In *Women and the Politics of Empowerment* eds. Ann Bookman and Sandra Morgen; Soraya Moore Coley, "'And Still I Rise': An Exploratory Study of Contemporary Black Private Household Workers;" Evelyn Nakano Glenn, *Issei, Nisei, War Brides: Three Generations of Japanese American Women in Domestic Service*.

7. In some cases, it was important to let women know that my own background had involved paid housework and that my mother and sister were currently employed full-time as private household workers. Sharing this information conveyed that my life had similarities to theirs and that I respected them. This sharing of information is similar to the concept of "reciprocity." R. Wax, "Reciprocity in Field Work," in *Human Organization Research: Field Relationships and Techniques*, eds. R. N. Adams and J. J. Preiss, 90–98.

8. Clark Knowlton, "Changing Spanish-American Villages of Northern New Mexico," pp. 455–75.

9. Nancie Gonzalez, *The Spanish-Americans of New Mexico*, p. 123.

10. William W. Winnie, "The Hispanic People of New Mexico."

11. Thomas J. Malone, "Recent Demographic and Economic Changes in Northern New Mexico," pp. 4–14.

12. Barrett, Donald N., and Julian Samora, *The Movement of Spanish Youth from Rural to Urban Settings*.

13. Knowlton, "The Spanish Americans in New Mexico," pp. 448–54.

14. See Paul A. Walter, "The Spanish-Speaking Community in New Mexico," pp. 150–57; Thomas Weaver, "Social Structure, Change and Conflict in a New Mexico Village;" Florence R. Kluckhohn and Fred L. Stodtbeck, *Variations in Value Orientations*; Frank Moore, "San Jose, 1946: A Study in Urbanization;" Barrett and Samora, *The Movement of Spanish Youth*.

15. Margaret Mead, "Household Help," p. 42.

16. Jane Addams, "A Belated Industry," p. 545.

17. Susan Tucker, *Telling Memories among Southern Women: Domestic Workers and Their Employers in the Segregated South*, p. 231.

18. Katzman, *Seven Days a Week*, p. 269–70.

19. See Margaret Mead, *Male and Female: A Study of the Sexes in a Changing World*; Aban Mehta, *The Domestic Servant Class*; Karen Tranberg Hansen, *Distant Companions*.

Chapter 2

1. For further elaboration on the significance of household labor see Sarah Fenstermaker Berk, *The Gender Factory*.

2. Concepts like "wageless housewives" or "unpaid household laborers" were developed to draw an analogy between women and racial minorities. Although popular comparisons between gender and racial oppression were intended to highlight the seriousness of sexist acts and comments in everyday interactions between men and women, the analogy at the same time devalued the experiences of women of color who suffer from both racism and sexism. Analogies do not take into account the fusion of racial and sexual hierarchies. This point becomes particularly important in the discussion of women of color and domestic service.

3. For example see Juliet Mitchell, *Women's Estate*, p. 14; Nona Glazer, "Everyone Needs Three Hands: Doing Unpaid and Paid Work," in *Women and Household Labor*, ed. S. F. Berk; Mariarosa Dalla Costa and Selma James, "Women and the Subversion of the Community," p. 19.

4.   Ann Oakley, *Women's Work: The Housewife, Past and Present.*

5.   Glazer, "Everyone Needs Three Hands."

6.   Women are generally found in jobs demanding skills and talents similar to those developed in the home, and as with household labor, these skills are devalued and unrecognized. The ideology that women have an innate ability to do the monotonous, repetitive work characteristic of housework has been replicated in assembly lines and offices. Moreover, in certain respects women's wage work, such as nursing and cleaning, is little more than "industrialized housework." Recent trends in the labor market reveal the continuing "feminization" of low-skilled occupations.

7.   Paul Smith, "Domestic Labour and Marx's Theory of Value," in *Feminism and Materialism: Women and Modes of Production*, eds. Annette Kuhn and Ann Marie Wolpe, pp. 200–219; John Harrison, "The Political Economy of Housework," pp. 35–51; Wally Secomb, "The Housewife and Her Labour Under Capitalism," pp. 3–24; Lise Vogel, "The Earthly Family," pp. 9–50; Ira Gerstein, "Domestic Work and Capitalism," pp. 101–28; Jean Gardinar, "Women's Domestic Labour," pp. 47–57; Jean Gardinar, S. Himmelweit and M. MacKintosh, "Women's Domestic Labour," pp. 1–11; S. Himmelweit and S. Mohun, "Domestic Labour and Capital," pp. 15–31; M. Coulson, B. Magas, and H. Wainwright, "The Housewife and Her Labour Under Capitalism: A Critique," pp. 59–71; I. Gought and J. Harrison, "Unproductive Labour and Housework Again," pp. 1–7; Terry Fee, "Domestic Labor: An Analysis of Housework and Its Relation to the Production Process," pp. 1–17.

8.   Annette Kuhn and others have pointed out the significance of the argument that wages should be paid for housework. For instance, see Ellen Malos ed., *The Politics of Housework*, p. 23; Peggy Morton, "A Woman's Work is Never Done," in *From Feminism to Liberation*, ed. E. H. Altbach. There are also those who have challenged aspects of the domestic labor theory in reference to modes of production and its application to human reproduction. See L. Beneria, "Reproduction, Production and the Sexual Division of Labor," pp. 203–225; J. Humphries, "Protective Legislation, the Capitalist State and Working Class Men," pp. 1–33; C. D. Deere, J. Humphries and M. D. de Leal, "Class and Historical Analysis for the Study of Women and Economic Change," in *Women's Roles and Population Trends in the Third World*, eds. R. Anker et al. (eds.), pp. 87–114; Maxine Molyneux, "Beyond the Domestic Labour Debate," pp. 3–37; Deborah Fehy Bryceson and Ulla Vuorela, "Outside the Domestic Labour Debate: Towards a Theory of Modes of Human Reproduction," pp. 137–166.

9.   H. Hartmann, "The Family as the Locus of Gender, Class and Political Struggle: The Example of Housework," p. 383.

10.   Martin Meissner, Elizabeth Humphrys, Scott Meis, and William Scheu, "No Exit for Wives: Sexual Division of Labor and the Cumulation of Household Demands," pp. 424–39; Richard A. Berk and Sarah Fenstermaker Berk, *Labor and Leisure at Home: Consent and Organization of the Household Day*; William R. Beer, *Househusbands: Men and Housework in American Families;* Kathryn Walker, "Time Spent by Husbands in Household Work," pp. 8–11.

11.   Berk and Berk, "A Simultaneous Equation Model for the Division of Household Labor," pp. 431–68.

12.   Julie A. Matthaei, *An Economic History of Women in America*, p. 305.

13.   Ann Game and Rosemary Pringle, *Gender at Work*, p. 126.

14.   Pat Mainardi, "The Politics of Housework," in *The Politics of Housework*, ed. Ellen Malos, p. 100.

15.   Betty Friedan, *The Feminine Mystique*, p. 233.

16.   Ibid., p. 235.

17.   Ann Oakley, *Subject Women*, p. 176.

18.   Ibid., p. 100. Also see Meg Luxton, *More Than a Labour of Love. Three Generations of Women's Work in the Home.*

19.   Oakley, *Women's Work*, p. 92.

20.   It is important to keep in mind that employment gives women another source of identity to

draw from. See Myra Marx Ferree, "Working-Class Jobs: Housework and Paid Work as Sources of Satisfaction," pp. 431–441; E. Mostow, "A Comparative Study of Work Satisfaction of Females with Full-Time Employment and Full-Time Housekeeping," pp. 538–48; Lillian Breslow Rubin, *Worlds of Pain: Life in the Working-Class Family*; Arlie Hochschild, *The Second Shift: Working Parents and the Revolution at Home*.

21. Oakley, *Women's Work*, p. 92.

22. Ibid., p. 91.

23. Ibid., p. 26.

24. Luxton, *More Than a Labour of Love*, p. 117.

25. Game and Pringle, *Gender at Work*, p. 127.

26. Diana Leonard Barker and Sheila Allen, *Dependence and Exploitation in Work and Marriage*, p. 2.

27. Oakley, *Women's Work*, pp. 6–7.

28. In *Gender*, Ivan Illich identifies two examples in the United States in which women's organizations attempted to change the term. In 1936, the Long Island Federation Women's Club suggested the change to "homemakers," and in 1942 there was a push in Kansas City to change the term to "household executive" (p. 47).

29. Lewis Coser, *Greedy Institutions*, p. 94. Furthermore, he notes that "in achievement and instrumentally oriented societies, those who do household work are led to consider it demeaning since it is symbolically downgraded as not 'real work.'" (p. 93).

30. Rae Andre, *Homemakers: The Forgotten Workers*, p. 50.

31. Oakley, *Women's Work*, p. 4. See also Berk, *The Gender Factory*, for further discussion on defining housework, particularly from a methodological standpoint.

32. Matthaei, *An Economic History*, p. 275.

33. M. A. Ferber and B. G. Birnbaum, "Housework: Priceless or Valueless?" pp. 387–400; see also Kathryn E. Walker and William Gauger, "The Dollar Value of Household Work;" Bettina Berch, *The Endless Day: The Political Economy of Women and Work*, pp. 94–96. However, "Average estimates of the annual value of a household worker can range from $15,000 to $20,000 depending upon the size of the family and the number of tasks routinely undertaken" (S. F. Berk, "Women's Unpaid Labor: Home and Community," in *Women Working: Theories and Facts in Perspective*, Ann H. Stromberg and Shirley Harkess eds., p. 293).

34. Ivan Illich, *Shadow Work*, p. 1–2. See also Illich, *Gender*.

35. Naomi Gerstel and Harriet Engel Gross, eds., *Families and Work*, p. 5.

36. K. E. Walker and M. Woods, *Time Use: A Measurement of Household Production of Goods and Services*; Joanne Vanek, "Time Spent in Housework," pp. 116–20; Berk and Berk, *Labor and Leisure at Home*; Ruth Schwartz Cowan, *More Work for Mother*.

37. Friedan, *The Feminine Mystique*, p. 239.

38. Oakley, *Women's Work*, p. 95.

39. See S. F. Berk, *The Gender Factory* for a critique of research's assessment of family contribution to housework. Also, idem., "Women's Unpaid Labor: Home and Family;" Laurie Davidson and Laura Kramer Gordon, *The Sociology of Gender*, pp. 43–44.

40. Shelly Coverman, "Gender, Domestic Labor Time and Wage Inequality," pp. 623–36; Sara Yogev, "Do Professional Women Have Egalitarian Marital Relationships?" pp. 865–71; E. Haavio-Mannila, "The Position of Finnish Women," pp. 339–47; C. F. Epstein, "Law Partners and Marital Partners," pp. 564–69; L. L. Holmstrom, *The Two-Career Family*; R. Rapoport and R. Rapoport, *Dual Career Families Re-Examined: New Integrations of Work and Family*; M. Meissner, E. W. Humphrey, S. M. Meiss, and W. J. Scheu, "No Exit for Wives: Sexual Division of Labour and the Accumulation of Household Demands," pp. 424–59; J. N. Hedges and J. K. Barnett, "Working Women and the Division of Household Tasks," pp. 9–13; Catherine White Berheide, and Sarah Fenstermaker Berk, and Richard A. Berk, "Household Work in the Suburbs: The Job and Its Partic-

ipants," pp. 491–518; Alexander Szalai, Philip E. Converse, Pierre Feldheim, Erwin K. Scheuch and Philip F. Stone, eds., *The Use of Time: Daily Activities of Urban and Suburban Populations in Twelve Countries.* However, the time spent by married women employed outside the home tends to differ from the amount spent by full-time housewives. The time absorbed by housework and child care depends upon both the type of labor force participation and number of small children. See L. Waite, "Working Wives and Family Life Cycle," pp. 272–94; S. Coverman, "Gender, Domestic Labor Time and Wage Inequality," pp. 623–37; Kathryn E. Walker and Margaret E. Woods, *Time Use: A Measure of Household Production of Family Goods and Services.*

41. Matthaei, *An Economic History*, p. 306; Myra Marx Ferree, "Sacrifice, Satisfaction and Social Change: Employment and the Family," in *My Troubles Are Going to Have Trouble with Me*, eds. Karen Sacks and Dorothy Remy, pp. 61–79.

42. For examples see Marabel Morgan, *Total Woman*; May Miller, *Happiness is Homemaking.*

43. Coser, "Servants: The Obsolescence of an Occupational Role"; David Chaplin, "Domestic Service and Industrialization," pp. 97–127; Vilhelm Aubert, "The Housemaid—An Occupational Role in Crisis," pp. 149–158.

44. Coser, p. 32.

45. Ibid., p. 32.

46. Ibid., p. 33.

47. Aaron Levenstein, *Why People Work*, p. 38.

48. Coser, p. 31.

49. Levenstein, p. 38.

50. Harold Wool, *The Labor Supply for Lower-Level Occupations*, p. 69–70.

51. Susan Tucker, *Telling Memories*, p. 248–49.

52. Investigating the social mobility among French servants, Theresa McBride's study of European servants concluded that significant intergenerational mobility was obtained (McBride, *The Domestic Revolution: The Modernization of Household Service in England and France, 1820–1920*; idem., "Social Mobility for the Lower Class: Domestic Servants in France," pp. 63–78). Similar conclusions were reached by George Stigler in an economic analysis of intergenerational mobility among foreign-born domestics in the United States between 1900 and 1940, (Stigler, *Domestic Servants in the United States, 1900–1940*).

53. For instance, David Katzman argued that live-in work situations were particularly beneficial in introducing the women to a "more American and modern environment" (*Seven Days a Week*, p. 171).

54. Ibid., p. 171.

55. Lenore Davidoff, "The Rationalization of Housework," in *Dependence and Exploitation in Work and Marriage*, eds. Diana Leonard Baker and Shelia Allen, p. 123.

56. Linda Martin and Kerry Segrave, *The Servant Problem: Domestic Workers in North America*, p. 70.

57. Judith Rollins, *Between Women*; Soraya Moore Coley, " 'And Still I Rise' "; Bonnie Thornton Dill, " 'Making Your Job Good Yourself': Domestic Service and the Construction of Personal Dignity"; Tucker, *Telling Memories*; Shellee Colen, " 'Just a Little Respect': West Indian Domestic Workers in New York City."

58. Rollins, *Between Women*, p. 183.

59. Ibid., p. 131.

60. Ibid., p. 156.

61. Dill, " 'Making Your Job'," p. 37–38.

62. Jacklyn Cock, *Maids and Madams: A Study in the Politics of Exploitation*, p. 11.

63. Recent discussions of the Marxist debate over whether domestic labor should be considered productive or unproductive labor as it applies to domestic service can be found in the study by Thelma Galvez and Rosalba Todaro of domestic service in Chile and in Jacklyn Cock's study of

domestics in South Africa (Thelma Galvez and Rosalba Todaro, "Housework for Pay in Chile: Not Just Another Job," pp. 307–21; Jacklyn Cock, *Maids and Madams*).

64. Althusser, Louis, *Lenin and Philosophy and Other Essays*, trans. Ben Brewster.

65. Callinicos argues that even if she does not work, "with the surplus, the wife can then accumulate petty capital and consume luxury goods," (L. Callinicos, "Domesticating Workers," *South African Labour Bulletin*, 2 [1975], p. 65; cited in Jacklyn Cock, *Maids and Madams*, p. 314).

66. Karen Tranberg Hansen, *Distant Companions: Servants and Employers in Zambia, 1900–1985*, p. 15.

67. Although Evelyn Glenn characterizes domestic service as preindustrial, she does locate the conflict and struggle between employer and employee within the work process (*Issei, Nisei, War Bride: Three Generations of Japanese American Women in Domestic Service*, p. 161).

68. Silvia Federici, "Wages Against Housework," in *The Politics of Housework*, Ellen Malos ed., p. 221.

69. Shulamith Firestone, *The Dialect of Sex: The Case for Feminist Revolution*, p. 207–8; Caroline Freeman, "When Is a Wage not a Wage?" pp. 166–73.

70. Glenn found an extremely rigid sexual division of labor in the homes of *issei* household workers.

71. Glenn notes a similar occurrence in her study. "Several women felt that their husbands made substantial contributions to household maintenance through yard work and other outdoor chores" (*Issei, Nisei, War Bride*, p. 223).

72. Oakley, *Women's Work*; Illich, *Gender*.

73. Japanese American household workers reported similar circumstances. Glenn, *Issei, Nisei, War Brides*, p. 235–6.

74. Glenn notes that children, particularly daughters, were a source of assistance to Japanese American household workers.

75. Glenn found that *issei* and *nisei* household workers relied on friends, neighbors, older children and husbands to babysit. See pp. 210 and 221. The strategies for child care among *nisei* women included arranging work schedules around school hours and leaving older children in charge of younger children (*Issei, Nisei, War Brides*, p. 221).

76. Rollins also found that African American domestics protected themselves from the degrading aspects of domestic service by separating their "selves" from their work roles.

77. Oakley, *Women's Work*, p. 4.

78. Rollins, *Between Women*, p. 24.

79. As Roger Sanjek and Shellee Colen maintain: "The domestic work context, we argue however, reinforces such differences by marking both populations with the inherent inequality it contains. This is possible, we believe, because there is something in the nature of domestic work in all class societies that results in stigma. Household labor, and we mean primarily housecleaning, kitchen work, and clothes washing, is seen as lowly, devalued work, associated with dirt and disorder" ("At Work In Homes," p. 23).

80. Ellen Malos, ed. *The Politics of Housework*, p. 36.

81. Matthaei, *Economic History of Women*, p. 29.

Chapter 3

1. For a detailed discussion see Christine Stansell, *City of Women: Sex and Class in New York, 1789–1860*.

2. L. A. Tilly and J. W. Scott, *Women, Work and Family*, p. 12.

3. Rhonda Rapoport and Robert Rapoport, "Work and Family in Contemporary Society," in *The Family and Change*, John N. Edwards, ed., p. 385.

4. Julie A. Matthaei, *An Economic History of Women in America*, p. 35.

5. Ibid., p. 31.

6. According to H. J. Neiboer, "the position held by the women of a tribe determines to some extent whether or not slaves are wanted. Where the drudgery is performed, and can be performed by the women, and men do not want to relieve them of it, there is not great use of slave labour. But where women enjoy high consideration, the men are more likely to procure slaves who are to assist the women in their work" (*Slavery as an Industrial System*, p. 388). See Judith Rollins, *Between Women*, pp. 21–59, for an excellent overview of the history of domestic service.

7. Lenore Davidoff and Ruth Hawthorn, *A Day in the Life of a Victorian Domestic Servant*.

8. Rollins, p. 25.

9. For a further discussion of "patriarchalism" see Reinhard Bendix, *Max Weber: An Intellectual Portrait*, p. 330–2.

10. Davidoff and Hawthorn, *A Day in the Life*.

11. Cited in Russell Lynes, "How America 'Solved' The Servant Problem," p. 50.

12. The choice to leave the service was not always voluntary. Pamela Horn points out that Lord North levied a tax against "keeping male servants" in 1777 in order to force more men into the factories (*The Rise and Fall of the Victorian Servant*, p. 9).

13. Ibid., p. 7.

14. Ibid., p. 11.

15. Theresa McBride, *Domestic Revolution*, p. 36.

16. Ibid., p. 48.

17. Ibid., p. 18.

18. Ibid., p. 18.

19. Rollins, *Between Women*, p. 35.

20. Ibid., p. 33.

21. McBride, *Domestic Revolution*, p. 28.

22. Lucy Salmon, *Domestic Service*, pp. 54, 61.

23. Glenna Matthews, *"Just a Housewife": The Rise and Fall of Domesticity in America*, p. 3.

24. See for instance J. K. Galbraith, *Economics and the Public Purpose*.

25. Stansell, *City of Women*, p. 11.

26. Ruth Schwartz Cowan's observation illustrates the impact of the division between economic and family activity: "The word 'housework,' which distinguishes work done at home from work done in other places, was not even part of the language until the middle of the nineteenth century" ("Women's Work, Housework, and History: The Historical Roots of Inequality in Work-Force Participation," in *Families and Work*, Naomi Gerstel and Harriet Engel Gross, eds., p. 165). Also see Ivan Illich, *Gender*, p. 47. In *City of Women*, Christine Stansell notes that some women did participate in commodity production, "as helpers to their husbands" and were most frequently found in sewing trades (p. 15).

27. Stansell, *City of Women*, p. 22.

28. J. Gardinar, "Women's Domestic Labour," pp. 47–58.

29. For a discussion of the doctrine of separate spheres see Barbara Welter, "The Cult of True Womanhood, 1820–1860," pp. 151–74, Kathryn Kish Sklar, *Catherine Beecher: A Study in American Domesticity*.

30. Meg Luxton, *More than a Labour of Love: Three Generations of Women's Work in the Home*, p. 11.

31. It follows that full-time homemaking became a symbol of femininity and served as a symbol of masculinity for their husbands who could afford the privilege of an unemployed wife. Only upper- and middle-class men and women had the means to fulfill the requirements of their new gender roles.

32. Gerda Lerner, *The Majority Finds Its Past: Placing Women in History*, p. 26, citing Thorstein Veblen, *The Theory of the Leisure Class* (New York [1899] 1962), pp. 70–1, 231–2.

33. Matthaei, *An Economic History*, p. 124. However, Stansell's study of working-class women

in New York City suggests that the amount of commodity production may be overestimated: "Poorer women lacked the steady income, the space or the facilities to engage in household crafts" (*City of Women*, p. 46).

34. I have borrowed Matthaei's term of the "separate sexual spheres of activity" to describe the sexual division of labor that relegated women to homemaking and family life and men to economic activity outside the home (*An Economic History*, p. 121–6).

35. Stansell, *City of Women*, p. 46.

36. Ibid., p. 52. For a detailed discussion, see chapter three ("Women in the Neighborhoods").

37. Matthews, *"Just a Housewife"*, p. 38. Citing Ralph Waldo Emerson, "Domestic Life," *Emerson's Complete Works,* vol. 7 (Boston: Houghton Mifflin, 1893), pp. 108f.

38. As quoted in Faye Dudden, *Serving Women: Household Service in Nineteenth-Century America*, p. 155 (from Mrs. A. J. Graves, *Women in America*, p. 79).

39. Barbara Welter, "The Cult of True Womanhood, 1820–1860."

40. Gerda Lerner, *The Majority Finds Its Past: Placing Women in History.*

41. Stansell, *City of Women*, p. 159.

42. Dudden, *Serving Women*, p. 155.

43. Ibid., p. 44.

44. Matthews, *"Just a Housewife,"* p. 30.

45. Dudden, *Serving Women*, p. 156.

46. Stansell, *City of Women*, p. 163.

47. Dudden, *Serving Women*, p. 168.

48. Ibid., p. 168.

49. Ibid., pp. 140–1.

50. Ibid., p. 159.

51. Ibid., p. 165.

52. Matthews, *"Just a Housewife,"* p. 151.

53. Ibid., p. 143.

54. Matthaei, *An Economic History*, p. 158.

55. Ibid., p. 159.

56. Dudden, *Serving Women*, p. 176.

57. Ibid., p. 178.

58. Ibid., p. 179.

59. Matthews, *"Just a Housewife,"* p. 14.

60. Ann Oakley, *Subject Women*, p. 172; J. Vanek, "Time Spent on Housework," p. 116.

61. Dudden, *Serving Women*; B. Ehrenreich and D. English, "The Manufacture of Housework," pp. 5–40; S. Ewen, *Captains of Consciousness: Advertising and the Social Roots of the Consumer Culture*; Christine Bose, "Technology and Changes in the Division of Labour in the American Home," pp. 226–38; V. K. Oppenheimer, *The Female Labor Force in the United States: Demographic and Economic Factors Governing Its Growth and Changing Composition*; S. Strasser, *Never Done: A History of American Housework*. See the following articles by R. S. Cowan: "The 'Industrial Revolution' in the Home: Household Technology and Social Change in the Twentieth Century," pp. 1–23; "Two Washes in the Morning and a Bridge Party at Night: The American Housewife Between Wars," pp. 147–71; "A Case Study of Technology and Social Change: The Washing Machine and Working Wife," pp. 245–53.

62. Lucy Salmon, *Domestic Service*, pp. 224–5.

63. David Katzman, *Seven Days a Week*, p. 233.

64. Ibid., p. 271.

65. Salmon, *Domestic Service*, p. 200.

66. Dudden, *Serving Women*, p. 127.

67. Ibid., p. 138.

68.   Cowan, "Women's Work, Housework, and History," p. 167.

69.   Dudden, *Serving Women*, p. 138.

70.   Barbara Ehrenreich and Deidre English, "The Manufacture of Housework"; Heidi Hartmann, "Capitalism and Women's Work in the Home, 1900–1930"; Ann Oakley, *Women's Work: The
Housewife Past and Present*; Robert Smuts, *Women and Work in America*; Joan Vanek, "Time Spent
in Housework," pp. 116–20; Susan Strasser, *Never Done: A History of American Housework*.

71.   Dudden, *Serving Women*, p. 141.

72.   Vanek, "Time Spent in Housework"; Catherine White Berheide and Sarah Fenstermaker
Berk and Richard A. Berk, "Household Work in the Suburbs: The Job and Its Participants," pp. 491–
518; C. E. Bose, P. L. Bereano and M. Malloy, "Household Technology and the Social Construction
of Housework," pp. 53–82.

73.   Ann Oakley, *Subject Women*, p. 171.

74.   Cowan, "Two Washes in the Morning"; Hildegard Kneeland "Limitations of Scientific Management in Household Work," pp. 311–4; Charlotte P. Gilman, *Women and Economics*.

75.   See Katzman, *Seven Days a Week*; Dudden, *Serving Women*.

76.   Katzman, *Seven Days a Week*, p. 275.

77.   Dudden, *Serving Women*, p. 156.

78.   Ibid., p. 7.

79.   Stansell, *City of Women*, p. 162.

80.   Susan Strasser, "Mistress and Maid, Employer and Employee: Domestic Service Reform in
the United States, 1897–1920," p. 63.

81.   Stansell, *City of Women*, p. 213.

82.   Horn, *Rise and Fall of the Victorian Servant*, p. 24.

83.   Katzman, *Seven Days a Week*, p. 271.

84.   George Stigler, *Domestic Servants in the United States: 1900–1940*, p. 1.

85.   Stansell, *City of Women*, p. 160.

86.   Ibid., pp. 160–1.

87.   Katzman, *Seven Days a Week*, p. 134.

88.   Stansell, *City of Women*, p. 156.

89.   Salmon, *Domestic Service*, pp. 140–50.

90.   C. Mackenzie, "Katie Is Leaving Again," *New York Times Magazine*, 31 August, 1941, p.
10; quoted in Martin and Segrave, *The Servant Problem: Domestic Workers in North America*,
p. 42.

91.   G. Fox, "Women Domestic Workers in Washington, D.C.," *Monthly Review* 54 (1942), p.
349; quoted in Martin and Kerry, *The Servant Problem: Domestic Workers in North America*, p. 37.

92.   Katzman, *Seven Days a Week*, p. 273.

93.   Stansell, *City of Women*, pp. 155, 157.

94.   Martin and Segrave, *The Servant Problem*, p. vii.

95.   Stansell, *City of Women*, p. 166.

96.   Henrietta Roelofs, "The Road to Trained Service in the Household," YWCA Commission
on Household Employment *Bulletin*, no. 2, n.d. [1915–16], pp. 12–3; quoted in Susan Strasser,
"Mistress and Maid," p. 59.

97.   Strasser, "Mistress and Maid," p. 61.

98.   I. M. Rubinow, "The Problem of Domestic Service," p. 514.

99.   Katzman, *Seven Days a Week*, p. 271.

100.   Ibid., p. 111.

101.   Elizabeth Clark-Lewis, "'This Work Had an End': The Transition From Live-in to Day
Work," p. 21.

102.   Katzman, *Seven Days a Week*, p. 270.

103.   Ibid., p. 90.

104.   Matthaei, *An Economic History*, p. 265.
105.   Ibid., p. 273. Black women had a continued presence in the labor force, and their numbers have continued to increase. As Matthaei observed: "The labor-force participation rate of non-white women with husbands present has risen continually—from 27.3% in 1940, to 31.8% in 1950, to 40.5% in 1960, to 50% in 1970—and has consistently remained higher than that of whites" (p. 253).
106.   Ibid., p. 282.
107.   Stiger, *Domestic Servants in the United States: 1900–1940*, p. 36.
108.   Martha Sterns (1951), "Castle in the Air with Maid," *Catholic World* 173, (1951), pp. 358–65; cited by Martin and Segrave, *The Servant Problem*, p. 20.
109.   D. Allen (1977) "Household Technicians Organize," *In These Times* 1 (376): 16; quoted in Martin and Segrave, *The Servant Problem*, p. 159.
110.   David Chaplin, "Domestic Service and the Negro," in *Blue Collar World*, A. B. Shostak and W. Gomberg, eds., pp. 527–36.
111.   Martin and Segrave, *The Servant Problem*, p. vii.
112.   D. Thompson (1960) "Are Women Bad Employers of Other Women?" *Ladies Home Journal* 77 (1960), p. 2; quoted in Martin and Kerry, *The Servant Problem*, p. 25.
113.   Portes, "The Informal Sector," p. 157.
114.   Matthaei, *An Economic History*, p. 282.
115.   Rosanna Hertz, *More Equal Than Others: Women and Men in Dual-Career Marriages*; see also Laura Lein, "Parental Evaluation of Childcare Alternatives," pp. 11–6.
116.   Carol Kleinman, "Maid Services Clean Up as Demand Escalates."

Chapter 4

1.   U.S. Census Bureau, Census of the Population and Housing: Provisional Estimate of Social, Economic and Housing Characteristics, pp. 25–30.
2.   Susan Tucker, *Telling Memories among Southern Women: Domestic Workers and Their Employers in the Segregated South*, p. 155.
3.   Lucy Salmon, *Domestic Service*, p. 16.
4.   Soraya Moore Coley, "'And Still I Rise'," p. 30.
5.   Ibid., p. 37.
6.   Charles S. Johnson, *Patterns of Negro Segregation*, p. 81.
7.   Ulrich B. Phillips, *American Negro Slavery: A Survey of the Supply, Employment and Control of Negro Labor as Determined by the Plantation Regime*, p. 402.
8.   Angela Davis, "Reflections on the Black Woman's Role in the Community of Slaves," pp. 2–15.
9.   Julie Matthaei, *An Economic History of Women in America*, p. 92.
10.   Jessie W. Parhurst, "The Role of the Black Mammy in the Plantation Household," *The Journal of Negro History*, p. 351.
11.   John B. Cade, "Out of the Mouths of Ex-Slaves," pp. 294–337; Eugene D. Genovese, "Life in the Big House," in *A Heritage of Her Own*, Nancy F. Cott and Elizabeth H. Pleck, pp. 290–97; American Anti-Slavery Society, *American Slavery as It Is: Testimony of a Thousand Witnesses*.
12.   Elizabeth Fox-Genovese, *Within the Plantation Household, Black and White Women of the Old South*, p. 35.
13.   Carter G. Woodson, "The Negro Washerwoman, A Vanishing Figure," p. 270.
14.   Judith Rollins, *Between Women: Domestics and Their Employers*, p. 51.
15.   Ibid., p. 50.
16.   Salmon, *Domestic Service*, p. 61.
17.   Alexis De Tocqueville, *Democracy in America*, p. 190.
18.   Ibid., p. 194.
19.   Ibid., p. 183.

20. Nancy Cott, *Bonds of Womanhood: "Woman's Sphere" in New England, 1780–1835*, p. 28.

21. Faye Dudden, *Serving Women: Household Service in Nineteenth-Century America*, pp. 42–3.

22. Ibid., p. 39.

23. Ibid., p. 44.

24. Salmon, *Domestic Service*, p. 59; citing Thomas Grettan, *Civilized America*, 2 vol. (London, 1859), p. 259.

25. Although there were class and racial distinctions between Indians and Hispanos in New Mexico, Dudden's description of native-born free laborers in Northern U.S. cities can be extended to the experience of domestics employed outside the *patron* system. Frequently, "helpers" were members of the extended kinship groups, such as nieces or cousins. The daughters of nearby neighbors also served as helpers. In some areas, Indian women served as helpers or domestics and later married into the family. The community had a well defined role for unmarried older women: the "spinster" included the care of her younger siblings and aging parents. The phrase *era como una criada* was a common way of describing such spinsters. However, under the *patron* system, even modest *haciendas* and missions were built with live-in accommodations for servants. Live-in arrangements included but were not restricted to young single women employed as chambermaids and cooks. Entire families were retained by the *patron*. In a typical situation, mothers might serve as cooks and daughters as chambermaids and laundress, while fathers and sons worked on the ranch or farm. Families with money, *los ricos*, hired married women as day workers to do the laundry or to help other servants. Widows often worked as washerwomen, collecting the laundry and returning to their homes in nearby villages where the clothes were washed and ironed. See Deena J. Gonzalez, "The Spanish-Mexican Women of Santa Fe: Patterns of Their Resistance and Accommodation, 1820–1880."

26. Cited by Glenna Matthews, *"Just a Housewife,"* p. 96.

27. Salmon, *Domestic Service*, pp. 62–5. Another event not included in Salmon's or Katzman's analysis was the Mexican American War.

28. Ibid., p. 62.

29. David M. Katzman, *Seven Days a Week: Women and Domestic Service in Industrializing America*, p. 49.

30. Ibid., p. 55.

31. June Oxford and Herman Levin, *Social Welfare: A History of the American Response to Need*, p. 27.

32. Susan Strasser, "Mistress and Maid, Employer and Employee: Domestic Service Reform in the United States, 1897–1920," p. 55.

33. Katzman, *Seven Days a Week*, p. 69–70.

34. Blaine Edward McKinley, "The Stranger in the Gates: Employer Reactions Toward Domestic Servants in America, 1825–1875," Ph.D. diss. Michigan State University.

35. Katzman, *Seven Days a Week*, p. 170.

36. Ibid., p. 172.

37. Ibid., p. 206.

38. Ibid., p. 24.

39. Ibid., p. 188.

40. Ibid., p. 192.

41. Ibid., p. 192.

42. Ibid., p. 204.

43. Ibid., p. 199.

44. See Mario Barrera, *Race and Class in the Southwest: A Theory of Racial Inequality*, for discussion on the application of the colonial labor system.

45. Albert Camarillo, *Chicanos in a Changing Society: From Mexican Pueblos to American Barrios in Santa Barbara and Southern California, 1848–1930*, p. 219.

46. Deena Gonzalez, "The Spanish-Mexican Women of Santa Fe: Patterns of Their Resistance and Accommodation, 1820–1880," p. 161. Also, see idem. "The Widowed Women of Santa Fe: Assessments on the Lives of an Unmarried Population, 1850–1880," pp. 65–90.

47. Salmon, *Domestic Service*, p. 173.

48. However, Deutsch suggests the underrepresentation of Chicana domestics in private households in Colorado was the function of workers' preferences. She argues that domestic service may have been too closely associated with Indian slaves and therefore, Chicanas sought other jobs. She explains that a third of the women in the coal-mining town of Trinidad, Colorado, took in boarders and one-fourth did laundry rather than day work because Chicanas rejected domestic service. *No Separate Refuge. Culture, Class and Gender on an Anglo-Hispanic Frontier in the American Southwest, 1880–1940.*

49. Victor S. Clark, *Mexican Labor in the United States*, p. 496.

50. For an excellent review of Americanization and Mexican immigrant women see George Sanchez, "'Go After the Women': Americanization and the Mexican Immigrant Women, 1915–1929." 51. Howard L. Scamehorn, *Pioneer Steelmaker in the West: The Colorado Fuel and Iron Company, 1872–1903*, p. 152.

52. Deutsch, *No Separate Refuge*, pp. 156–7.

53. Emory S. Bogardus, "The Mexican Immigrant," pp. 470–88; cited in Mario Garcia, *Desert Immigrants: The Mexicans of El Paso, 1880–1920*, p. 253.

54. Paul Taylor, *Mexican Labor in the United States*, p. 225.

55. Deutsch, *No Separate Refuge*, p. 323.

56. Ibid., p. 146.

57. Ibid., p. 146.

58. Nan Elsasser, Kyle MacKenzie, and Yvonne Tixier y Vigil, *Las Mujeres: Conversations with the Hispanic Community*, p. 29.

59. Deutsch, *No Separate Refuge*, p. 180.

60. Coley, "And Still I Rise," p. 131.

61. Katzman, *Seven Days a Week*, pp. 58–76.

62. Ibid., p. 72.

63. For further discussion on migration and domestic service among African American women, Carole Marks, "The Bone and Sinew of the Race: Black Women, Domestic Service and Labor Migration." African American household workers experienced a brief period of competition during the depression when white native and immigrant women were forced back into service because their husbands were unable to find work. Lorenzo Greene characterized the era: "White workers rushed in, and either divided the work with the Negroes, or else thrust them out of such employment altogether" (Lorenzo J. Green, "Economic Conditions among Negroes in the South, 1930," p. 269). The figures tell the story. Between 1910 and 1920, the ratio of native white women in the domestic labor force dropped from 23 to 17 percent, while that of foreign-born women dropped from 46 to 36 percent. The depression reversed this trend, so that by 1930, native white women had increased their share of the domestic labor market to 20 percent and foreign-born women had gone back up to 41 percent. Thus, in the early thirties, we find the anomalous situation in which three out of every five domestics in the deep South were white. This was a temporary perturbation of the dominant trend, however, by 1940, native white women had returned to their families or found better jobs and comprised only 11 percent of the domestic labor force.

64. Barrera, *Race and Class in the Southwest*, p. 95.

65. Mario Garcia, "The Chicana in American History: The Mexican Women of El Paso, 1880–1920," pp. 315–37.

66. Deutsch, *No Separate Refuge*, p. 180.

67. Katzman, *Seven Days a Week*, p. 271.

68. Deutsch, *No Separate Refuge*, p. 329; citing Dorothy Overstreet, "Problems and Progress among Mexicans of Our Own Southwest," *Home Mission Monthly* 32 (November 1917).

69. Ibid., p. 148.

70. C. H. Moses, "I Never Want A Maid Again," *House Beautiful* 87 (November 1945), p. 152 (article pp. 152, 157–8, 160); cited in Martin and Segrave, *The Servant Problem*, p. 6.

71. Grace A. Farrell, "Homemaking with 'Other Half' along Our International Border," p. 417.

72. Merton E. Hill, *The Development of an Americanization Program*, p. 28.

73. Gilbert Gonzalez, "The System of Public Education and its Function within the Chicano Communities, 1920–30." Gonzalez's study of the Americanization of Mexican women showed that schools in Los Angeles and other cities with high enrollments of Mexican children offered predominately vocational training curricula between 1910 and the 1940s. See also idem. "The Americanization of Mexican Women of Their Families During the Era of De Jure School Segregation, 1900–1950," in *Ethnic and Gender Boundaries in the United States: Studies of Asian, Black, Mexican and Native Americans*, Sucheng Chan, ed., pp. 212–37.

74. Mario Garcia, *Desert Immigrants*, p. 112.

75. Deutsch, *No Separate Refuge*, pp. 328–9.

76. See Phyllis Palmer's *Domesticity and Dirt: Housewives and Domestic Servants in the United States, 1920–1945* for an excellent discussion of African American women and the WPA programs.

77. Emory Bogardus, *The Mexican in the United States*, p. 43.

78. Deutsch, *No Separate Refuge*, p. 182.

79. Florence Kerr, "Training for Household Employment I: The WPA Program," *Journal of Home Economics*, (September, 1940), p. 437; cited in Martin and Segrave, *The Servant Problem*, p. 82.

80. L. Doman, "Training Courses for Household Employees," *Journal of Home Economics* (1941), p. 711; cited in Martin and Segrave, *The Servant Problem*, p. 42.

81. Deutsch, *No Separate Refuge*, p. 182.

82. Ibid., p. 183.

83. Sarah Deutsch, "Culture, Class, and Gender: Chicanas and Chicanos in Colorado and New Mexico, 1900–1940," p. 397.

84. Coley, "And Still I Rise," pp. 130–144.

85. G. Fox, "Women Domestic Workers in Washington, D.C.: 1940," *Monthly Labor Review* 54 (February 1942), p. 338; as quoted in Martin and Segrave, *The Servant Problem*, p. 37.

86. Mary T. Waggamon, "Wartime Job Opportunities for Women Household Workers in Washington, D.C.," p. 576.

87. Tucker, *Telling Memories*, p. 105.

88. Elizabeth McLean Petras, "Jamaican Women in the US Health Industry: Caring, Cooking and Cleaning," pp. 304–23.

89. Rollins, *Between Women*, p. 56.

90. U.S. Census Bureau, Census of the Population, Selected Characteristics of Employed Persons by Occupation, Industry and Sex, 1980, pp. 1–3.

91. Martin and Segrave, *The Servant Problem*, p. 105.

92. Gladys Hawkins, Jean Soper, and Jane Henry, *Your Maid from Mexico*, p. 6.

93. Ibid., p. ix.

94. Ibid., p. 6.

95. Ibid., p. 11.

96. Ibid., p. 16.

97. Ibid., p. 6.

98. Ibid., p. 24.

99. Ibid., p. 1–2.

100. Erving Goffman, *The Presentation of Self in Everyday Life*, p. 151.

101. Hawkins, et al. *Your Maid from Mexico*, p. 8.

102. Ibid., p. 9.

103. Katzman, *Seven Days a Week*, p. 188.

104. Hawkins, et al. *Your Maid from Mexico*, p. 3.

105. Ibid., pp. 3–4.

106. Ibid., p. 5.

107. Ibid., p. 8.

108. Ibid., p. 11.

109. Ibid., p. 21.

110. David Katzman, "Domestic Service: Women's Work," in *Women Working: Theories and Facts in Perspective*, Ann Stromberg and Shirley Harkess, eds., p. 385. In an interview with the head of a Haitian women's program for the American Friends Service Committee in New York, Maria Laurino was told that "sexual harassment is so common that many women ask to work for elderly couples" (Maria Laurino, "'I'm Nobody's Girl': New York's New Indentured Servants," p. 18).

111. Katzman, *Seven Days a Week*, p. 242.

112. In her study of domestics in the Boston area, Judith Rollins found that ten- and twelve-hour days are not necessarily "a thing of the distant past" (*Between Women*, p. 72).

113. *El Paso Times*, 25 September 1953; *El Paso Herald Post*, 12, 15, 30 October and 9, 18 November 1953.

114. Rosalia Solorzano Torres, "Women, Labor, and the U.S.-Mexico Border: Mexican Maids in El Paso, Texas," in *Mexicanas at Work in the United States*, ed., Margarita Melville, p. 77.

115. Mary Wilson Warton, "Methodism at Work among the Spanish-Speaking People of El Paso, Texas," p. 15.

116. Sasha G. Lewis, *Slave Trade Today: American Exploitation of Illegal Aliens*, p. 83.

117. Ibid., pp. 89–90.

118. Ibid., p. 53.

119. Michael Quintanilla and Peter Copeland, "Mexican Maids: El Paso's Worst-Kept Secret," (special report, "The Border," *El Paso Herald Times*, summer, 1983), p. 83.

120. Ibid., p. 83.

121. Ibid., p. 84.

122. Jill Nelson, "I'm Not Your Girl,", p. 146.

123. U.S. Department of Labor (Women's Bureau), *Private Household Workers*, p. 2.

124. Sherrie A. Rossoudji and Susan I. Rainey, "The Labor Market Earnings of Female Migrants: The Case of Temporary Mexican Migrants to the U.S.," pp. 1120–43.

125. Pierrette Hondagneu-Sotelo, "Gender and the Politics of Mexican Undocumented Immigrant Settlement"; idem., "Advocacy Research for Immigrant Women Domestic Workers."

126. Judith Ann Warner and Helen K. Henderson, "Latina Women Immigrant's Waged Domestic Labor: Effects of Immigration Reform on the Link between Private Households and the International Labor Force."

127. Leslie Salzinger, "A Maid by Any Other Name: The Transformation of 'Dirty Work' by Central American Immigrants."

128. Jacklyn Cock, *Maids and Madams, A Study in the Politics of Exploitation*, p. 265.

129. James Bossard, *The Sociology of Child Development*, p. 250.

130. Ibid., p. 250.

131. Hawkins, et al., *Your Maid from Mexico*, p. 2.

Chapter 5

1. Ann Oakley, *Woman's Work: The Housewife, Past and Present*; Nona Glazer, "Everyone Needs Three Hands: Doing Unpaid and Paid Work," pp. 249–73; Mariarosa Dalla Costa and Selma James, "Women and the Subversion of the Community," pp. 67–102.

2. Robert Coles and Jane Hallowell Coles, *Women of Crisis: Lives of Struggle and Hope*, p. 239.

3. Margaret M. Poloma and T. Neal Garland, "The Married Professional Woman: A Study in the Tolerance of Domestication," pp. 531–40; Constantina Safilos-Rothchild, "The Influence of the Wife's Degree of Work Commitment upon Some Aspects of Family Organization and Dynamics," pp. 681–91; Naomi Gerstel and Harriet Gross, *Commuter Marriage*; Rosanna Hertz, *More Equal Than Others*; Arlie Hochschild, *The Second Shift: Working Parents and the Revolution at Home*.

4. Linda Martin and Kerry Segrave, *The Servant Problem: Domestic Workers in North America*, pp. 32–33.

5. Viva, "Maid in New York. How to Get and Keep Help," p. 35.

6. Hertz, *More Equal Than Others*, p. 178.

7. R. Dimanno (1979) "To Serve and Protest," *The Canadian*, September 15–16, p. 4; cited in Martin and Segrave, *The Servant Problem*, p. 78.

8. In *The Hidden Injuries of Class*, Richard Sennett and Jonathan Cobb suggest that workers rank jobs lower when "their functions are felt to be more dependent on and more at the mercy of others" (p. 236). This is certainly applicable to domestic service.

9. Nan Elsasser, Kyle MacKenzie and Yvonne Tixier y Vigil, *Las Mujeres: Conversations from a Hispanic Community*, p. 70–1.

10. For instance, Daniel Sutherland gave the following reasons for nineteenth-century American women hiring servants: "The physical strain of housework was the principal one. Many women simply could not accomplish their innumerable household tasks without help. Almost as important were the roles and responsibilities assigned to American women, especially their roles as 'house-keepers' and 'ladies.' Status was the third reason for having servants, tradition yet another" (*Americans and Their Servants: Domestic Service in the United States from 1800 to 1920*, p. 10).

11. Lewis Coser, "Servants: The Obsolescence of an Occupational Role," p. 39.

12. Elaine Kaplan, "'I Don't Do No Windows': Competition between the Domestic Worker and the Housewife," in *Competition A Feminist Taboo?* Valerie Miner and Helen E. Longino, eds., p. 94.

13. Kathy Dobie, "Black Women, White Kids, A Tale of Two Worlds," p. 23.

14. Soraya Moore Coley, "'And Still I Rise': An Exploratory Study of Contemporary Black Private Household Workers," p. 213.

15. Shellee Colen, "With Respect and Feelings: Voices of West Indian Domestic Workers in New York City," p. 46.

16. Ibid., p. 56.

17. Ibid., p. 56.

18. Ibid., p. 47.

19. Hertz, *More Equal Than Others*, p. 64.

20. Studs Terkel, *Working: People Talk About What They Do All Day and How They Feel About What They Do*, p. 118.

21. Evelyn Nakano Glenn, *Issi, Nisei, War Bride: Three Generations of Japanese American Women in Domestic Service*, p. 160.

22. Ibid., p. 161.

23. However, Hertz reported that dual-career couples listed supervising the housekeeper as one of the wife's duties (*More Equal Than Others*, p. 105).

24. Terkel, *Working*, p. 118.

25. Ibid., p. 112–8.

26. Rollins, *Between Women*, p. 142.

27. Susan Tucker, *Telling Memories among Southern Women Domestic Workers and Their Employers in the Segregated South*, p. 88.

28. Dill, "Making the Job Good Yourself," p. 40.

29. Glenn, *Issei, Nisei, War Bride*, p. 155.
30. Coley, "And Still I Rise," p. 196.
31. Judith Rollins, *Between Women, Domestics and Their Employers*, p. 120.
32. Tucker, *Telling Memories*, p. 135.
33. Ibid., p. 239.
34. Hertz, *More Equal Than Others*, p. 160.
35. Bonnie Thornton Dill, "I Like What I Do and I'm Good at It," p. 70.
36. Coley, "And Still I Rise," p. 195.
37. Phyllis McGinley, "Help!" p. 64.
38. Hertz, *More Equal Than Others*, p. 162.
39. Glenn, *Issei, Nisei, War Bride*, p. 159.
40. Rollins, *Between Women*, p. 167.
41. Kaplan, "I Don't Do No Windows," p. 101.
42. Ibid., p. 101.
43. Rollins, *Between Women*, p. 189.
44. Tucker, *Telling Memories*, p. 162.
45. Rollins, *Between Women*, p. 174.
46. Tucker, *Telling Memories*, pp. 100–1.
47. Judith Ann Warner and Helen K. Henderson, "Latina Women Immigrant's Waged Domestic Labor: Effects of Immigration Reform on the Link between Private Households and the International Labor Force," p. 17.
48. Tucker, *Telling Memories*, p. 178.
49. Dobie, "Black Women, White Kids," p. 25.
50. Rollins, *Between Women*, p. 192.
51. Ibid., p. 192.
52. Tucker, *Telling Memories*, pp. 161–60.
53. Kaplan, "I Don't Do No Windows," p. 98.
54. Dobie, "Black Women, White Kids," p. 25.
55. Coley, "And Still I Rise," p. 182
56. "Guide to Household Help," *House and Garden* 153 (February, 1981), p. 22.
57. Ibid., p. 22.
58. Dobie, "Black Women, White Kids," p. 21.
59. Tucker, *Telling Memories*, p. 131.
60. Coley, "And Still I Rise," p. 229.
61. Rollins, *Between Women*, p. 156.
62. Ibid., p. 129.
63. Tucker, *Telling Memories*, p. 269.
64. Ibid., p. 269.
65. Martin and Segrave, *The Servant Problem*, p. 3.
66. Coley, "And Still I Rise," p. 238.
67. Kaplan, "I Don't Do No Windows," p. 98.
68. Ibid., p. 98.
69. Dobie, "Black Women, White Kids," p. 24.
70. Glenn, *Issei, Nisei, War Bride*, p. 158.
71. Colen, "With Respect and Feelings," p. 57.
72. David Katzman, "Domestic Service: Woman's Work," p. 384.
73. Ibid., p. 384.
74. Rollins, *Between Women*, p. 162.
75. Claude Brown, *Manchild in the Promised Land*, p. 286.
76. Rollins, *Between Women*, p. 160.
77. Terkel, *Working*, pp. 112–8.

78. Laurino, "I'm Nobody's Girl," p. 24.
79. Tucker, *Telling Memories*, p. 234.
80. Shellee Colen, "'Just a Little Respect': West Indian Domestic Workers in New York City."
81. Laurino, "I'm Nobody's Girl," p. 21.
82. Tucker, *Telling Memories*, p. 94.
83. Dill, "I Like What I Do," p. 71.
84. Rollins, *Between Women*, p. 164.
85. Trudier Harris, *From Mammies to Militants: Domestics in Black American Literature*, p. 15.
86. Rollins, *Between Women*, pp. 207–8.
87. Erving Goffman, *The Presentation of Self in Everyday Life*, p. 2.
88. Colen, "With Respect and Feelings," p. 58.
89. Ibid., p. 58.
90. Tucker, *Telling Memories*, p. 221.
91. Colen, "With Respect and Feelings," p. 58.
92. Coley, "And I Still Rise," pp. 203–4.
93. Glenn, *Issei, Nisei, War Bride*, p. 453.
94. Tucker, *Telling Memories*, p. 208.
95. See Leslie Salzinger, "A Maid by any Other Name: The Transformation of 'Dirty Work' by Central American Immigrants"; Warner and Henderson, "Latina Women Immigrant's Waged Domestic Labor"; Pierrette Hondagneu-Sotelo, "Advocacy Research for Immigrant Women Domestic Workers"; idem., "Gender and the Politics of Mexican Undocumented Immigrant Settlement."
96. Tucker, *Telling Memories*, p. 204.
97. Ibid., p. 257.
98. Coley, "And Still I Rise," pp. 248–9.
99. Glenn, *Issei, Nisei, War Bride*, p. 155.
100. Laurino, "I'm Nobody's Girl," p. 21.
101. Ibid., pp. 248–9.
102. Ibid., p. 239.
103. Tucker, *Telling Memories*, pp. 200–1.
104. Rollins, *Between Women*, p. 176.
105. Hertz, *More Equal Than Others*, p. 178.
106. Coley, "And Still I Rise," p. 207.
107. Tucker, *Telling Memories*, p. 216.
108. Ibid., p. 153.
109. E. Kaplan, "I Don't Do No Windows," p. 98.
110. Alice Childress, *Like One of the Family*. For a brilliant analysis of Childress's character, Mildred, see Trudier Harris's "Beyond the Uniform," chapter six in *From Mammies to Militants*.
111. Ibid., p. 1.
112. Ibid., p. 2.
113. Ibid., p. 3.
114. Coley, "And Still I Rise," p. 199.
115. Ibid., p. 198.
116. For a discussion of this strategy as used by flight attendants, see Arlie Russell Hochschild, *The Managed Heart: Commercialization of Human Feeling*, p. 182.
117. Glenn, *Issei, Nisei, War Bride*, p. 156.
118. Coley, "And Still I Rise," p. 197.
119. Rollins, *Between Women*, p. 174.
120. Ibid., pp. 67–8.
121. Coley, "And Still I Rise," p. 245.
122. Ibid., p. 247.
123. Viva, "Maid in New York," p. 35. Housewives have a history of complaining about do-

mestic's demands and shortage problems. The history is well documented in popular journals. See Martin and Segrave, *The Servant Problem.*

124. Tucker, *Telling Memories*, p. 154.
125. Hochschild, *The Managed Heart*, p. 172.
126. Ibid., p. 173.
127. Ibid., p. 172.
128. Bonnie Thornton Dill, "Across the Boundaries of Race and Class: An Exploration of the Relationship Between Work and Family among Black Female Domestic Servants," p. 94.

Chapter 6

1. Bonnie Thornton Dill, "Making Your Job Good Yourself," p. 35.
2. Susan Tucker, *Telling Memories*, p. 237.
3. Susan Tucker, *Telling Memories*, pp. 248–49.
4. Judith Rollins, *Between Women*, pp. 212–213.
5. Tucker, *Telling Memories*, p. 197.
6. Dill, "Making Your Job Good Yourself," p. 51.
7. Colen, "Just a Little Respect," p. 187.
8. Rollins, *Between Women*, pp. 231–32.
9. Ibid., p. 227.
10. Ibid., p. 227.
11. Dill, "Making Your Job Good Yourself," p. 50.
12. Dill, "Across the Boundaries of Race and Class: An Exploration of the Relationship Between Work and Family Among Black Female Domestic Servants," p. 103.
13. Tucker, *Telling Memories*, p. 106.
14. Ibid., p. 197.
15. Shellee Colen, "'Just a Little Respect': West Indian Domestic Workers in New York City," p. 187. Although Colen's account of domestics' resistance included "defining their own tasks and airing grievances," refusing "to perform certain tasks," and quitting, she does not describe their actions in the same detail as other studies. Therefore, it is difficult to make any comparisons with other studies.
16. Colen, "With Respect and Feelings," p. 64.
17. Jacklyn Cock, *Maids and Madams: A Study in the Politics of Exploitation*, p. 103.
18. Ibid., p. 103.
19. David Katzman characterized the "hourly 'cleaning lady,'" as replacing "the uniformed maid who was part of the household," ("Domestic Service: Woman's Work," p. 378).
20. Evelyn Nakano Glenn, *Issei, Nisei, War Bride*, p. 143.
21. Coley, "And Still I Rise," p. 255.
22. Ibid., p. 260.
23. Glenn, *Issei, Nisei, War Bride*, p. 162.
24. Pierrette Hondagneu-Sotelo, "Gender and the Politics of Mexican Undocumented Immigrant Settlement," idem., "Advocacy Research for Immigrant Women Domestic Workers."
25. Coley, "And Still I Rise," p. 267.
26. See Coley, "And Still I Rise," p. 268. Glenn states, "It was an especially difficult step for the issei and older nisei because resigning was an admission of defeat and violated the principle of *gaman* ("endurance")" (*Issei, Nisei, War Bride*, p. 164).
27. Glenn, *Issei, Nisei, War Bride*, p. 160.
28. Ibid., p. 161.
29. Judith Ann Warner and Helen K. Henderson also refer to household labor as precapitalistic

social relations ("Latina Women Immigrant's Waged Domestic Labor: Effects of Immigration Reform on the Link Between Private Households and the International Labor Force").

30.   Glenn, *Issei, Nisei, War Bride*, p. 154.

31.   Ibid., p. 155.

32.   Coley, "And Still I Rise," p. 276.

33.   Ibid., p. 261.

34.   Ibid., p. 277.

35.   Leslie Salzinger's ethnography of two cooperatives identified the different structure resulting in improving working conditions and wages ("A Maid by Any Other Name: The Transformation of 'Dirty Work' by Central American Immigrants").

36.   Ibid., p. 142.

37.   Interviewees cited in Tucker's narratives also mention this practice. They refer to the replacement as "keeping a job going" (*Telling Memories*, pp. 109 and 154).

38.   Similar findings were reported in the following studies: Glenn, *Issei, Nisei, War Bride*; Salzinger, "A Maid by Any Other Name"; Hondagneu-Sotelo, "Advocacy Research for Immigrant Women Domestic Workers"; Terry A. Repak, "Labor Market Experiences of Central American Migrants in Washington, D.C."

39.   Several studies have reported that immigrant women employed as domestics in the United States held white collar and professional jobs in their mother countries before migrating. None of the Chicanas I interviewed had ever held such jobs. See Colen, "With Respect and Feelings," and Salzinger, "A Maid by Any Other Name."

40.   See G. Reid, "Job Search and the Effectiveness of Job-Finding Methods," pp. 479–95; F. E. Katz, "Occupational Contract Network," pp. 52–55; T. Caplow and R. McGee, *The Academic Marketplace*.

41.   Evelyn Nakano Glenn, "Occupational Ghettoization: Japanese American Women and Domestic Service, 1905–1970," p. 380.

42.   Hondagneu-Sotelo reported competition among the women for domestic jobs. Competition for jobs was not reported by the women I interviewed.

43.   Coley also found that domestic service seemed "'the best of all possibilities' in their world of limited options" ("And Still I Rise," p. 270).

44.   Tucker also found that the flexible schedule was an important issue for domestics with children (*Telling Memories*, p. 152).

45.   Interviewees in Tucker's study discuss taking their children to jobs: see pp. 119 and 152. This is also a practice cited in Ximena Bunster and Elsa M. Chaney eds., *Sellers and Servants: Working Women in Lima, Peru*, p. 141. They found that some of the live-out maids with preschool children took the children to work.

46.   Richard Sennett and Jonathan Cobb, *Hidden Injuries of Class*, p. 236.

47.   Howard Becker, "Career of the Chicago Public Schoolteacher," p. 470.

48.   Other researchers have also noted that private household workers negotiate working conditions. The titles of articles indicate negotiations: "I Do Not Do Windows,"; "Making Your Job Good Yourself." See the following for descriptions of negotiations: Hertz, *More Equal Than Others*; Hondagneu-Sotelo, "Advocacy Research for Immigrant Women Domestic Workers"; Salzinger, "A Maid by Any Other Name."

49.   Presently, Mexican immigrants do not represent competition; nevertheless, Chicanas indicated they are incorporating Mexican women into their networks and urge them not to lower standards. However, several women expressed concern over Vietnamese immigrants' willingness to work for less pay as well as to include gardening along with household chores. For the most part, Chicanas experienced a domestics' market and therefore, used the latitude to select employers who showed respect and professional behavior.

50.   Hondagneu-Sotelo also found women employed in domestic service as a second job.

51. Warner and Henderson reported that fifty-five percent of the 200 Mexican immigrants surveyed did not receive social security.

52. Hondagneu-Sotelo reported a preference for getting paid by the job.

53. Glenn, *Issei, Nisei, War Bride*, p. 163.

54. Salzinger also points out that "It is easier to construct a house as a workplace when it contains only workers (or more likely a single worker), than it is when it is shared with those for whom it is 'home'" ("A Maid by Any Other Name," p. 156).

55. In her interview with Susan Tucker, Linda Barron states: "I really would say I'm a domestic engineer because of the fact that if you're an engineer, you've got to put all kinds of stuff together. You're going from the lower part of work to the higher part of work. I think it's a profession." (*Telling Memories*, p. 258).

56. Glenn, *Issei, Nisei, War Bride*, p. 161.

57. Tucker cites an incident in which a domestic found someone to work for her and referred to the practice as "keeping the job going" (*Telling Memories*, p. 152).

58. See the following for a discussion on the problems workers face in female-dominated occupations lacking authority: Dee Ann Spencer, "Public Schoolteaching: A Suitable Job for a Woman," pp. 167–186; G. Ritzer, *Working; Conflict and Change*.

59. Coley, "And Still I Rise," p. 171.

60. Coley also describes a similar apprenticeship and recognized the important socialization role it played.

61. Salzinger, "A Maid by Any Other Name," p. 153.

62. Along with working for numerous employers, Hondagneu-Sotelo lists other factors affecting immigrant women's ability to negotiate better working conditions: legal status, English skills and transportation ("Advocacy Research").

63. Phyllis Palmer, *Domesticity and Dirt: Housewives and Domestic Servants in the United States, 1920–1945*.

64. Salzinger's study supports much of my analysis of the structure of work. By comparing two social service agencies aimed at finding employment for Central American immigrant women in domestic service, it became apparent how the different approaches to the way the work is structured resulted in different working conditions.

65. Hertz, *More Equal Than Others*, p. 163.

66. Ibid., p. 195.

Chapter 7

1. Faye Dudden, *Serving Women: Household Service in Nineteenth-Century America*, p. 43.

2. Mary Ann Mason, *The Equality Trap, Why Working Women Shouldn't Be Treated Like Men*, p. 150.

BIBLIOGRAPHY

Adams, R. N., and J. J. Preiss, eds. 1960. *Human Organization Research: Field Relationships and Techniques*. New York: Dorsey.

Addams, Jane. 1896. "A Belated Industry," *American Journal of Sociology* 1:536–50.

Althusser, Louis. 1971. *Lenin and Philosophy and Other Essays*, (translated by Ben Brewster.) New York: Monthly Review Press.

American Anti-Slavery Society. [1839] 1968. *American Slavery as It Is: Testimony of a Thousand Witnesses. New York Times*; reprint, New York: Arno Press.

Andre, Rae. 1981. *Homemakers: The Forgotten Workers*. Chicago: University of Chicago Press.

Aubert, Vilhelm. 1955–56. "The Housemaid—An Occupational Role in Crisis," *Acta Sociologica* 1:149–58.

Barker, Diana Leonard, and Sheila Allen. 1976. *Dependence and Exploitation in Work and Marriage*. New York: Longman.

Barrera, Mario. 1979. *Race and Class in the Southwest: A Theory of Racial Inequality*. Notre Dame, Ind.: University of Notre Dame Press.

Barrett, Donald N., and Julian Samora. 1963. *The Movement of Spanish Youth from Rural to Urban Settings*. Washington, D.C.: National Committee for Children and Youth.

Becker, Howard. 1952. "Career of the Chicago Public Schoolteacher," *American Journal of Sociology* 57 (5):470–77.

Beer, William R. 1983. *Househusbands: Men and Housework in American Families*. New York: Praeger.

Bendix, Reinhard. 1960. *Max Weber: An Intellectual Portrait*. Garden City, N.Y.: Doubleday.

Beneria, L. 1979. "Reproduction, Production and the Sexual Division of Labor," *Cambridge Journal of Economics* 3 (2):203–25.

Benson, Margaret. 1980. "The Political Economy of Women's Liberation," In *The Politics of Housework*, edited by Ellen Malos, 119–29. New York: Allison & Busby.

Berch, Bettina. 1982. *The Endless Day: The Political Economy of Women and Work.* New York: Harcourt Brace Jovanovich.

Berheide, Catherine White, Sarah Fenstermaker Berk, and Richard A. Berk. 1976. "Household Work in the Suburbs: The Job and Its Participants," *Pacific Sociological Review* 19:491–518.

Berk, Richard A. and Sarah Fenstermaker Berk. 1978. "A Simultaneous Equation Model for the Division of Household Labor," *Sociological Methods and Research* 6:431–68.

———. 1983. *Labor and Leisure at Home: Consent and Organization of the Household Day.* Beverly Hills, Calif.: Sage.

Berk, Sarah Fenstermaker. 1985. *The Gender Factory. The Apportionment of Work in American Households.* New York: Plenum.

———. 1988. "Women's Unpaid Labor: Home and Community," In *Women Working: Theories and Facts in Perspective,* edited by Ann H. Stromberg and Shirley Harkess, 287–302. Mountain View, Calif.: Mayfield.

Bogardus, Emory S. 1926–27. "The Mexican Immigrant," *Sociology and Social Research* 2:470–88.

———. 1934. *The Mexican in the United States.* School of Research Studies no. 5. Los Angeles: University of Southern California Press.

Bose, C. E., P. L. Bereano, and M. Malloy. 1983. "Household Technology and the Social Construction of Housework," *Technology and Culture* 25:53–82.

Bose, Christine. 1982. "Technology and Changes in the Division of Labour in the American Home," In *The Changing Experience of Women,* edited by Elizabeth Whitelegg et al., 226–38. Oxford: Martin Robertson.

Boserup, Ester. 1970. *Women's Role in Economic Development.* New York: St. Martin's.

Bossard, James. 1954. *The Sociology of Child Development,* 2nd ed. New York: Harper.

Brown, Claude. 1965. *Manchild in the Promised Land.* New York: Macmillan.

Bryceson, Deborah Fahy, and Ulla Vuorela. 1984. "Outside the Domestic Labour Debate: Towards a Theory of Modes of Human Reproduction," *Review of Radical Political Economics* 16:137–66.

Bunster, Ximena, and Elsa M. Chaney. 1985. *Sellers and Servants: Working Women in Lima, Peru.* New York: Praeger.

Cade, John B. 1935. "Out of the Mouths of Ex-Slaves," *The Journal of Negro History* 20 (July):294–337.

Camarillo, Albert. 1979. *Chicanos in a Changing Society: From Mexican Pueblos to American Barrios in Santa Barbara and Southern California, 1848–1930.* Cambridge: Harvard University Press.

Caplow, T., and R. McGee. 1958. *The Academic Marketplace.* New York: Basic.

Chaplin, David. 1964. "Domestic Service and the Negro," In *Blue Collar World,* edited by A. B. Shostak and W. Gomberg, 527–36. Englewood Cliffs, N. J.: Prentice-Hall.

———. 1978. "Domestic Service and Industrialization," *Comparative Studies In Sociology* 1:97–127.

Childress, Alice. 1986. *Like One of the Family: Conversations from a Domestic's Life.* Boston: Beacon.

Clark, Victor. 1908. *Mexican Labor in the United States.* United States Labor Bureau Bulletin no. 78, Washington, D.C.: U.S. Department of Labor.

Clark-Lewis, Elizabeth. 1985. "'This Work Had an End': The Transition from Live-in to Day Work," Southern Women: The Intersection of Race, Class and Gender Series Working Paper no. 2. Center for Research on Women, Memphis: Memphis State University.

Cock, Jacklyn. 1980. *Maids and Madams: A Study in the Politics of Exploitation.* Johannesburg: Raven Press.

Colen, Shellee. 1986. "With Respect and Feelings: Voices of West Indian Domestic Workers in New York City," In *All American Women: Lines That Divide and Ties That Bind,* edited by Johnnetta B. Cole, 46–70. New York: Free Press.

―――. 1989. "'Just a Little Respect': West Indian Domestic Workers in New York City," In *Muchachas No More: Household Workers in Latin America and the Caribbean*, edited by Elsa M. Chaney and Mary Garcia Castro, 171–94. Philadelphia: Temple University Press.

Coles, Robert, and Jane Hallowell Coles. 1978. *Women of Crisis: Lives of Struggle and Hope*. New York: Delacorte.

Coley, Soraya Moore. 1981. "'And Still I Rise': An Exploratory Study of Contemporary Black Private Household Workers," Ph.D. diss., Bryn Mawr College.

Coser, Lewis. 1974. "Servants: The Obsolescence of an Occupational Role," *Social Forces* 52:31–40.

Cott, Nancy. 1977. *Bonds of Womanhood: "Woman's Sphere" in New England, 1780–1835*. New Haven: Yale University Press.

Coulson, M., B. Magas, and H. Wainwright. 1975. "The Housewife and Her Labour under Capitalism: A Critique," *New Left Review* 89:59–71.

Coverman, Shelly. 1983. "Gender, Domestic Labor Time and Wage Inequality," *American Sociological Review* 48:623–36.

Cowan, Ruth Schwartz. 1974. "A Case Study of Technology and Social Change: The Washing Machine and Working Wife," In *Clio's Consciousness Raised: New Perspectives on the History of Women*, edited by Mary Hartman and Lois Banner, 245–53. New York: Harper and Row.

―――. 1976a. "The 'Industrial Revolution' in the Home: Household Technology and Social Change in the Twentieth Century," *Technology and Culture* 17 (1):1–23.

―――. 1976b. "Two Washes in the Morning and a Bridge Party at Night: The American Housewife between Wars," *Women's Studies* 3 (2):147–71.

―――. 1983. *More Work For Mother: The Ironies of Household Technology from the Open Hearth to the Microwave*. New York: Basic.

―――. 1987. "Women's Work, Housework, and History: The Historical Roots of Inequality in Work-Force Participation," In *Families and Work*, edited by Naomi Gerstel and Harriet Engel Gross, 164–77. Philadelphia: Temple University Press.

Dalla Costa, Mariarosa, and Selma James. 1972. "Women and the Subversion of Community," *Radical America* 6 (1):67–102.

Davidoff, Lenore. 1976. "The Rationalization of Housework," In *Dependence and Exploitation in Work and Marriage*, edited by Diana Leonard Barker and Sheila Allen, 121–51. New York: Longman.

Davidoff, Lenore, and Ruth Hawthorn. 1976. *A Day in the Life of a Victorian Domestic Servant*. London: George Allen & Unwin.

Davidson, Laurie, and Laura Kramer Gordon. 1979. *The Sociology of Gender*. Chicago: Rand McNally.

Davis, Angela. 1971. "Reflections on the Black Woman's Role in the Community of Slaves," *Black Scholar* 3 (44):2–15.

Deere, C. D., J. Humphries, and M. D. de Leal. 1982. "Class and Historical Analysis for the Study of Women and Economic Change," In *Women's Roles and Population Trends in the Third World*, edited by Richard Anker, Mayra Buvinic, and Nadia H. Youssef, pp. 87–114. London: Croom Helm.

Deutsch, Sarah. 1985. "Culture, Class, and Gender: Chicanas and Chicanos in Colorado and New Mexico, 1900–1940," Ph.D. diss., vols. 1 and 2. Yale University.

―――. 1987. *No Separate Refuge. Culture, Class and Gender on an Anglo-Hispanic Frontier in the American Southwest, 1880–1940*. New York: Oxford University Press.

Dill, Bonnie Thornton. 1979. "Across the Boundaries of Race and Class: An Exploration of the Relationship between Work and Family among Black Female Domestic Servants," Ph.D. diss., New York University.

―――. 1981. "I Like What I Do and I'm Good at It," *Southern Exposure* 9 (4):70–72.

―――. 1988. "'Making Your Job Good Yourself': Domestic Service and the Construction of Personal Dignity," In *Women and the Politics of Empowerment*, edited by Ann Bookman and Sandra Morgen, 33–52. Philadelphia: Temple University Press.

Ditto, Helen. 1974. "Diet and Style of Food Preparation as a Measure of Cultural Change in Cordova, New Mexico," Senior thesis, Colorado College.

Dobie, Kathy. 1988. "Black Women, White Kids, A Tale of Two Worlds," *Village Voice*, 12 January, 20–27.

Dudden, Faye. 1983. *Serving Women: Household Service in Nineteenth-Century America*. Middletown, Conn.: Wesleyan University Press.

Ehrenreich, B., and D. English. 1975. "The Manufacture of Housework," *Socialist Revolution* 5 (26):5–40.

El Paso Herald Post. 1953. October 12, 15, 30; November 9, 18.

El Paso Times. 1953. September 25.

———. 1983. "The Border."

Elsasser, Nan, Kyle MacKenzie, and Yvonne Tixier y Vigil. 1980. *Las Mujeres: Conversations with the Hispanic Community*. Old Westbury, N.Y.: Feminist Press.

Epstein, C. F. 1971. "Law Partners and Marital Partners," *Human Relations* 4:564–69.

Ewen, Stuart. 1976. *Captains of Consciousness: Advertising and the Social Roots of the Consumer Culture*. New York: McGraw-Hill.

Farrell, Grace A. 1929. "Homemaking with the 'Other Half' along Our International Border," *Journal of Home Economics* 12:413–18.

Federici, Silvia. 1980. "Wages against Housework," In *The Politics of Housework*, edited by Ellen Malos, 221. New York: Allison & Busby.

Fee, Terry. 1976. "Domestic Labor: An Analysis of Housework and Its Relation to the Production Process," *Review of Radical Political Economics* 8 (1):1–17.

Ferber, M. A., and B. G. Birnbaum. 1980. "Housework: Priceless or Valueless?" *Review of Income and Wealth* 26:387–400.

Ferree, Myra Marx. 1976. "Working-Class Jobs: Housework and Paid Work as Sources of Satisfaction," *Social Problems* 23:431–41.

———. 1984. "Sacrifice, Satisfaction and Social Change: Employment and the Family," In *My Troubles Are Going to Have Trouble with Me: Everyday Trials and Triumphs of Women Workers*, edited by Karen Brodkin Sacks and Dorothy Remy, 61–79. New Brunswick, N.J.: Rutgers University Press.

Firestone, Shulamith. 1970. *The Dialectic of Sex: The Case for Feminist Revolution*. New York: Bantam Books.

Fox-Genovese, Elizabeth. 1988. *Within the Plantation Household. Black and White Women of the Old South*. Chapel Hill: University of North Carolina Press.

Freeman, Caroline. 1980. "When Is a Wage Not a Wage?" In *The Politics of Housework*, edited by Ellen Malos, 166–73. New York: Allison & Busby.

Friedan, Betty. 1963. *The Feminine Mystique*. New York: Norton.

Galbraith, John Kenneth. 1973. *Economics and the Public Purpose*. Boston: Houghton Mifflin.

Galvez, Thelma, and Rosalba Todaro. 1989. "Housework for Pay in Chile: Not Just Another Job," In *Muchachas No More: Household Workers in Latin America and the Caribbean*, edited by Elsa M. Chaney and Mary Garcia Castro, 307–21. Philadelphia: Temple University Press.

Game, Ann, and Rosemary Pringle. 1983. *Gender at Work*. Boston: George Allen & Unwin.

Garcia, Mario. 1980. "The Chicana in American History: The Mexican Women of El Paso, 1880–1920," *Pacific Historical Review* 9 (2):315–37.

———. 1981. *Desert Immigrants: The Mexicans of El Paso, 1880–1920*. New Haven: Yale University Press.

Gardinar, Jean. 1975. "Women's Domestic Labour," *New Left Review* 89:47–57.

Gardinar, Jean, S. Himmelweit, and M. MacKintosh. 1975. "Women's Domestic Labour," *Bulletin of the Conference of Socialist Economists* 4 (2):1–11.

Genovese, Eugene D. 1979. "Life in the Big House," In *A Heritage of Her Own: Toward a New Social History of American Women*, edited by Nancy F. Cott and Elizabeth H. Pleck. New York: Simon and Schuster.

Gerstein, Ira. 1973. "Domestic Work and Capitalism," *Radical America* 7 (4–5):101–28.

Gerstel, Naomi, and Harriet Engel Gross, eds. 1984. *Commuter Marriage*. New York: Guilford.

———. 1987. *Families and Work*. Philadelphia: Temple University Press.

Gilman, Charlotte P. [1898] 1966. *Women and Economics*. Boston: Small, Maynard & Co.; reprint, New York: Harper and Row.

Glazer, Nona. 1980. "Everyone Needs Three Hands: Doing Unpaid and Paid Work," In *Women and Household Labor*, edited by Sarah Fenstermaker Berk, 249–73. Beverly Hills, Calif.: Sage.

———. 1984. "Paid and Unpaid Work: Contradictions in American Women's Lives Today," In *Women and Household Labor: Effects on Families*, edited by Kathryn M. Borman, Daisy Quaim, and Sarah Gideonse, 169–86. Norwood, N.J.: Ablex.

Glenn, Evelyn Nakano. 1981. "Occupational Ghettoization: Japanese American Women and Domestic Service, 1905–1970," *Ethnicity* 7 (4):352–86.

———. 1986. *Issei, Nisei, War Bride: Three Generations of Japanese American Women in Domestic Service*. Philadelphia: Temple University Press.

Goffman, Erving. 1959. *The Presentation of Self in Everyday Life*. Garden City, N.Y.: Doubleday Anchor.

Gonzalez, Deena J. 1985. "The Spanish-Mexican Women of Santa Fe: Patterns of Their Resistance and Accommodation, 1820–1880," Ph.D. diss., University of California, Berkeley.

———. 1988. "The Widowed Women of Santa Fe: Assessments on the Lives of an Unmarried Population, 1850–1880," In *On Their Own: Widows and Widowhood in the American Southwest, 1848–1939*, edited by Arlene Scadron, 65–90. Urbana, Ill.: University of Illinois Press.

Gonzalez, Gilbert. 1974. "The System of Public Eduction and Its Function within the Chicano Communities, 1920–30," Ph.D. diss., University of California, Los Angeles.

———. 1989. "The Americanization of Mexican Women and Their Families during the Era of De Jure School Segregation, 1900–1950," In *Ethnic and Gender Boundaries in the United States: Studies of Asian, Black, Mexican and Native Americans*, edited by Sucheng Chan, 212–37. Lewiston, N.Y.: Edwin Mellen Press.

Gonzalez, Nancie. 1967. *The Spanish-Americans of New Mexico*. Albuquerque: University of New Mexico Press.

Gought, I., and J. Harrison. 1975. "Unproductive Labour and Housework Again," *Bulletin of the Conference of Socialist Economists* 3 (1):1–7

Green, Lorenzo J. 1979. "Economic Conditions among Negroes in the South, 1930," *The Journal of Negro History* 64:265–73.

Haavio-Mannila, E. 1969. "The Position of Finnish Women," *Journal of Marriage and Family* 31:339–47.

Hansen, Karen Tranberg. 1989. *Distant Companions: Servants and Employers in Zambia, 1900–1985*. Ithaca, N.Y.: Cornell University Press.

Harris, Trudier. 1982. *From Mammies to Militants: Domestics in Black American Literature*. Philadelphia: Temple University Press.

Harrison, John. 1973. "The Political Economy of Housework," *Bulletin of the Conference of Socialist Economists* 4:35–51.

Hartmann, Heidi. 1974. "Capitalism and Women's Work in the Home, 1900–1930," Ph.D. diss., Yale University.

———. 1981. "The Family as the Locus of Gender, Class and Political Struggle: The Example of Housework," *Signs* 6 (31):366–94.

Hawkins, Gladys, Jean Soper, and Jane Henry. 1959. *Your Maid from Mexico*. San Antonio, Tex.: Naylor.

Hedges, J. N., and J. K. Barnett. 1972. "Working Women and the Division of Household Tasks," *Monthly Labor Review* 95:9–13.

Hertz, Rosanna. 1986. *More Equal Than Others: Women and Men in Dual-Career Marriages.* Berkeley: University of California Press.

Hill, Merton E. 1928. *The Development of an Americanization Program.* Ontario, Calif.: The Board of Trustees of the Chaffey Union High School and the Chaffey Junior College.

Himmelweit, S., and S. Mohun. 1977. "Domestic Labour and Capital" *Cambridge Journal of Economics* 1 (1):15–31.

Hochschild, Arlie. 1983. *The Managed Heart: Commercialization of Human Feeling.* Berkeley: University of California Press.

———. 1989. *The Second Shift: Working Parents and the Revolution at Home.* New York: Viking.

Holmstrom, L. L. 1972. *The Two-Career Family.* Cambridge: Schenkman.

Hondagneu-Sotelo, Pierrette. 1990. "Gender and the Politics of Mexican Undocumented Immigrant Settlement," Ph.D. diss., University of California, Berkeley.

———. 1991. "Advocacy Research for Immigrant Women Domestic Workers," Paper presented at the 1991 Annual Meeting of the Society for the Study of Social Problems, Cincinnati, Ohio.

Horn, Pamela. 1975. *The Rise and Fall of the Victorian Servant.* New York: Saint Martin's.

House and Garden. 1981. "Guide to Household Help." 153:22.

Humphries, J. 1981. "Protective Legislation, the Capitalist State and Working Class Men," *Feminist Review* 7:1–33.

Illich, Ivan. 1980. *Shadow Work.* Cape Town: University of Cape Town.

———. 1982. *Gender.* New York: Pantheon.

James, Selma. 1975. "Wageless of the World," In *All Work and No Pay*, edited by Wendy Edmonds and Suzie Fleming, 25–34. Bristol: Falling Wall Press.

Johnson, Charles S. 1943. *Patterns of Negro Segregation.* New York: Harper and Brothers.

Kaplan, Elaine. 1987. "'I Don't Do No Windows': Competition between the Domestic Worker and the Housewife," In *Competition: A Feminist Taboo?*, edited by Valerie Miner and Helen E. Longino, 92–105. New York: Feminist Press.

Katz, F. E. 1958. "Occupational Contract Networks," *Social Forces* 37:52–54.

Katzman, David. 1978. "Domestic Service: Women's Work," In *Women Working: Theories and Facts in Perspective*, edited by Ann Stromberg and Shirley Harkess, 377–91. Palo Alto: Mayfield.

———. 1981. *Seven Days a Week. Women and Domestic Service in Industrializing America.* Chicago: University of Illinois Press.

Kleinman, Carol. 1986. "Maid Services Clean Up as Demand Escalates," *Chicago Tribune*, 17 August, sect. 8, 1.

Kluckhohn, Florence R., and Fred L. Stodtbeck. 1961. *Variations in Value Orientations.* Evanston, Ill.: Row, Peterson.

Kneeland, Hildegard. 1966. "Limitations of Scientific Management in Household Work," *Journal of Home Economics* 20: 311–14.

Knowlton, Clark. 1961. "The Spanish Americans in New Mexico," *Sociology and Social Research* 45 (4):448–54.

———. 1969. "Changing Spanish-American Villages of Northern New Mexico." *Sociology and Social Research* 53 (4):455–75.

Landes, Joan. 1975. "Wages for Housework: Subsidizing Capitalism?" *Quest* 2 (2):17–30.

Laurino, Maria. 1986. "'I'm Nobody's Girl': New York's New Indentured Servants," *Village Voice* 31 (41):17–18, 20–22, 24.

Lein, Laura. 1979. "Parental Evaluation of Childcare Alternatives." *Urban and Social Change Review* 12:11–16.

Lerner, Gerda. 1979. *The Majority Finds Its Past: Placing Women in History.* New York: Oxford University Press.

Levenstein, Aaron. 1962. *Why People Work*. New York: Crowell.

Lewis, Sasha G. 1979. *Slave Trade Today: American Exploitation of Illegal Aliens*. Boston: Beacon.

Luxton, Meg. 1980. *More than a Labour of Love. Three Generations of Women's Work in the Home*. Toronto: Women's Press.

Lynes, Russell. 1963. "How America 'Solved' the Servant Problem." *Harper's Magazine* 227 (1358):46–54.

Mainardi, Pat. 1980. "The Politics of Housework." In *The Politics of Housework*, edited by Ellen Malos, 99–104. New York: Allison & Busby.

Malone, Thomas J. 1964. "Recent Demographic and Economic Changes in Northern New Mexico." *New Mexico Business* 17 (9):4–14.

Malos, Ellen, ed. 1980. *The Politics of Housework*. New York: Allison & Busby.

Marks, Carole. 1987. "The Bone and Sinew of the Race: Black Women, Domestic Service and Labor Migration." Paper presented at the Delaware Seminar in Women's Studies, University of Delaware.

Martin, Linda, and Kerry Segrave. 1985. *The Servant Problem: Domestic Workers in North America*. Jefferson, N.C.: McFarland.

Mason, Mary Ann. 1988. *The Equality Trap. Why Working Women Shouldn't Be Treated Like Men*. New York: Simon & Schuster.

Matthaei, Julie A. 1982. *An Economic History of Women in America: Women's Work, the Sexual Division of Labor and the Development of Capitalism*. New York: Schocken.

Matthews, Glenna. 1987. *"Just a Housewife": The Rise and Fall of Domesticity in America*. New York: Oxford University Press.

McBride, Theresa. 1974. "Social Mobility for the Lower Class: Domestic Servants in France." *Journal of Social History* 8:63–78.

———. 1976. *The Domestic Revolution: The Modernization of Household Service in England and France, 1820–1920*. London: Croom Helm.

McGee, Samuel, Jr. 1935. *Labor in Colonial New York, 1664–1776*. New York: Ira J. Friedman.

McGinley, Phyllis. 1963. "Help!" *Ladies Home Journal* 80:64.

McKinley, Blaine Edward. 1969. "The Stranger in the Gates: Employer Reactions Toward Domestic Servants in America, 1825–1875." Ph.D. diss., Michigan State University.

Mead, Margaret. 1955. *Male and Female: A Study of the Sexes in a Changing World*. New York: New American Library.

———. 1976. "Household Help." *Redbook Magazine*, October, 42, 45, 47.

Mehta, Aban. 1950. *The Domestic Servant Class*. Bombay: Popular Book Depot.

Meissner, Martin, Elizabeth Humphrys, Scott Meis, and William Scheu. 1975. "No Exit for Wives: Sexual Division of Labor and the Cumulation of Household Demands." *Review of Canadian Sociology and Anthropology* 12:424–39.

Miller, May. 1974. *Happiness is Homemaking*. Harrisonburg, Va.: Choice Books.

Mitchell, Juliet. 1966. "Women: The Longest Revolution." *New Left Review* 40 (November-December): 11–37.

———. 1971. *Women's Estate*. Harmondsworth, England: Penguin.

Molyneux, Maxine. 1979. "Beyond the Domestic Labour Debate." *New Left Review* 16:3–27.

Moore, Frank. 1947. "San Jose, 1946: A Study in Urbanization." Master's thesis, University of New Mexico.

Morgan, Marabel. 1975. *Total Woman*. New York: Pocket Books.

Morton, Peggy. 1971. "A Woman's Work Is Never Done." In *From Feminism to Liberation*, edited by E. H. Altbach, 211–27. Cambridge, Mass.: Schenkman.

Mostow, E. 1975. "A Comparative Study of Work Satisfaction of Females with Full-Time Employment and Full-Time Housekeeping." *American Journal of Orthopsychiatry* 45:538–48.

Neiboer, H. J. 1971. *Slavery as an Industrial System*. New York: Lenox Hill.

Nelson, Jill. 1980. "I'm Not Your Girl." *Essence*, November, 146.

Oakley, Ann. 1974. *Woman's Work: The Housewife, Past and Present*. New York: Pantheon.

———. 1981. *Subject Women*. New York: Pantheon.

Oppenheimer, V. K. 1972. *The Female Labor Force in the United States: Demographic and Economic Factors Governing its Growth and Changing Composition*. Westport, Conn.: Greenwood.

Oxford, June, and Herman Levin. 1975. *Social Welfare: A History of the American Response to Need*. New York: Harper and Row.

Palmer, Phyllis. 1989. *Domesticity and Dirt: Housewives and Domestic Servants in the United States, 1920–1945*. Philadelphia: Temple University Press.

Parhust, Jessie W. 1938. "The Role of the Black Mammy in the Plantation Household." *The Journal of Negro History* 23:349–69.

Petras, Elizabeth McLean. 1989. "Jamaican Women in the US Health Industry: Caring, Cooking and Cleaning." *International Journal of Urban and Regional Research* 13:304–23.

Pettengill, Lillian. 1903. *Toilers of the Home: The Record of a College Woman's Experience as a Domestic Servant*. New York: Doubleday.

Phillips, Ulrich B. 1918. *American Negro Slavery: A Survey of the Supply, Employment and Control of Negro Labor as Determined by the Plantation Regime*. New York: D. Appleton.

Poloma, Margaret M., and T. Neal Garland. 1971. "The Married Professional Woman: A Study in the Tolerance of Domestication." *Journal of Marriage and the Family* 33 (3):531–40.

Portes, Alejandro. 1983. "The Informal Sector: Definition, Controversy, and Relation to National Development." *Review* 8 (1):151–74.

Rapoport, Rhonda and Robert Rapoport. 1969. "Work and Family in Contemporary Society." In *The Family and Change*, edited by John N. Edwards, 385–408. New York: Knopf.

———. 1976. *Dual Career Families Re-Examined: New Integrations of Work and Family*. New York: Harper & Row.

Reid, G. 1972. "Job Search and the Effectiveness of Job-Finding Methods." *Industrial and Labor Relations Review* 25:479–95.

Repak, Terry A. 1991. "Labor Market Experiences of Central American Migrants in Washington, D.C.," Paper presented at the Latin American Studies Association Meetings, Washington, D. C.

Ritzer, G. 1977. *Working: Conflict and Change*. Englewood Cliffs, N.J.: Prentice-Hall.

Rollins, Judith. 1985. *Between Women: Domestics and Their Employers*. Philadelphia: Temple University Press.

Rossoudji, Sherrie A., and Susan I. Rainey. 1984. "The Labor Market Earnings of Female Migrants: The Case of Temporary Mexican Migrants to the U.S." *International Migration Review* 28:1120–43.

Rubin, Lillian Breslow. 1976. *Worlds of Pain: Life in the Working-Class Family*. New York: Basic.

Rubinow, I. M. 1906. "The Problem of Domestic Service," *Journal of Political Economy* 14:502–84.

Safilos-Rothchild, Constantina. 1970. "The Influence of the Wife's Degree of Work Commitment upon Some Aspects of Family Organization and Dynamics." *Journal of Marriage and the Family* 32 (4):681–691.

Salmon, Lucy. [1901] 1972. *Domestic Service*. New York: Macmillan; reprint, New York: Arno Press.

Salzinger, Leslie. 1991. "A Maid by Any Other Name: The Transformation of 'Dirty Work' by Central American Immigrants." In *Ethnography Unbound: Power and Resistance in the Modern Metropolis*, edited by Michael Buraway et al., 139–60. Berkeley: University of California Press.

Sanchez, George. 1984. "'Go After the Women': Americanization and the Mexican Immigrant Woman, 1915–1929." Working Papers Series, vol. 6, Stanford Center for Chicano Research Center, Stanford University.

Sanjek, Roger, and Shellee Colen. 1988. "At Work in Homes." Unpublished.

Scamehorn, Howard L. 1976. *Pioneer Steelmaker in the West: The Colorado Fuel and Iron Company, 1872–1903*. Boulder, Colo.: Pruett.

Secombe, Wally. 1974. "The Housewife and Her Labour under Capitalism." *New Left Review* 83 (January–February): 3–24.

Sennett, Richard, and Jonathan Cobb. 1973. *The Hidden Injuries of Class*. New York: Vintage.

Sklar, Kathryn Kish. 1973. *Catherine Beecher: A Study in American Domesticity*. New Haven: Yale University Press.

Smith, Paul. 1978. "Domestic Labour and Marx's Theory of Value." In *Feminism and Materialism: Women and Modes of Production*, edited by Annette Kuhn and Ann Marie Wolpe, 200–19. London: Routledge and Kegan Paul.

Smuts, Robert. 1971. *Women and Work in America*. New York: Schocken.

Solorzano-Torres, Rosalia. 1988. "Women, Labor, and the U.S.-Mexico Border: Mexican Maids in El Paso, Texas." In *Mexicanas at Work in the United States*, edited by Margarita Melville, 75–83. Mexican American Studies Monograph no. 5, Mexican American Studies Program, University of Houston.

Spencer, Dee Ann. 1987. "Public Schoolteaching: A Suitable Job for a Woman." In *The Worth of Women's Work; A Qualitative Synthesis*, edited by Anne Statham, Elaanor M. Miller, and Hans O. Mauksch, 167–86. Albany: State University of New York Press.

Stansell, Christine. 1986. *City of Women. Sex and Class in New York, 1789–1860*. Chicago: University of Illinois Press.

Stigler, George J. 1946. *Domestic Servants in the United States, 1900–1940*. Occasional Paper no. 24. New York: National Bureau of Economic Research.

Strasser, S. 1982. *Never Done: A History of American Housework*. New York: Pantheon.

———. "Mistress and Maid, Employer and Employee: Domestic Service Reform in the United States, 1897–1920." *Marxist Perspectives* 1 (4):52–67.

Sutherland, Daniel. 1981. *Americans and Their Servants: Domestic Service in the United States from 1800 to 1920*. Baton Rouge: Louisiana State University Press.

Szalai, Alexander, Philip E. Converse, Pierre Feldheim, Erwin K. Scheuch, and Philip F. Stone, eds. 1972. *The Use of Time: Daily Activities of Urban and Suburban Populations in Twelve Countries*. The Hague: Mouton.

Taylor, Paul. 1929. *Mexican Labor in the United States*. vol. 1. of University of California Publications in Economics. Los Angeles: University of California.

Terkel, Studs. 1974. *Working: People Talk about What They Do All Day and How They Feel about What They Do*. New York: Pantheon.

Tilly, L. A., and J. W. Scott. 1978. *Women, Work and Family*. New York: Holt, Rinehart and Winston.

Tocqueville, Alexis De. [1841] 1963. *Democracy in America*, vol. 2. First edition, J. & H. G. Landley; New York: Knopf.

Tucker, Susan. 1988. *Telling Memories among Southern Women: Domestic Workers and Their Employers in the Segregated South*. Baton Rouge: Louisiana State University Press.

U.S. Census Bureau. 1980. Census of the Population and Housing; Provisional Estimate of Social, Economic and Housing Characteristics, 25–30. Washington, D.C.: U.S. Department of Commerce.

———. 1980. Census of the Population. Selected Characteristics of Employed Persons by Occupation, Industry and Sex, 1–3. Washington, D.C.: U.S. Department of Commerce.

U.S. Department of Labor. 1978. *Private Household Workers*. Women's Bureau. Washington, D.C.: U.S. Department of Labor.

Vanek, Joanne. 1974. "Time Spent in Housework." *Scientific American* 231:116–20.

Viva. 1986. "Maid in New York. How to Get and Keep Help." *Village Voice*, 9 September, 35.

Vogel, Lise. 1973. "The Earthly Family." *Radical America* 7 (4–5):9–50.

Waggamon, Mary T. 1945. "Wartime Job Opportunities for Women Household Workers in Washington, D.C." *Monthly Labor Review* 60:575–84.

Waite, L. 1980. "Working Wives and Family Life Cycle." *American Journal of Sociology* 85: 272–94.

Walker, Kathryn. 1970. "Time Spent by Husbands in Household Work." *Family Economics Review* 4:8–11.

Walker, Kathryn, and William Gauger. 1973. "The Dollar Value of Household Work." Information Bulletin 60, Consumer Economics and Public Policy no. 5. Ithaca, N.Y.: Cornell University.

Walker, Kathryn, and Margaret Woods. 1976. *Time Use: A Measurement of Household Production of Goods and Services.* Washington, D.C.: American Home Economics Association.

Walter, Paul A. 1939. "The Spanish-Speaking Community in New Mexico." *Sociology and Social Research* 24:150–57.

Warner, Judith Ann, and Helen K. Henderson, "Latina Women Immigrants' Waged Domestic Labor: Effects of Immigration Reform on the Link between Private Households and the International Labor Force." Paper presented at the 1990 Meetings of the American Sociological Association.

Warton, Mary Wilson. 1950. "Methodism at Work among the Spanish–Speaking People of El Paso, Texas." Master's thesis, Texas Western College.

Wax, R. 1960. "Reciprocity in Field Work." In *Human Organization Research: Field Relationships and Techniques*, edited by R. N. Adams and J. J. Preiss, 90–98. New York: Dorsey.

Weaver, Thomas. 1965. "Social Structure, Change and Conflict in a New Mexico Village," Ph.D. diss., University of California.

Welter, Barbara. 1966. "The Cult of True Womanhood, 1820–1860." *American Quarterly* 17:151–74.

Winnie, William W. 1955. "The Hispanic People of New Mexico." Master's thesis, University of Florida.

Woodson, Carter G. 1930. "The Negro Washerwoman. A Vanishing Figure." *The Journal of Negro History* 15 (3):269–77.

Wool, Harold. 1976. *The Labor Supply for Lower-Level Occupations.* New York: Praeger.

Yogev, Sara. 1981. "Do Professional Women Have Egalitarian Marital Relationships?" *Journal of Marriage and the Family* 43:865–71.

Zaretsky, Eli. 1973. "Capitalism, the Family and Personal Life. Part I." *Socialist Revolution* 3 (1–2):69–125.

INDEX